EXORBITANT PRIVILEGE

EXORBITANT PRIVILEGE

The Rise and Fall of the Dollar and the Future
of the International Monetary System

Barry Eichengreen

OXFORD
UNIVERSITY PRESS
2011

OXFORD
UNIVERSITY PRESS

Oxford University Press, Inc., publishes works that further
Oxford University's objective of excellence
in research, scholarship, and education.

Oxford   New York
Auckland   Cape Town   Dar es Salaam   Hong Kong   Karachi
Kuala Lumpur   Madrid   Melbourne   Mexico City   Nairobi
New Delhi   Shanghai   Taipei   Toronto

With offices in
Argentina   Austria   Brazil   Chile   Czech Republic   France   Greece
Guatemala   Hungary   Italy   Japan   Poland   Portugal   Singapore
South Korea   Switzerland   Thailand   Turkey   Ukraine   Vietnam

Copyright © 2011 by Barry Eichengreen

Published by Oxford University Press, Inc.
198 Madison Avenue, New York, NY 10016

www.oup.com

Oxford is a registered trademark of Oxford University Press

Library of Congress Cataloging-in-Publication Data
Eichengreen, Barry J.
Exorbitant privilege : The Rise and Fall of the Dollar and the Future
of the International Monetary System / Barry Eichengreen.
p.   cm.
Includes bibliographical references and index.
ISBN 978-0-19-975378-9
1. Money—United States—History—20th century.
2. Devaluation of currency—United States—History—21st century.
3. United States—Economic policy—2009–
4. Financial crises—United States—21st century.
I. Title.
HG540.E33   2010
332.4′973—dc22   2010018239

5 7 9 8 6 4

Printed in the United States of America
on acid-free paper

CONTENTS

1   Introduction   1

2   Debut   9

3   Dominance   39

4   Rivalry   69

5   Crisis   97

6   Monopoly No More   121

7   Dollar Crash   153

Notes   179

References   199

Acknowledgments   207

Index   209

EXORBITANT PRIVILEGE

CHAPTER I

INTRODUCTION

The Counterfeiters, an award-winning German film set in 1940s Europe, opens with the concentration camp survivor Salomon Sorowitsch, played by the Austrian actor Karl Markovics, sitting fully clothed on the beach holding a suitcase full of dollars. The war has just ended, and he intends to put that currency, of dubious provenance, to work on the tables of Monte Carlo. That it is dollars rather than French francs is essential to the authenticity of the scene. In post–World War II Europe it was the dollar, the currency of the only major economy still standing, that people in all countries wanted. Dollars were the only plausible currency that a Holocaust survivor might carry into a casino in 1945.

Fast forward now 50-odd years. In *City of Ghosts*, a 2002 thriller set in contemporary Cambodia, the hero, a crooked insurance salesman played by Matt Dillon, uses a suitcase full of dollars to ransom his partner and mentor, played by James Caan, who has been kidnapped by business associates. More than half a century of cinematic time has passed and the location is now developing Asia rather than Europe, but the suitcase still contains dollars, not Japanese yen or Chinese renminbi. That any self-respecting kidnapper would expect the ransom to be paid in dollars is so obvious as to go unstated.

The suitcase full of dollars is by now a standard trope of mystery novels and Hollywood screenplays. But this artistic convention reflects a common truth. For more than half a century the dollar has been the world's monetary lingua franca. When a senator from the Republic of Kalmykia is caught shaking down a Russian airline, he is apprehended with a suitcase containing $300,000 in marked U.S. bills. When Somali pirates ransom a ship, they demand that the ransom money be parachuted to them in dollars. As the *Wall Street Journal* has put it, "In the black market, the dollar still rules."[1] The fact that nearly three-quarters of all $100 bills circulate outside the United States attests to the dollar's dominance of this dubious realm.

But what is true of illicit transactions is true equally of legitimate business. The dollar remains far and away the most important currency for invoicing and settling international transactions, including even imports and exports that do not touch U.S. shores. South Korea and Thailand set the prices of more than 80 percent of their trade in dollars despite the fact that only 20 percent of their exports go to American buyers. Fully 70 percent of Australia's exports are invoiced in dollars despite the fact that fewer than 6 percent are destined for the United States. The principal commodity exchanges quote prices in dollars. Oil is priced in dollars. The dollar is used in 85 percent of all foreign exchange transactions worldwide. It accounts for nearly half of the global stock of international debt securities.[2] It is the form in which central banks hold more than 60 percent of their foreign currency reserves.

This situation is more than a bit peculiar. It made sense after World War II when the United States accounted for more than half of the combined economic output of the Great Powers.[3] America being far and away the largest importer and main source of trade credit, it made sense for imports and exports to be denominated in dollars. Since the United States was the leading source of foreign capital, it made sense that international financial business was transacted in dollars. And with these same considerations encouraging central banks to stabilize their currencies against the dollar, it made sense that they should hold dollars in reserve in case of a problem in foreign exchange markets.

But what made sense then makes less sense now, when both China and Germany export more than the United States. Today the U.S. share of global exports is only 13 percent. The United States is the source of less than 20 percent of foreign direct investment, down from nearly 85 percent between 1945 and 1980.[4]

These two changes are both manifestations of the same fact: the United States is less dominant economically than 50 years ago. This fact reflects the progress of other economies, first Europe, then Japan, and most recently emerging markets like China and India, in closing the per capita income gap. Economists refer to this narrowing as catch-up or convergence. It is entirely natural insofar as there is no intrinsic reason that U.S. incomes and levels of labor productivity should be multiples of those in the rest of the world. This process of catch-up is one of the great achievements of the late twentieth and early twenty-first centuries in that it has begun lifting out of poverty the majority of the world's population. But it also means that the United States accounts for a smaller share of international transactions. And this fact creates an uneasy tension with the peculiar dominance of the dollar.

This dominance is something from which we Americans derive considerable benefit. An American tourist in New Delhi who can pay his cab driver in dollars is spared the inconvenience of having to change money at his hotel. The widespread international use of the dollar is similarly an advantage for American banks and firms. A German company exporting machine tools to China and receiving payment in dollars incurs the additional cost of converting those dollars into euros, the currency it uses to pay its workers and purchase its materials. Not so a U.S. exporter of machine tools. Unlike firms in other countries, the U.S. producer receives payment in the same currency, dollars, that it uses to pay its workers, suppliers, and shareholders.

Similarly, a Swiss bank accepting deposits in francs but making foreign loans in dollars, since that's what its customers want, has to worry about the risk to its profits if the exchange rate moves.[5] That risk can be managed, but doing so is an added cost of business. Our Swiss bank can protect itself by buying a forward contract that converts the receipts on its dollar loan into francs when the loan matures, at a rate agreed when the loan is made. But that additional transaction has an additional cost. American banks that make foreign loans in dollars as well as taking deposits in dollars are spared the expense of having to hedge their foreign currency positions in this way.

A more controversial benefit of the dollar's international-currency status is the real resources that other countries provide the United States in order to obtain our dollars. It costs only a few cents for the Bureau of Engraving and Printing to produce a $100 bill, but other countries have to pony up $100 of actual goods and services in order to obtain one. (That difference between what it costs the government to print the note and a foreigner to procure it is known as "seignorage" after the right of the medieval lord, or *seigneur*, to coin money and keep for himself some of the precious metal from which it was made.) About $500 billion of U.S. currency circulates outside the United States, for which foreigners have had to provide the United States with $500 billion of actual goods and services.[6]

Even more important is that foreign firms and banks hold not just U.S. currency but bills and bonds that are convenient for international transactions and at the same time have the attraction of bearing interest. Foreign central banks hold close to $5 trillion of the bonds of the U.S. treasury and quasi-governmental agencies like Fannie Mae and Freddie Mac. They add to them year after year.

And insofar as foreign banks and firms value the convenience of dollar securities, they are willing to pay more to obtain them. Equivalently, the interest rate they require to hold them is less. This effect is substantial: the interest that the United States must pay on its foreign liabilities is two to three percentage points less than the rate of return on its foreign investments.[7] The U.S. can run an external deficit in the amount of this difference, importing more than it exports and consuming more than it produces year after year without becoming more indebted to the rest of the world. Or it can scoop up foreign companies in that amount as the result of the dollar's singular status as the world's currency.

This has long been a sore point for foreigners, who see themselves as supporting American living standards and subsidizing American multinationals through the operation of this asymmetric financial system. Charles de Gaulle made the issue a *cause célèbre* in a series of presidential press conferences in the 1960s. His finance minister, Valéry Giscard d'Estaing, referred to it as America's "exorbitant privilege."

Not that this high-flown rhetoric led to changes in the actual existing system. In international finance as in politics, incumbency is an advantage. With other countries doing the bulk of their transactions in dollars, it was impossible for any individual country, even one as critical of America's exorbitant privilege as France, to move away from the currency. And what was true in the 1960s remained true for the balance of the twentieth century.

But today, in the wake of the most serious financial crisis in 80 years, a crisis born and bred in the United States, there is again widespread criticism of

America's exorbitant privilege. Other countries question whether the United States should have been permitted to run current account deficits approaching 6 percent of GDP in the run-up to the crisis. Emerging markets complain that as their economies expanded and their central banks felt compelled to augment their dollar reserves, they were obliged to provide cheap finance for the U.S. external deficit, like it or not. With cheap foreign finance keeping U.S. interest rates low and enabling American households to live beyond their means, poor households in the developing world ended up subsidizing rich ones in the United States. The cheap finance that other countries provided the U.S. in order to obtain the dollars needed to back an expanding volume of international transactions underwrote the practices that culminated in the crisis. The United States lit the fire, but foreigners were forced by the perverse structure of the system to provide the fuel.

If this was not injustice enough, there is the fact that America's international financial position was actually strengthened by the crisis. In the course of 2007 the dollar weakened by about 8 percent on the foreign exchange market.[8] But since our debts are denominated in our own currency, there was no impact on their dollar value. In contrast, our foreign investments, whether in bonds or factories, became more valuable as the dollar fell.[9] The interest and dividends they threw off were worth more when converted back into dollars.

The dollar's depreciation thereby improved the U.S. external position by almost $450 billion.[10] This largely offset the increase in U.S. indebtedness to the rest of the world that would have otherwise resulted from our $660 billion current account deficit. It was almost enough to keep our debts to other countries stable, despite our consuming 6 percent more than we produced. Then in 2008, in the throes of the most serious financial crisis in 80 years, the federal government was able to borrow vast sums at low interest rates because foreigners figured that the dollar was the safest currency to be in at a time of great turmoil. And again in the spring of 2010, when financial volatility spiked, investors fled into the most liquid market, that for U.S. treasury bonds, pushing down the cost of borrowing for the U.S. government and, along with it, the mortgage interest rates available to American households. This is what exorbitant privilege is all about.

But now, as a result of the financial mismanagement that spawned the crisis and growing dissatisfaction with the operation of the international monetary system, the dollar's singular status is in doubt. The U.S. government has not been a worthy steward of an international currency, its critics complain. It looked the other way while the private sector produced the mother of all financial crises. It ran enormous budget deficits and incurred a gigantic debt. Foreigners have lost faith in the almighty dollar. They are moving away from it as a unit in which to invoice and settle trade, denominate commodity prices, and conduct international financial transactions. The dollar is at risk of losing its exorbitant privilege to the euro, the renminbi, or the bookkeeping claims issued by the International Monetary Fund known as Special Drawing Rights (SDRs).

Or so it is said. It is said by no less an authority than Sarah Palin on her Facebook page, who warned in October 2009 that talk that the Gulf countries might shift to pricing oil in a basket of currencies "weakens the dollar and renews fears about its continued viability as an international reserve currency."[11]

That this issue has flashed across the radar screens of politicians who are not exactly renowned for their financial expertise reflects the belief that larger things are at stake. It is thought that widespread international use of a currency confers on its issuer geopolitical and strategic leverage. Because the country's financial position is stronger, its foreign policy is stronger. Because it pays less on its debts, it is better able to finance foreign operations and exert strategic influence. It does not depend on other people's money. Instead, it has leverage over other countries that depend on its currency. Compare the nineteenth century, it is said, when Britannia ruled the waves and the pound dominated international financial markets, with the post–World War II period, when sterling lost its dominance and the United States, not Britain, called the foreign-policy shots.

Were all this right, there would have been no reason for me to write this book or for you to read it. In fact, however, much of what passes for conventional wisdom on this subject is wrong. To start, it has cause and effect backward. There may be an association between the economic and military power of a country and the use of its currency by others, but it is a country's position as a great power that results in the international status of its currency. A currency is attractive because the country issuing it is large, rich, and growing. It is attractive because the country standing behind it is powerful and secure. For both reasons, the economic health of the country issuing the currency is critical for its acquisition and retention of an international role.

But whether its currency is used internationally has at best limited implications for a country's economic performance and prospects. Seignorage is nice, but it is about number 23 on the list of factors, ranked in descending order of importance, determining the place of the United States in the world. That said, how the country does economically, and whether it avoids policy blunders as serious as those that led to the financial crisis, will determine the dollar's fate. Sterling lost its position as an international currency because Britain lost its great-power status, not the other way around. And Britain lost its great-power status as a result of homegrown economic problems.

The conventional wisdom about the historical processes resulting in the current state of affairs—that incumbency is an overwhelming advantage in the competition for reserve currency status—is similarly wrong. It is asserted that the pound remained the dominant international currency until after World War II, long after the United States had overtaken Britain as the leading economy, reflecting those self-same advantages of incumbency. In fact, the dollar already rivaled sterling as an international currency in the mid-1920s, only 10 short years after the establishment of the Federal Reserve System. It did so as a result of some very concrete actions by the Fed to promote the dollar's international role. This fact has very different implications than the conventional wisdom for how and when the Chinese renminbi might come to rival the dollar. It suggests that the challenge may come sooner rather than later.

Finally, the idea that the dollar is now doomed to lose its international currency status is equally wrong. The dollar has its problems, but so do its rivals. The euro is a currency without a state. When the euro area experiences economic and financial problems, as in 2010, there is no powerful executive branch with the power to solve them, only a collection of national governments more inclined to pander to their domestic constituencies. The only euro-area institution capable of quick action is the European Central Bank. And if quick action means printing money to monetize government debts, then this is hardly something that will inspire confidence in and international use of the euro. The renminbi, for its part, is a currency with too much state. Access to China's financial markets and international use of its currency are limited by strict government controls. The SDR is funny money. It is not, in fact, a currency. It is not used to invoice and settle trade or in private financial transactions. As a result, it is not particularly attractive for use by governments in their own transactions.

The United States, whatever its other failings, is still the largest economy in the world. It has the largest financial markets of any country. Its demographics imply relatively favorable growth prospects.

But the fundamental fallacy behind the notion that the dollar is engaged in a death race with its rivals is the belief that there is room for only one international currency. History suggests otherwise. Aside from the very peculiar second half of the twentieth century, there has always been more than one international currency. There is no reason that a few years from now countries on China's border could not use the renminbi in their international transactions, while countries in Europe's neighborhood use the euro, and countries doing business with the United States use the dollar. There is no reason that only one country can have financial markets deep and broad enough to make international use of its currency attractive. There may have been only one country with sufficiently deep financial markets in the second half of the twentieth century, but not because this exclusivity is an intrinsic feature of the global financial system.

The world for which we need to prepare is thus one in which several international currencies coexist. It was with this world in mind that the euro was created. A world of several international currencies is similarly what China is after. China has no interest in "dethroning" the dollar. To the contrary, it has too much invested in the greenback. But preserving its investment in the dollar is entirely compatible with creating a more consequential international role for its own currency. And where the renminbi leads, other emerging market currencies, such as the Indian rupee and Brazilian real, could eventually follow.

Serious economic and financial mismanagement by the United States is the one thing that could precipitate flight from the dollar. And serious mismanagement, recent events remind us, is not something that can be ruled out. We may yet suffer a dollar crash, but only if we bring it on ourselves. The Chinese are not going to do it to us.

But this is to get ahead of the story.

CHAPTER 2

DEBUT

When in 1620 a landing party of English religious dissidents led by William Bradford and Myles Standish came ashore near what is today Provincetown, Massachusetts, they brought with them English money and a custom of expressing values in pounds, shillings, and pence. The colonists were not a wealthy band, and it was not many years before they had expended their English money on supplies from the Old World. Finding a substitute was not easy in a colony without a mint or the permission to establish one, and with England prohibiting the export of coin (the English monarchs husbanding all the precious metal they possessed for fighting expensive wars).

Commodity currency was the obvious alternative. Every schoolchild learns about the colonists' use of wampum. Native Americans valued the purple and white quahog and whelk shells strung in the form of necklaces and ornamental belts and were willing to part with furs, skins, and other commodities in order to obtain them.[1] The colonists with their tools were efficient producers of necklaces and belts. From trade with the natives the use of wampum spread to transactions among the colonists themselves. In 1637 wampum was made legal tender, officially recognized money for paying debts, in the Massachusetts Bay Colony at a rate of six white beads or three purple beads per penny.

But there were only so many snail and clam shells to go around. So the colonists turned to other commodities for use in their barter transactions: corn, codfish, and beaver in the north, tobacco and rice in the south. These items were used in transactions because they were the dominant products of the region. Local governments allowed residents use corn or tobacco to discharge their tax obligations.[2] The next step was to declare that the commodity in question should be accepted not just in public payments but by private parties. Massachusetts made corn legal tender. Connecticut did the same for wheat, Virginia for tobacco.[3]

Making these commodities legal tender had some awkward consequences. When Virginia gave tobacco legal-tender status, there was an incentive to increase production, of the lowest grades in particular. With more tobacco chasing the same goods, the purchasing power of tobacco declined. Farmers complained of low prices. The General Assembly of Burgesses, the representatives of Virginia's agricultural districts, considered measures to restrict tobacco cultivation but could not agree. In 1682, farmers angry over low crop prices took matters into their own hands, rampaging through the fields and destroying their neighbors' tobacco plants. The government mustered the militia. The rioters carried out their work under cover of darkness. Order was restored only after several months of police action.

Farm products like tobacco had further disadvantages as media of exchange, stores of value, and means of payment—most obviously bulk, lack of uniformity, and spoilage. There understandably developed a preference for coin. Since the English authorities did not permit the colonies to operate a mint, such coin as circulated had to be imported.[4] English coin could be obtained by exporting other merchandise, although London with its prohibitions did not make this easy. Closer at hand, coin could be obtained in the West Indies, silver coins being abundant there as a result of Spain's prolific Mexican and Peruvian mines. The North American colonists sold dried fish, whale oil, pickled beef, and grain in return for coin. Exportation of many of these products to destinations other than other English colonies and the mother country being prohibited, much of this was smuggled. Coin earned by exporting merchandise was supplemented by that acquired through piracy, an important industry for the seventeenth-century colonists in the established English tradition.[5] The pirates spent much of their booty, which included Spanish coin, while on shore leave in the northern colonies.

The most popular coins, weighing 423.7 grains of silver were known as "pesos." Valued at eight Spanish reals, they were referred to as "pieces of eight."[6]

Dealers in foreign exchange in London referred to them as "dollars" or "Spanish dollars," the Bohemian state of Joachimsthal having produced a coin of similar size and content known as the *Joachimsthaler*, or as anglicized the "Joachimsdollar." In addition, gold *johannes* were imported from Portugal, louis d'or from France, sequins from Venice. But on the eve of the colonies' war of independence, Spanish silver coins were the dominant part of the coinage.

Coin was supplemented with bills of credit—paper money issued via public loans.[7] It was issued, that is, when the colonists' English overseers permitted, Parliament prohibiting the practice starting in 1751. This ban was among the economic grievances setting the stage for the American Revolution. No less a figure than Benjamin Franklin objected to it in testimony to the British Parliament in 1766.

ALL ABOUT THE BENJAMINS

The colonies' war of independence was necessarily improvised, but nowhere more than in the monetary sphere. Delegates to the Continental Congress, not being able to commit their principals, lacked the power to raise taxes. They sought to pay for the war by issuing IOUs, continental bills or "continentals" for short. Bills issued under the authority of the Continental Congress were supplemented by bills issued by each colony. The consequences predictably included bills trading at a confusing variety of different prices, inflation, and the disappearance of gold and silver from circulation.

It took the leaders of the new nation some time to regularize this irregular situation. In 1785 the Congress passed a resolution declaring that the "money unit of the United States of America be one dollar" and that the dollar should be divided according to the decimal system. Thomas Jefferson, having been exposed to the advantages of decimalization in France, insisted on the provision. A resolution adopted in August 1786 then referred to the hundredth part of a dollar as a cent and a tenth part as a dime. It defined the dollar in terms of grains of silver and gold at a ratio of 15.253 to 1.

In September 1786, Congress then ordered the establishment of a mint. In its initial months of operation, only a few one-half-, one-, and two-cent copper coins were produced, minting being an activity with which the locals had little experience. A number of states also engaged in coining. The Constitution, which came into force in March 1789, then asserted the power of Congress to coin money and regulate its value while prohibiting the states from coining money or emitting IOUs that circulated like money.[8]

The last phase of the birthing process was the Coinage Act of 1792, for which Alexander Hamilton was midwife. Hamilton, one of the three members of President George Washington's first cabinet, believed fervently in the need to bind the thirteen states together. He saw a uniform currency as an effective form of glue. His *Report on the Establishment of a Mint*, submitted to the Congress in January 1791, offered detailed proposals for a mint and a uniform coinage to encourage commerce not just within but across the newly independent states.

Hamilton was a proponent of bimetallism, in which gold coins were used for large-value trade, silver coins for petty transactions. In the course of preparing his report, he examined the tables that Sir Isaac Newton prepared in 1717, when as master of the mint Newton had specified the pound's value in terms of the two metals. The 1792 act based on Hamilton's report similarly defined the dollar in terms of both gold and silver. It defined smaller denominations using the decimal system, dubbing them the quarter, dime, and cent.

To determine the silver content of the dollar, Hamilton had the Treasury weigh a sample of Spanish dollars. Their average silver content was 371.25 grains, not the official Spanish figure of 377, coins circulating in the United States being clipped and worn. The Americans being nothing if not pragmatic, 371.25 grains was adopted as the official silver content of the dollar. Drawing inspiration once more from Newton's 1717 report, the ratio of silver to gold was set at fifteen to one.[9]

Acceptance of the new U.S. dollar was swift because of its resemblance to the Spanish dollars already in circulation. Indeed, Spanish dollars, notably those coined in Mexico, continued to circulate because of the slow progress of the mint. So widely did they circulate that in 1793 Congress recognized the most important ones as legal tender. Many remained in circulation until the middle of the nineteenth century. One enduring legacy of the Spanish coins that constituted the bulk of the circulation is the dollar sign. The sign "$" derives from the peso, the two parallel lines being the vertical portions of "P," and the "S" indicating the plural. This explains why the "$" symbol is also used in countries whose currency is the peso—in Argentina, for example.

O CANADA

Over the balance of the nineteenth century the dollar had a colorful history, but it was almost entirely a domestic history. Canada was the one place outside the United States where it circulated. The British colonies of Upper and Lower Canada, like their colonial counterparts to the south, had no currency of their own. English, French, and Spanish coins all circulated. In the 1830s one writer complained that the coinage had "more the appearance of the fifteenth than the nineteenth century. All the antiquated cast-off rubbish, in the whole world, finds it way here, and remains. This Colony is literally the Botany Bay for all the condemned coins of other countries; instead of perishing in the crucible, as they ought to do, they are banished to Canada, where they are taken in hand."[10]

These coins had legal tender status at values that depended on their gold and silver content. As trade with the newly independent United States expanded, they were increasingly supplemented by dollars. While the merchants of Upper and Lower Canada still did their accounting in pounds, shillings, and pence, their transactions increasingly were in dollars and cents.

In the 1850s, with U.S. coins in widespread use, a groundswell developed to give them official status in Canada. Francis Hincks, the onetime banker and railway speculator who served as prime minister from 1851 to 1854, endorsed the campaign, and in 1853 an act was passed recognizing not just pounds, shillings, and pence but also dollars and cents as units of Canadian currency. Simply shifting to the decimal system would have been easier, but the prospect excited fears that doing so would somehow lead to annexation by the United States. Finally in 1857, suppressing these exaggerated worries, the Canadian Parliament passed an act specifying that the accounts of provincial governments should be expressed in dollars and cents. In 1858 the English Royal Mint stamped the first Canadian silver coins in denominations of 5, 10, and 20 cents.

But even after confederation in 1867 and the issuance of a dominion currency, U.S. dimes, quarters, and half-dollars continued to circulate. The bullion content of these U.S. coins was typically 2.5 percent less than their face value. While they might be accepted at face value by merchants and individuals, banks accepted them only at a discount.

This lack of uniformity was a considerable nuisance. In 1868 the dominion government sought to eliminate it by exporting to New York the U.S. silver coins that had come into its possession. This making only a small dent in the problem, in 1870 it agreed to provide the banks a commission in return for buying up the remaining U.S. coin and to pay the cost of exporting it to New York.[11] This was Hincks at work again, his having returned as finance minister in 1869 after a period as imperial governor in Barbados and British Guiana. The dominion government then issued full-bodied silver coins in 25- and 50-cent denominations to replace the U.S. coin that now finally disappeared from circulation. The dollar's international role north of the border thereby came to an ignominious end.

OTHER PEOPLE'S MONEY

Not only did little U.S. money circulate outside the United States, especially after it was expelled from Canada, but the dollar played virtually no role in financing America's own import and export trade. Whether an American merchant needed credit to purchase imports or to extend credit to a foreign purchaser of American goods, he secured it not in New York but in London or, less frequently, Paris or Berlin. It followed that this credit was denominated not in dollars but in pounds, francs, or marks.

Why London dominated this business is no mystery. Britain was the first industrial economy and the leading trading nation. With economic growth and development came the growth of financial markets. Already in the mid-nineteenth century Britain had a well-developed banking system. It had the Bank of England, chartered in 1694 to raise money for war with France, which had come to assume the functions of a modern central bank. It had stable money as a result of being on the gold standard.

It had not always been so. Traditionally the Royal Mint had been run by the Company of Moneyers, descended from the medieval gild of coiners, whose members were notorious for self-dealing, corruption, and drunkenness. Practices at the mint had so deteriorated by the end of the seventeenth century that the government took the extraordinary step of appointing the country's premier scientist, the efficient and scrupulously honest Isaac Newton, as Warden of the Mint. Saddled with financial difficulties, Newton was happy to accept, since the position came with a salary. He addressed the personnel problem. He did his detailed study of the coinage. He put Britain on the gold standard in 1717.

By the nineteenth century, London had become the premier financial center. Because it was where members of the British Empire serviced their debts, London had developed efficient clearing mechanisms that could also be used by other countries. Britain was the leading foreign investor. And when one of its banks made a loan to a foreign borrower, that loan was naturally in the form of its own currency, the pound sterling. With so many loans denominated in sterling, it became natural for governments, when borrowing in London, to maintain accounts there in order to conveniently service their debts. These accounts were what subsequently came to known as "reserves."

Because Britain was the leading importer of industrial raw materials and food, the most important commodity exchanges—the Manchester Cotton Exchange, the Liverpool Corn Market, and of course the London Gold Market— were located there. Britain was also an efficient provider of trade-related services such as shipping and insurance. All this made London an obvious place to obtain credit for those engaged in international trade. And for reasons of their own convenience, the credit provided by British banks was denominated in sterling. It followed that upwards of 60 percent of world trade was invoiced and settled in British pounds.[12]

No Credit

When a businessman ships a batch of goods, he needs cash. He goes to his bank with papers showing that he has shipped the goods and what he will be paid in the future. If his credit—and the credit of the buyer—is good, he can get his money immediately rather than having to wait for the goods to arrive in the foreign market and for the buyer's payment to arrive in the United States. The papers in question are known as "trade acceptances." In purchasing them at a discount from their face value, a bank is said to "discount" them.

But having to rely on London for trade credit, as U.S. importers and exporters did, made the process positively labyrinthine. Picture the requirements facing a New York coffee roaster importing beans from Brazil.[13] The importer first had to go to his bank to obtain a letter of credit specifying the terms of the transaction, the goods to be shipped, and the insurance on the shipment. In issuing the letter, his bank committed to paying out funds when receiving confirmation that the transaction was complete. The bank then sent a copy of the letter to the London bank guaranteeing payment of the bill. It gave the importer the original and a second copy.

The importer next sent the original letter of credit to the Brazilian dealer, authorizing him to draw on the London bank against his shipment of coffee. The dealer shipped the coffee and, with documents attached, presented his draft on the London bank to his Brazilian bank. The willingness of his Brazilian bank to purchase (or "discount") the draft reflected the expectation that it would be "accepted" by a reputable British bank that would pay out the specified amount of cash when the draft matured.

After discounting the draft, the Brazilian bank sent one duplicate set of documents to the New York bank and another, along with its draft, to its correspondent bank in London. The correspondent could hold the accepted draft until it matured, at which point the correspondent would present it to the accepting bank and be paid, or sell it to another party. In practice other interested parties included not just banks but also business enterprises and individuals seeking to invest in relatively safe short-term assets. When presented with the draft for payment, the accepting bank in London checked it against the letter of credit it had received from New York. Finding everything in order, it sent the papers accompanying the draft back to the New York bank.

At this point the American importer, in order to obtain the bill of lading sent to the New York bank by the London bank as part of the documentation accompanying the draft, signed a trust receipt committing to hold the goods in trust for the bank as its property and to turn over to it the proceeds of his sales as they applied to the acceptance. An accepted bill was generally drawn to mature in 90 days, giving the importer time to sell the shipment. Prior to the draft maturing, the importer delivered the funds to his New York bank, which sent them on to the London bank. The London bank paid the holder of the acceptance on its maturity, and the transaction was complete.

One's first reaction on encountering this exhaustingly long list of procedures is that the transaction could have been completed more easily had it not required multiple communications with London. American merchants complained of having to pay not just a fee to their New York bank for the letter of credit but also a collection charge to the bank in London. Since London banks preferred lending in sterling, the practice also exposed American merchants to the risk that the sterling-dollar exchange rate would move against them, which was an additional cost of doing business.[14]

These practices had still further disadvantages for American business. To the extent that finance and commercial services like shipping and insurance came bundled together, American providers of the latter found it more difficult to compete. Familiarity with facilities for providing trade credit similarly made London the obvious place to source other financial services—to underwrite bond issues, for example.

Prominent by Its Absence

Great Britain was a small windswept island off the northeast coast of Europe. The United States, in contrast, was a continental economy. By 1870 it had pulled ahead of Britain in the production of goods and services. By 1912 it had pulled ahead as an exporter of merchandise.

It was thus anomalous that the United States continued to depend on London for trade finance and that the dollar played no international role. Part of the explanation lay in regulations preventing American banks from branching overseas. Extending credit to foreign merchants required information on their activities, something that British banks, with their far-flung branch networks, were in a position to gather. French, German, and Dutch banks similarly had foreign branch networks. But not so national banks in the United States, which were prohibited from branching not just internationally but even across state lines. In some states they were prohibited from branching at all.[15]

An exception was the International Banking Corporation, a specialized institution created to engage in foreign banking but which, to prevent it from using this advantage to dominate the domestic market, was prohibited from engaging in banking business in the United States. IBC was organized in 1901 by Marcus Hartley, owner of the Remington Arms Company, to promote and finance the expansion of American trade with Asia, the Spanish-American War having brought the region to his attention. Hartley and his partners copied the structure and raided the personnel of British banks already active in the Far East.[16] By 1910 IBC had sixteen branches, mostly in Asia.[17]

In addition, some states allowed trust companies (bank-like companies that oversaw the affairs of trust funds and estates) to operate foreign branches.

Foreign branches made it easier to invest in foreign bonds. But the only trust companies with foreign branches were the Farmers' Loan and Trust Company, the Trust Company of America, the Guaranty Trust Company, the Empire Trust Company, and the Equitable Trust Company. Farmers' Trust had two foreign branches, the others just one. Such was the extent of foreign branching by American financial institutions.[18]

Until the passage of the Federal Reserve Act in 1913, national banks were even prohibited from dealing in trade credit.[19] The National Banking Act of 1863 and associated legislation included no provisions authorizing them to do so. And the courts, suspicious of banks encroaching into new areas, ruled that national banks could not engage in the business without express congressional authorization.[20]

Before putting too much weight on these legal restrictions, it is worth recalling that all the great accepting banks in London were private. The United States also had private banks that did not need state or federal charters and hence were free of regulatory restrictions. These included names like J.P. Morgan and Company, Brown Brothers and Company, and Lazard Frères. In principle, nothing prevented these banks from dealing in acceptances. Many had sister firms and offices across the water to provide market intelligence. J.P. Morgan had Morgan, Grenfell and Company. Lazard Frères had offices in London and Paris.

But even private banks contributed to the finance of U.S. foreign trade only to a very limited extent. Evidently something else made it hard for American banks, even private banks not inhibited by regulatory restrictions, to break into the market.

That something else was a cost disadvantage. London banks had a well-developed population of investors to whom trade acceptances might be resold, which made risks less and interest rates lower. With so many investors active on this market, it was possible to buy and sell these instruments without moving prices. To put it in the language of finance, the London market was exceptionally liquid. There was little uncertainty about the price one could obtain when discounting a bill. This encouraged yet more investors to come to London, adding further to the market's liquidity. It made the decision of whether to ask for a draft on a well-known British house or an unfamiliar American competitor a no-brainer for our Brazilian coffee dealer. It was possible to engage in a large volume of business without moving prices.

And what worked for individual investors worked for governments and central banks. The liquidity of its market made London an attractive place for governments and central banks to hold reserves. And the more bills on London they substituted for gold—which, its other attractions notwithstanding, bore no interest—the greater was the liquidity of the market. This was the advantage of the incumbent international currency, the so-called "first-mover advantage" that enables it to hang on even when the country issuing it has gone into decline.

But the fact that France and Germany were able to enter the market suggests that Britain's first-mover advantage was not insurmountable. Other factors must have been holding America back. One handicap was the volatility of its financial markets. By one count, the United States experienced fourteen financial crises in the century preceding World War I, of which 1907 was the worst. Interest rates spiked, and for many borrowers credit became unavailable at any price. This was not a market on which many people, given a choice, would finance their trade.

Then there was the fact that it proved impossible for the United States to keep both gold and silver coins in circulation, given that the market price of the two metals was changing continuously. Even after 1879, when the United States formally went onto the gold standard, its commitment remained uncertain. This was notably true in the 1890s, when the inflationist free-silver movement was given voice by William Jennings Bryan. Our Brazilian coffee dealer would have been reluctant to accept a contract in which he would receive dollars sometime in the future, given the risk that additional silver might be coined and the dollar might depreciate against currencies more firmly tied to gold.

BIDDLE'S FOLLY

Finally there was the fact that the United States had no central bank to stabilize the market. When London banks needed cash, they could raise it by reselling to the Bank of England some of the securities that they had purchased previously. (The practice was known, for self-evident reasons, as "rediscounting" at the Bank.) At the end of the nineteenth century, the Bank of England was the single largest purchaser of bills on the London market, sometimes accounting for the majority of all transactions.[21]

America had nothing resembling these arrangements. A proto-central bank, the Bank of the United States, had been founded in Philadelphia in 1791. The Bank of the United States was another Alexander Hamilton invention, Hamilton having educated himself about the advantages accruing to Britain from the existence of the Bank of England. Created over the objections of Thomas Jefferson and James Madison, who feared that it would lead to elite control of American finances, the Bank of the United States was the new nation's largest financial institution and the only one permitted to operate in more than one state. It kept the Treasury Department's accounts. By refusing to accept the notes of banks that did not pay out the designated amount in gold or silver, it maintained the link between the money stock and supply of precious metal. It provided a check on local monopoly power by offering an alternative to local banks charging exorbitant rates.

These other institutions predictably registered their displeasure when the charter of the Bank of the United States came up for renewal in 1810. They complained that the Bank was less than vigilant in refusing to accept the notes of a non-specie-paying bank when politically influential individuals or its own investors were among its shareholders. Jeffersonian Democrats interpreting the Constitution literally insisted that the Congress had no power to charter a bank. The bill to recharter was defeated.

State banks were thus freed of discipline on their note-issuing activities. The next years saw a massive lending boom fueled by a flood of state banknotes, leading first to inflation and then, inevitably, to a crash. In 1816 this unhappy experience caused the Congress to reverse itself and charter a second Bank of the United States, again with a head office in Philadelphia and again for 20 years.

The policies of the Second Bank attracted little notice under its initial presidents, the unremarkable William Jones and Langdon Cheves. This changed in 1823 when Cheves was succeeded by Nicholas Biddle. Biddle was exceptionally smart and knew it, having completed his studies at Princeton at the age of fifteen and being selected to deliver the valedictory address. His self-confidence was matched only by his commitment to federalism, which traced back to his Princeton days, and by his belief that a strong government needed a strong central bank.

As a young member of the Pennsylvania State Senate, Biddle had fought unsuccessfully to mobilize support for rechartering the First Bank. Now, as the president of the Second Bank, he expanded its operations. He increased its loans and investments. He enlarged its branch network and again used it to discipline other banks. And he made no secret of his contempt for his fellow bankers, most of whom did not measure up to his exalted standards.

This approach did not exactly smooth relations with the country's other financial institutions, whose owners complained to their elected representatives. Biddle sought to buy congressional support with campaign contributions and bribes, but these proved less effective than they might have been in softer hands.

In 1832, 4 years ahead of schedule and with Biddle's encouragement, the eventual Whig candidate for president, Henry Clay, introduced into the Senate a bill to recharter the Bank. When Clay's bill was passed by the Congress, the president, Andrew Jackson, promptly vetoed it. A Tennessean, Jackson was wedded to the increasingly anachronistic Jeffersonian ideal of an agrarian republic. He saw the Bank as favoring an elite circle of bankers and industrialists and favoring the Northeast over the South and West. Jackson was therefore quite happy to make his opposition to the Bank a central issue in his 1832 reelection campaign.

Biddle was confident, given what he took as the lessons of 1811–15, that the issue would be a winner for Clay. The voters, having shorter memories and being less enamored of the Bank's hard-money policies, proved him wrong. There was also the opposition of the New York financial community, which was not fond of an arrangement that made Philadelphia the seat of financial power. Once reelected, Jackson made clear that the Bank would be rechartered only over his dead body.

In 1836, its federal charter expiring, the second Bank of the United States took out a state charter and became the United States Bank of Pennsylvania. Biddle attempted to establish his state-chartered bank as a platform for building a market in bills of exchange in Philadelphia. But with no equivalent of the Bank of England to backstop the market, even a formidable state bank lacked the resources. Biddle attempted to secure a line of credit from the Bank of England for his operation but, not surprisingly, was rebuffed. At that point the 1836–37 financial crisis put an end to his plan.[22]

More than three-quarters of a century would pass before the United States again possessed a central bank. Among the consequences was an international monetary system in which the dollar played no role. For central banks and governments, sterling, not the dollar, was "as good as gold." Not just the French franc, German mark, Swiss franc, and Dutch guilder but even the Italian lira, Belgian franc, and Austrian shilling all ranked ahead of the dollar on the international pecking order on the eve of World War I, despite the fact that the United States was far and away the largest economy.[23] Sterling accounted for roughly half of all of the foreign exchange reserves of central banks and governments, the French franc 30 percent, the German mark 15 percent. In addition, small amounts of Dutch guilder and Swedish krona were held as foreign exchange reserves. But not dollars.

ENTER THE FED

After the 1907 financial crisis, concern over the instability of American finance fused with the desire to create a U.S. market in trade credits. The 1907 panic was caused, the experts explained, by the fact that financial transactions in New York were nothing more than stock market speculation, as opposed to the kind of wholesome investments backed by import and export business that dominated in London. Then there was the fact that, in the absence of a central bank, the major financial institutions had been forced to rely on Wall Street's dominant figure, the supremely confident and supremely rich J. Pierpont Morgan, to organize a rescue. This was not entirely reassuring, since it was unclear whether Morgan or someone like him would be there the next time crisis struck.

This pointed to the need for a permanent mechanism for managing monetary problems. To investigate solutions, a National Monetary Commission was set up in 1908. It included eighteen members of Congress under the chairmanship of the brusque and intimidating senior senator from Rhode Island, Nelson Aldrich. Although descended from an old New England family (his forbearers included John Winthrop and Roger Williams), Aldrich's parents were not rich; he married money rather than inheriting it. Politically, he worked his way up, starting with the Providence City Council. Economically, he put his wife's money to work by investing in the Providence street railway system. (The two endeavors were clearly not unrelated.) From city council Aldrich moved to the Rhode Island House of Representatives, the U.S. House, and finally, in 1881, the Senate.

By 1910 Aldrich had been in the Senate for close to 30 years. Having risen to the chairmanship of the Finance Committee, he was used to getting his way and not much inclined to defer to his senatorial colleagues. A conservative Republican, he had previously concentrated on securing tariff protection for U.S. manufacturing. But the 1907 crisis convinced Aldrich of the need for a stronger monetary framework, much as the monetary turmoil experienced by the new nation had convinced Hamilton of the need for the Bank of the United States.

The question was what kind of monetary framework. As head of the investigatory commission, Aldrich hired advisors. He consulted experts. He led a mission to Europe to study arrangements there. The trip convinced him of the need for a European-style money market backed by a central bank. The upshot was the Aldrich Plan, proposing the creation of a National Reserve Association at whose center would be a central bank with the power to influence financial conditions and lend to banks in distress.

The author of the Aldrich Plan's technical provisions, who was to play an important role in the dollar's subsequent rise to international prominence, was the German-born financier Paul Warburg. Warburg had started his career working for Simon Hauer, an importer and exporter in Hamburg. After further seasoning working for bankers in London and Paris, he moved to the family banking firm of M.M. Warburg and Company.

Warburg was thus intimately familiar with the mechanics of international finance. He was also connected with the higher echelons of American banking. At the end of a round-the-world tour in 1892, he had met the charming and talented Nina Loeb, who just happened to be the daughter of one of the founders of the prominent New York bank Kuhn, Loeb and Co. One thing led to another, and the two were married in 1895. After 7 years in Hamburg, the couple relocated to New York, and Warburg took up a position with his father-in-law's firm. It was on a visit to Kuhn, Loeb in preparation for his mission to Europe that Aldrich encountered Warburg, who seemed uniquely well informed about European finance. By this time Warburg had become a proponent of an American central bank to support the development of a market in trade acceptances. He in turn was impressed by broad-shouldered Aldrich, who he took as the embodiment of monetary reform. Warburg began writing Aldrich about his ideas. Again, one thing led to another.[24]

Shy and self-effacing, Warburg preferred working out of the public eye. With a thick German accent, he was not a natural public speaker. But the 1907 financial crisis made him a man with a mission. By the end of the year, he was publishing in the *New York Times* on the need for a European-style central bank to stabilize American financial markets. He was not deterred by letters abusing him for his "un-American views." By 1908 he was giving speeches on financial crises. He was soon testifying before Congress and serving as head of the National Citizens' League for the Promotion of Sound Banking, a lobby for monetary reform.

In November 1910, Warburg and Aldrich, together with A. Piatt Andrew, assistant secretary of the treasury and a former assistant professor at Harvard who had served as special assistant to Aldrich's monetary commission, and three Wall Street titans—Benjamin Strong, head of Bankers Trust; Frank Vanderlip, a onetime financial journalist and former assistant secretary of the treasury newly appointed as president of National City Bank, the largest bank in the country; and Henry Davison, senior partner and in-house fixer at J.P. Morgan & Company—snuck off to Jeckyll Island off the Georgia coast to draft a blueprint for a central bank.[25] That Andrew's participation was not known even to his boss, Secretary of the Treasury Franklin MacVeagh, testifies to the boldness of the expedition. J. P. Morgan himself had regularly taken hunting vacations on Jeckyll Island, explaining the venue. The six conspirators traveled by private railcar, disguised as duck hunters, to prevent their movements from being traced. To avoid having their identities learned by porters, Vanderlip and Davison adopted the further artifice of referring to one another as Orville and Wilber.

After the New Year, the Jeckyll Island blueprint was announced as the Aldrich Plan. To reassure those fearful of overweening government control, it proposed a more decentralized central banking structure than existed in Europe. It described a National Reserve Association with fifteen regional branches, each with the authority to discount trade acceptances. To ensure what the plan's authors saw as proper democratic control, it recommended that their directors be elected by the commercial banks associated with each individual branch.

This was not obviously enough to surmount deep-seated popular and congressional concern over concentrated financial power. The notion that small business and the farmer were exploited by big finance still resonated power-fully, as in the days of Andrew Jackson. Attaching Aldrich's name to the plan also had the unfortunate consequence of exciting those suspicious of a Wall Street money trust. Aldrich's daughter, Abby, had married John D. Rockefeller Jr., only son of the oil magnate John D. Rockefeller, the single richest person in the country, causing Aldrich to be widely viewed as Rockefeller's mouthpiece. The governor of New Jersey and presidential hopeful Woodrow Wilson explained that, while had not read the Aldrich Plan, he disliked anything bearing the senator's name.

Then there was the fact that Frank Vanderlip, another member of the Jeckyll Island traveling party, had already begun to position the institution he headed, National City Bank (forerunner of today's Citigroup), to capitalize on the opportunities created by monetary reform. Vanderlip established the National City Company, a holding-company affiliate, to buy up state banks and trust companies and engage in activities prohibited of a national bank. The prospect of a megabank monopoly excited not just local bankers but also farmers and businessmen long suspicious of big finance. Congressman Charles A. Lindbergh Sr. of Minnesota, a leading critic of the financial establishment, member of the House Committee on Banking and Currency, and father of the famous aviator, introduced a resolution to investigate the money trust. "Wall Street brought on the 1907 panic," Lindbergh thundered, and "got people to demand currency reform . . . and, if it dares, [it] will produce another panic to pass the Aldrich central bank plan. We need reform, but not at the hands of Wall Street."[26] Lindbergh had grown up on the Minnesota frontier in the hey-day of the Populist revolt against extortionate bankers and railroads. He was, it can be fairly said, obsessed with the money trust. Lindbergh was reported to have read all of the dozen-plus studies published by Aldrich's National Mone-tary Commission cover to cover and still found time to pen his own 318-page study of monetary reform.[27]

It took the better part of 2 years for something resembling the Aldrich Plan to wend its way through the Congress. To quiet the critics and satisfy him-self, the bill signed by President Woodrow Wilson provided for a system of regional reserve banks with locally appointed boards, not unlike that in Aldrich's plan, but supervised by a Federal Reserve Board whose seven members would be selected by the president and not by the bankers.

Lindbergh was not impressed. "This act establishes the most gigantic trust on earth," he railed. "When the president signs this bill, the invisible government by the Monetary Power will be legalized. The people may not know it immediately, but the day of reckoning is only a few years removed." That day came, of course, in 1929, although it did not take exactly the form that Lindbergh had in mind.

ACCEPT YOURSELF

The mandate of the new central bank was to provide an "elastic currency." It was to regulate the supply of credit to prevent disruptive interest rate spikes and market seizures like those of 1907. Among its techniques would be purchasing trade acceptances, the studies of the National Monetary Commission having shown that this was how the Bank of England smoothed rates.

Buying trade acceptances denominated in dollars assumed, of course, a supply of dollar-denominated trade acceptances to be bought. Providing them required American banks to go abroad. The Federal Reserve Act therefore authorized national banks with capital of at least $1 million to establish branches in foreign countries.[28] It allowed them to purchase trade acceptances up to a limit of 50 percent of their own funds.

How did this market get up and running, given the cost and reputational advantages possessed by London? The difference now was not just the Federal Reserve Act but also World War I. The war saw a dramatic expansion of U.S. export trade, as America became factory and grainery to the world. American multinationals established operations in Latin America and Asia. The United States was transformed from debtor to creditor nation.

The war also disrupted the provision of trade credit in Europe. As governments mobilized for war, capital for trade finance grew scarce. German and British banks turned to New York to accept endorsed bills for their clients' imports not just from North American but from Latin America and Asia as well. The credit they received was denominated in dollars because this was the currency with which the New York banks were familiar.

But this was not the only reason. Starting in 1915 sterling's value in terms of gold, still the standard measuring rod, oscillated violently. Contracting today for future payment in a currency whose value was uncertain was unappealing.

It was especially unappealing given the existence of an alternative, the dollar, still firmly pegged to gold. Not just American traders but also Brazilian exporters of coffee, and more generally importers and exporters throughout Latin America and Asia, concluded that the dollar was the more attractive unit in which to do business.

American banks, free now to deal in acceptances, scrambled to attract this business. The always expansion-minded National City Bank set up a Foreign Trade Department to provide exporters with information on the foreign demand for U.S. products and the creditworthiness of customers, packaging this advice with its financial services. National City was soon extending some $20 million of trade acceptances annually.[29]

In January 1916, with American support, the British government succeeded in pegging sterling to the dollar.[30] But even if the British authorities succeeded in stabilizing sterling for the moment, this did not create confidence that it would remain stable, given massive wartime budget deficits and the rapid rise of British prices. Predictably, the pound began falling when American support was withdrawn at the end of the war. Within a year it had lost a third of its value, more even than when Napoleon returned from Elba in 1815. All the while the dollar remained pegged to gold. It was not surprising that American importers and exporters saw the dollar as the more attractive unit in which to do business. And what was true of merchants and traders in the United States was true of those in other countries.

National City Bank under Frank Vanderlip was again in the vanguard of U.S. banks expanding abroad. Possessing a former financial journalist's mindfulness of the power of publicity, Vanderlip moved quickly to advertize his bank's ambitions. Immediately upon passage of the Federal Reserve Act, he had a questionnaire sent to 5,000 American firms soliciting their views on which foreign markets would benefit from the presence of a National City branch. The Du Pont Company, which, sensing the wartime demand for munitions, had opened a nitrate factory in Chile, replied that it was desirous of South American branches. National City set up a branch in Argentina followed by others in Brazil, Chile, and Cuba. In 1915 it acquired the International Banking Corporation, which it used to set up branches across Europe and Asia. Where the bank did not establish branches outright, it sent representatives to gather market intelligence and solicit business.

Other U.S. banks followed National City into the fray. By the end of 1920, American banking institutions operated 181 branches abroad.[31] Of those 181 branches, 100 were foreign offices of seven banks doing regular banking business in the United States, and 29 of those 100 branches were foreign offices of National City Bank or its subsidiary, the International Banking Corporation.[32]

These American banks operating in other countries encouraged importers there to accept drafts in dollars drawn on them by American exporters. Foreigners exporting to the United States could similarly draw in dollars on a U.S. bank instead of drawing drafts in London. Thus, it was not just U.S. importers and exporters who made use of the new acceptance market in New York but also foreign merchants linked to it by the foreign branches of American banks.

In Strong Hands

But the growth of the acceptance market in New York and its progeny, the international use of the dollar, entailed more than the miracle of the market. American banks were not yet capable of building a dollar acceptance market. Their costs were still too high, reflecting a dearth of other investors to whom to sell their acceptances. In their absence, banks were forced to hold the acceptances they originated on their own balance sheets. Doing so was expensive, since the yield to maturity on this paper was often less than what the banks themselves had to pay when borrowing money.

The obstacle was the lack of familiarity of investors with the asset class. And familiarizing them took time. As explained by the new industry's advocate, the American Acceptance Council (another Paul Warburg creation), the investor "would have to be educated, first as to the nature of a bankers' acceptance, second as to its attractiveness as an investment, and third, owing to its quality as a doubly secured risk [that it was guaranteed both by the original issuer and the accepting bank], that it would be offered at a lower rate than he had been accustomed to, when buying the best single name commercial paper."[33] Until this was done, dollar acceptance business would remain stunted.

Rather than relying on the invisible hand, the entirely visible hand of Benjamin Strong, now governor of the Federal Reserve Bank of New York, took hold of this problem. In the Hamiltonian tradition, Strong believed in the need for central control of financial affairs. His great-grandfather, also named Benjamin, had served as Alexander Hamilton's first clerk in the Treasury. The great-grandson grew up in modest circumstances. His father superintended a section of the New York Central Railroad, and Strong himself chose to forego college for financial reasons. Starting as a clerk (and for that purpose taking a remedial penmanship course to correct his borderline-illegible handwriting), Strong rose through the financial ranks before being tapped by Henry Davison, a country club acquaintance, to work for the newly formed Bankers Trust Company. When during the 1907 financial crisis J. P. Morgan organized the New York banks to rescue their weaker brethren, Morgan turned to Davison to manage the effort, and Davison turned to Strong. Strong's involvement in those 1907 rescue efforts made him an energetic advocate of financial reform and put him on the road to Jeckyll Island.

Like Warburg, who had helped recruit him to the governorship of the New York Fed, Strong saw the need for a trade acceptance market to stabilize America's finances. Fostering a market in actual merchandise transactions, as opposed to financial speculation, would help to prevent a recurrence of 1907-style financial excesses, he believed. As governor of the New York Fed, Strong also appreciated that the existence of a market in trade acceptances gave the Bank of England a handle with which to manage credit conditions. He saw development of this market as enhancing the competitiveness of American industry and expanding the country's foreign trade. He saw all this as a project that the Federal Reserve System should support.

Following Strong's lead, the Federal Reserve Board therefore instructed the system's regional branches to purchase acceptances for their own account.[34] The reserve banks purchased acceptances to stabilize and reduce discount rates, and the favorable behavior of discount rates in turn encouraged the growth of the market. In the first half of the 1920s the Federal Reserve Banks were the dealers' dominant counterparty. In addition, a few other knowledgeable investors were attracted to the market. The main ones were foreign banks, including foreign central banks, with large surplus balances in the United States for whom acceptances quickly became a favored investment. The July 1919 issue of the *Federal Reserve Bulletin* noted that most of the $10 million acquired by the Dutch Central Bank on behalf of Dutch sellers of flower bulbs and diamonds purchased by Americans in Holland was invested in bank acceptances.

Slowly dealers specializing in acceptance business appeared on the scene. The largest of them, the International Acceptance Bank, had as its chairman none other than one Paul M. Warburg. Warburg's motivation for launching IAB was to finance German grain imports and help rebuild Germany's war-torn economy. IAB was also a way for Warburg to help his brother Max, who still ran the family firm in Hamburg. IAB would work hand in glove with M. M. Warburg, giving the latter much-needed business in the straitened circumstances of the 1920s.[35] Slowly but surely other banks also created subsidiaries to purchase and sell acceptances and market them to retail investors.

Debut of the Dollar

The growth of this market in trade acceptances finally allowed the dollar to assume a meaningful international role. By the second half of the 1920s more than half of all U.S. imports and exports were financed by bank acceptances denominated in dollars.[36] The attractiveness of doing business in New York reflected the fact that the interest rate that importers and exporters had to pay was now as much as a full percentage point lower than in London. Not just those buying and selling goods to the United States but also merchants engaged in trade with other countries flocked to New York. By the end of the 1920s the value of dollar acceptances issued to finance trade between third countries, together with those backed by goods warehoused in foreign countries, approached that of acceptances issued to finance imports into the United States itself.

This trend was part of the growing importance of the United States in international transactions generally. Europe having been devastated by the war, the resource requirements of postwar reconstruction were immense. It followed that the continent looked abroad for finance. A United States flush with funds was the obvious place to look. To governments for whom this was not obvious, Strong drove home the point. He traveled to Europe to negotiate loans. From Poland to Romania he sent emissaries like the Princeton University money doctor Edwin Kemmerer to encourage countries to contract loans in the United States.

In doing so Strong competed with Montagu Norman, his counterpart at the Bank of England, who urged countries to seek assistance for financial stabilization not in the United States but through the League of Nations—of which the United States conveniently was not a member. A League loan in London might help a country stabilize its currency, but it would also encourage it to contract for further borrowing there. Negotiating bilaterally with the United States, in contrast, would lead to borrowing in New York. Although the two men were outwardly very different—where Strong was handsome and self-confident, Norman had the pinched features of a hypochondriac—they were friends and even vacationed together. Strong famously kept interest rates low in 1924–25 to support Norman's effort to return sterling to the gold standard. But if allied in other causes, they were rivals in this one. Strong used all his leverage to encourage countries to arrange their stabilization loans in New York.

All through the 1920s capital flowed from the United States, where it was abundant, to Europe, where it was scarce. American banks arranged bond issues for European governments and corporations, denominating them in dollars so they could be marketed to American investors. They opened store-fronts to pitch them to retail customers.

This high-pressure salesmanship should have been a warning. As inexperienced U.S. financial institutions rushed into the field, they extended increasingly dubious loans. One is reminded of the scramble of regional banks in the later stages of the boom into the subprime mortgage market. The title of Ilse Mintz's study *Deterioration in the Quality of Foreign Bonds Issued in the United States, 1920–1930* tells the tale.[37] Inexperienced U.S. banks enthusiastically underwrote, and their clients enthusiastically subscribed, bonds issued on behalf of German cities for the construction of municipal swimming pools, a form of liquidity that did not directly enhance the capacity to repay. Eighty years later American borrowers got even by selling German banks collateralized debt obligations backed by those same subprime loans.

Lending in Latin America by new entrants like the Chase Securities Company fared little better. A loan to Cuba for a highway spanning the island foundered on the inability of the contractors to complete more than isolated segments of pavement. It didn't help that, for political reasons, the government felt compelled to commence construction of separate segments in all five provinces. Investors were in the dark about the fact that the son-in-law of the Cuban president had been hired by the Cuban branch of the American bank during the period that the bank in question competed for the privilege of lending to the Cuban government.

When at the end of the 1920s new money to service old debts stopped flowing, the Ponzi-like nature of the scheme was revealed. The majority of the foreign bonds underwritten by American banks lapsed into default.

But these were problems for later. For now the main impact of these flows was to enhance the international role of the dollar. Before the war, the dollar exchange rate had been quoted in fewer financial centers than minor currencies like the Italian lira and the Austrian shilling. Now it was quoted more frequently than all rivals. By the second half of the 1920s, foreign acceptances in dollars exceeded foreign acceptances in sterling by a factor of two to one. By 1924 the dollar accounted for a larger share than the pound of the foreign exchange reserves of central banks and governments.

Incumbency is thought to be a powerful advantage in international currency competition. It is blithely asserted that another quarter of a century, until after World War II, had to pass before the dollar displaced sterling as the dominant international unit. But this supposed fact is not, in fact, a fact. From a standing start in 1914, the dollar had already overtaken sterling by 1925. This should be taken as a caution by those inclined to argue that incumbency gives the dollar formidable advantages today.

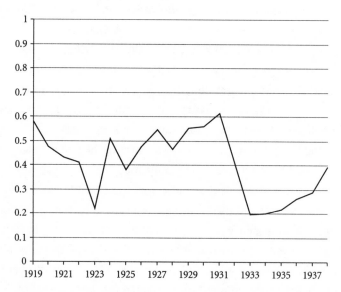

Figure 2.1. Fraction of Total Reserves Held in Dollars.
Source: Computed from data used in Eichengreen and Flandreau (2009).

To be sure, it took an exceptional shock, World War I, and the market-making efforts of the Fed to effect this changing of the guard. Still, it is not impossible to imagine something analogous today. For the wartime shock to sterling, substitute chronic U.S. budget deficits. And for the efforts of the Fed to establish a market in trade acceptances in New York, substitute the efforts of Chinese officials to establish Shanghai as an international financial center. The renminbi replacing the dollar may not be anyone's baseline scenario, but it is worth recalling the history of the 1920s before dismissing the possibility.

IT ALL COMES CRASHING DOWN

The financial flowering of the dollar, however, soon was all for naught. The Roaring Twenties gave way to the Great Depression. This mother of all depressions was global. It affected every country. One of its most destructive impacts was on international transactions. And with the decline in international transactions came a decline in the international role of the dollar.

Trade was bound to contract with so vicious a fall in output and spending. But this was not all: seeing spending collapse, governments slapped on tariffs and quotas in a desperate effort to bottle up the remaining demand. Not knowing what else to do, they used trade policy to shift spending toward domestically produced goods. In the United States, farmers who had endured depressed crop prices now allied with light industry along the Eastern Seaboard to push the Smoot-Hawley tariff through Congress. In the UK, the influential economist John Maynard Keynes had trumpeted the advantages of globalization in his 1919 best-seller, *The Economic Consequences of the Peace*. In 1931, seeing no alternative, he advised the British government to impose an across-the-board tariff in a last-ditch effort to boost spending on domestic goods. The result was the General Tariff of 1932.[38] Germany followed with an "equalizing tariff." The Netherlands abandoned its traditional free trade policy, raising import duties by 25 percent. And so on. Whereas global production of primary products and manufactures fell by 20 percent between 1929 and 1932, the volume of international trade fell by fully 36 percent.[39] There was correspondingly less demand for dollars to finance and settle trade.

The implosion of long-term foreign lending was even more dramatic. New long-term foreign loans by U.S. investors, having peaked at $1.2 billion annually in 1927 and 1928, fell to less than $200 million in 1931 and a scant $700,000 in 1932.[40] And since the dollars on which foreigners relied to purchase U.S. imports were no longer available, the tendency to hold balances in New York to service such obligations declined commensurately.

What made the Great Depression great, of course, was that it was allowed to destabilize banking systems. Banks that had extended loans not just to foreign governments and corporations but also to American firms, farmers, and municipalities now saw these investments go bad. As bank balance sheets deteriorated, depositors scrambled to withdraw their funds. A first wave of bank runs erupted in the final months of 1930. Most of the affected banks had links to the Nashville-based investment firm Caldwell and Company, which controlled the largest chain of banks in the South. These banks were all owned by Caldwell and Company itself or one of its affiliates, or else they were owned and operated by individuals with personal ties to the founder, Rogers Caldwell. Caldwell was the Michael Milken of his day, having established his firm in 1917 at the tender age of twenty-seven to underwrite the junk bonds of southern municipalities and sell them to retail investors.[41] His father, James Caldwell, had come to Nashville in 1870, where he went to work for a wholesale grocery. Finding himself one day unable to complete an order for millet seed (seed used to raise hay for horses), James had bought up the entire supply in the city, cornering the market and doubling his investment. From there it was a small step into insurance and banking. The son similarly moved into banking, and his operations were similarly dubious. Often the main and, indeed, only customers of Caldwell's banks were the same municipalities whose bonds Caldwell and Company underwrote and sold onward. When those municipalities experienced financial distress in 1930, so did Caldwell's banks.

But had it not been Caldwell it would have been someone else. The deterioration of economic conditions made banking problems inevitable. By 1931 there were bank runs in all parts of the United States. Nor was the problem limited to America: banking panics erupted in Argentina, Mexico, Austria, Belgium, France, Germany, Hungary, Romania, the Baltic states, Egypt, Turkey, and the UK. Where there were banks, there were panics. Scarcely a part of the world was immune.

In some cases these crises were compounded by the failure of the authorities to act, but in others they were worsened by the very fact that authorities did act. When officials provided banks with emergency assistance, as in Britain, they signaled that they attached higher priority to stabilizing the financial system than stabilizing the currency. British banks, under pressure from their new American competitors, had provided credit to German exporters on concessional terms. As the financial crisis now spread to Germany, Berlin froze repayments. This punched a hole in the balance sheets of the London banks and, as well, in Britain's balance of payments. Under other circumstances the Bank of England would have responded to the resulting gold losses by raising interest rates to attract capital from abroad. But it understood that higher rates would make funding their operations more expensive for the banks. So the Bank of England resisted the temptation to tighten. Some observers ascribed the Bank's failure to defend sterling to the fact that the governor, Montagu Norman, was indisposed. Exhausted by the crisis, he had sailed off for a Canadian holiday. In fact, however, Norman's seconds at the Bank knew exactly what they were doing. They were consciously choosing the stability of the banks over the stability of sterling.

Investors monitoring the Bank of England had no trouble seeing that currency depreciation was coming. Their self-preservation instincts kicking in, they scrambled to get their money out of the country before sterling's depreciation eroded the value of their claims. They converted their funds into foreign currency and redeposited them abroad.

Still the Bank of England stuck with its strategy, which was to do nothing. Aside from two small increases in the second half of July, it resisted the pressure to raise interest rates to defend the exchange rate. The decision to abandon the gold standard and allow the pound to depreciate followed, unavoidably, on September 20.

Not everyone was pleased. British tourists disembarking in Manhattan from the White Star Line's S.S. *Homeric* were shocked by how few dollars their pounds could buy. "A pound is still a pound in England," huffed one. "I shall carry my pounds home with me! A bit high this, something of a holdup, what?"[42] The response of industry, in contrast, was distinctively positive. "Bryan was right," as Clark H. Minor, the UK-based president of International General Electric, summarized the lesson, referring to William Jennings Bryan's campaign against gold. Minor was not the only one to draw the link; before long, the British Isles were engulfed in a "Britain for Bryan" boom.

Dollar Backlash

Sterling's devaluation raised questions about whether the dollar was secure, shifting financial pressure to New York. Not just private investors but central banks, with France, Belgium, Switzerland, Sweden, and the Netherlands in the vanguard, rushed to convert their dollars into gold before the moment passed. Conversions started on September 21, the first business day after sterling's devaluation. After waiting two weeks, the New York Fed raised its discount rate by a full percentage point to defend the dollar. A week later it raised the discount rate a second time, again by a full percentage point.

This was the sharpest increase in rates in such a short period in the history of the Federal Reserve. Not for 47 years, until 1978 and another episode of pronounced dollar weakness, would the Fed again raise rates so far so fast. Although the dollar exchange rate was stabilized by its aggressive action, the same cannot be said of the banking system. In October alone, 500 banks failed. In the six months from August 1931, nearly 2,000 went under. Such are the effects of raising interest rates in a financial crisis.

With the Fed stoutly defending the dollar, the pound/dollar exchange rate fell from $4.86 to $3.75 in a week. By December 1931 it had reached $3.25. Expensive British exports now became cheap. From $3.25, speculators concluded, the sterling exchange rate could only go up. Accordingly, it mounted a modest recovery. Freed to support the economy, the Bank of England could cut its discount rate to 2 percent, inaugurating the policy known as "cheap money." Ultimately this was the same escape route chosen by other countries, starting with Britain's Commonwealth and other trade partners, followed by the United States, which abandoned the gold standard in 1933, and concluding with France, Belgium, the Netherlands, and Switzerland, all members of the "gold bloc," so named because they continued against all odds to cling to the gold standard before finally abandoning it in 1935–36.

With less trade, less foreign borrowing, and less commitment to defending exchange rates, there was less need for central banks to hold foreign currencies. When governments and central banks sought to influence market outcomes, they were now more likely to do so by tightening controls than by buying and selling foreign exchange. This change in strategy permitted them to drastically reduce their foreign currency holdings. Prior to Britain abandoning gold, the National Bank of Belgium, which held reserves in London, had asked the Bank of England whether there was a danger that sterling might be devalued. The Bank of England had responded that this step was out of the question. Having been burned, the National Bank of Belgium now sold off not just its sterling but also, just in case, its dollars. The Bank of France and others followed suit.

Although the importance of both the dollar and the pound as reserve currencies was diminished by the crisis, the sale of foreign currencies by central banks was disproportionately a sale of dollars. By the end of 1931, dollars accounted for 40 percent of remaining foreign exchange reserves worldwide, but sterling nearly 50 percent.[43] This result might seem peculiar, given that the Fed was defending the dollar while the Bank of England was not doing likewise for sterling. But the U.S. depression was deeper and longer. The British economy began recovering in early 1932, but it took another year for activity to bottom out in the United States. The collapse in U.S. trade being even more severe, the volume of acceptance business fell off even more dramatically in New York.

That said, the single most important reason that sterling temporarily regained its lead as an international currency was the practice of the members of the Commonwealth and Empire of holding their reserves in London. For Commonwealth countries like Australia and New Zealand, doing so was more than a matter of economic logic. It was a demonstration of political solidarity. For the Empire it was not even a choice. The colonies did what they were told by the Foreign or Colonial Office. Because the United States lacked the same imperial prerogatives, the dollar did not enjoy the same support.

But with international transactions of all kinds depressed for the balance of the 1930s and with politics dominating economics, it was easy to miss that a changing of the guard had already taken place. It was easy to overlook that the dollar had overtaken sterling as the leading international currency. For anyone uncertain about the situation, however, World War II would clarify it soon enough.

CHAPTER 3

DOMINANCE

For a quarter of a century after World War II, the dollar reigned supreme. Only the United States emerged strengthened from the war. Its economy towered over the world like none other. It accounted for fully half of global industrial production.[1] Only its currency was freely traded.

As a result, barely two decades after its debut as an international currency the dollar was the dominant unit in which prices were quoted, trade was invoiced, and transactions were settled worldwide. For foreign central banks and governments the dollar was as good as gold, since the United States stood ready to sell gold at a fixed price of $35 an ounce.[2] The Articles of Agreement of the International Monetary Fund, the newly created steward of the international system, acknowledged the currency's unique status by authorizing countries to define their exchange rates in dollars. Other potential issuers of international currencies lacked either open financial markets, like Germany, or financial stability, like France. The UK lacked both. The dollar was not just the dominant international currency but, outside the British Commonwealth and Empire, effectively the only one.

Central banks still had the option of accumulating gold, but the supply of newly mined gold was limited. There was also the uncomfortable fact that since the Soviet Union and South Africa were the main producers, purchasing gold effectively subsidized two unsavory regimes.

These facts placed the dollar and the United States in a unique position. American consumers and investors could acquire foreign goods and companies without their government having to worry that the dollars used in their purchases would be presented for conversion into gold. Instead those dollars were hoarded by central banks, for which they were the only significant source of additional international reserves. America was able to run a balance-of-payments deficit "without tears," in the words of the French economist Jacques Rueff. This ability to purchase foreign goods and companies using resources conjured out of thin air was the exorbitant privilege of which French Finance Minister Valéry Giscard d'Estaing so vociferously complained.

STERLING HANGOVER

For reasons of history if nothing else, the pound remained the dollar's principal rival. The Commonwealth, Empire, and other members of the sterling area had given the UK an unlimited credit line during the war.[3] They supplied Britain and its army with resources and war matériel, taking British treasury notes as IOUs. Britain and its allies meanwhile ran down their dollar reserves to procure supplies from the United States. By the end of the war the accumulated sterling balances of central banks and governments thus exceeded their dollar balances by a factor of two to one.[4]

Superficially this created the impression that the pound was still the leading reserve currency. But two-thirds of overseas financial claims on the UK were in the hands of that small part of the world that comprised the sterling area.[5] Most of its members had accumulated sterling for wartime reasons. They maintained it now only because the controls imposed by Britain prevented them from exchanging it for goods or more useful currencies.

It was widely understood that holding sterling was a losing proposition. In the halcyon days before 1914, Britain's assets abroad had greatly exceeded its liabilities. There had been no question about the stability of sterling or the security of foreigners' investments. But now the country's net external sterling liabilities, at $15 billion, were nearly six times its gold and foreign currency holdings.

If foreigners were allowed to freely sell their claims on Britain, their value would drop like a stone. This danger became acute in 1946 when the United

States made the removal of Britain's currency controls a precondition for extending a loan for British reconstruction. This was the one great wartime failure of John Maynard Keynes. This greatest of British economists had served H.M. Treasury in a variety of wartime capacities and led negotiations with the Americans over the structure of the postwar international monetary system. Supremely self-confident, he believed that the U.S. government would provide its ally with a postwar loan free of onerous conditions once it heard his compelling arguments. Instead, the Americans demanded that Britain remove its controls. Doing so, they believed, would expand the market for U.S. exports.[6] For them the resumption of normal peacetime international financial relations was overdue.

Keynes's failure to head off this demand reflected his limited understanding of American politics. In the British system, a government with a parliamentary majority could do pretty much as it pleased. An enlightened Roosevelt-Truman administration, Keynes reasoned, could similarly push through its chosen policies, enjoying as it did a majority in both houses of Congress. He failed to reckon with the independence of American legislators or their isolationist tendencies. The further one moved from the Eastern Seaboard, the less Americans and their congressional representatives valued their supposed special relationship with Britain. When the administration pushed for concessions for the British, the Congress pushed back.

Keynes's failure to negotiate better terms may have also reflected his weakened physical state. He was suffering from a bacterial heart infection that subjected him to increasingly serious heart attacks. He tired easily and was frequently incapacitated. That the UK continued to rely on him to represent its interests, despite these problems, testifies to his singular intellectual capacity and stature.

The precise requirement laid down by the Americans was that all sterling now earned by foreigners should be freely usable in merchandise transactions within a year of the loan's approval by the Congress. When current account convertibility, as this condition was known, was duly restored on July 15, 1947, residents of other countries rushed to convert sterling into dollars to purchase American goods.[7] Britain's reserve losses in the first month exceeded $1 billion. For a country with less than $2.5 billion of gold and foreign exchange, the position was untenable. Anthony Eden, deputy leader of the Conservatives, likened it to "doing the splits over an ever-widening abyss."

With no choice, Britain slapped controls back on after just five weeks. So much for the idea that a convertible pound sterling might again play a leading international role.

British policymakers became understandably shy about current account convertibility. Not until 1959 would they try again. When 1959 arrived, sterling balances, still mainly in the hands of the Commonwealth and Empire, remained at the same level as a decade earlier. Dollar reserves, meanwhile, had more than tripled.[8] It was clear which currency countries wanted when they accumulated reserves. It was not the currency of Europe's sick man.

BATTLE OF ALGIERS

Nor were there other attractive options. The franc had once been an important reserve currency, but it never recovered from the political and financial chaos through which France suffered after World War I. France now also had its quagmire in Algeria. The aftermath of World War II saw bloody independence struggles around the world, but the Algerian conflict was especially violent. The Algerian National Liberation Front fought not just the French army but the rival Algerian National Movement. The army, under attack at home and abroad, split into two factions, with members of one plotting to overthrow the French government. There were massacres of civilians. Cafes in Paris were bombed. Torture was used to extract information from political prisoners.[9] Meanwhile successive French governments, each weaker than the last, vacillated.

The culmination in the spring of 1958 was a political crisis in which a cabal of dissident army officers seized control of Algeria to prevent it from being abandoned by an indecisive Paris. Paratroopers from the Algerian corps then landed in Corsica, taking over the island on May 24. They planned next to seize Paris and replace the government with one more firmly committed to control of Algeria. Their generals sent out the coded message to prepare for the invasion. ("The carrots are cooked. The carrots are cooked.") In Paris, the embattled government uncoiled rolls of barbed wire on the airfields to prevent the paratroops from landing. The public was not reassured.

Seeing their support dissolving, the leaders of the Fourth Republic agreed that the war hero, Charles de Gaulle, should be recalled to power. Only de Gaulle had the authority to put down the rebellion. His personal prestige was greater than that of "any Frenchman since Napoleon," one expert observed. (Certainly this was de Gaulle's own view.) The great man returned to Paris from his home village of Colombey-les-deux-églises. Granted emergency powers for six months, he brought the army into line.

This political crisis was also a financial crisis. The cost of the war was enormous, and the French central bank was forced to directly finance the government's budget deficit. Already in 1955–1957 the Bank of France had lost two-thirds of its reserves. The finance ministry responded by tightening import licensing requirements, restricting purchases of foreign securities, and limiting the amount of currency that residents could carry when traveling abroad.

These measures to bottle up the pressure proved inadequate, what with the Bank of France continuously pumping additional money into circulation to finance the budget deficit. On August 12, 1957, the government was forced to devalue. The country's militant trade unions, seeing the purchasing power of their earnings eroded, were not pleased. Buying them off required sharp wage increases, which dissipated the hoped-for improvement in competitiveness.[10] The first devaluation having failed, a second one, this time by 17 percent, followed in barely a year. To minimize embarrassment, de Gaulle waited until the end of December and after the presidential elections, in which he won 78 percent of the electoral college.

This second devaluation, being accompanied by budget-balancing measures, restored external balance.[11] But serial devaluation was not the behavior of a major power. It was not the behavior of a grand general. De Gaulle was imperious and preoccupied by the glory of France, not to mention his own glory. Presiding over the December devaluation rankled. That the French president subsequently became preoccupied with dethroning the dollar no doubt reflected his memories of this demoralizing episode.

Reluctant Powers

Germany was the one European country with a history as a reserve center and no significant balance-of-payments problems.[12] But memories of the first half of the 1920s, when it had experienced one of the most extreme hyperinflations in recorded history, were still fresh. German officials reacted now in almost Pavlovian fashion to the least whiff of inflation.

The problem was that each time the Bundesbank, West Germany's newly established central bank, tightened monetary policy with the goal of curbing inflation, its higher interest rates attracted capital from abroad, loosening credit conditions and reigniting inflation fears. To limit inflows, Germany therefore maintained restrictions on purchases of money market instruments by nonresidents.[13] Even had foreigners wished to use the deutschmark for international transactions, in other words, they would have been frustrated. Germany relaxed some of its controls in the late 1950s and 1960s but tightened them again in April 1970 and May 1971 in response to renewed capital inflows. None of this made the country an attractive place for foreigners to do financial business.

There was also the absence of competition from rising powers. In the third quarter of the twentieth century, Japan resembled today's China, an Asian nation growing three times as fast as the United States. By the 1970s it had become the second largest economy in the world, such being the miracle of compound interest. But the yen then, like the renminbi now, played essentially no international role. Neighboring Asia, where Japan sourced materials and sold manufactures, was an obvious place where the yen might have been used to quote prices, settle transactions, and serve as international reserves. But memories of Japanese colonialism and wartime brutality had not faded. Relying on the yen would have sat uneasily with the neighbors. It did not help that the most important of them, Mao's China, was cut off commercially and financially from the outside world.

And even had there been a desire to use the yen in international transactions, Japanese policymakers would have discouraged the practice. Their priority was export-led growth. They fostered export-oriented manufacturing using a hypercompetitive exchange rate and a battery of tax breaks and subsidies. They enlisted the Export-Import Bank of Japan and the Japan Development Bank, together with their influence over other financial institutions, to channel cheap investment finance to export industries.

Internationalizing the yen would have undermined those policies. Had banks been free to take money out of the country, they could have evaded government direction to lend to domestic producers at artificially low rates. Japanese financial markets had to be placed in an airtight compartment sealed off from the rest of the world. Allowing foreigners to invest in the country, as needed for reserve-currency status, would have subverted the industrial-policy strategy of the Ministry of International Trade and Industry (MITI). And allowing a foreign demand for yen to develop would have put upward pressure on the exchange rate, negating undervaluation as a tool of economic development. In order to internationalize its currency, Japan then, like China now, would have had to abandon its tried-and-true growth model.

Eventually in the 1980s it did. Japanese policymakers sought to transform Tokyo into an international financial center and cultivate an international role for the yen. But their so-called Big Bang reforms, which removed restrictions on domestic and international financial transactions, did not work as planned. The Big Bang allowed large Japanese companies to access the corporate bond market. Seeing that they were losing their corporate clients, the banks scrambled for other customers, whom they found in real estate developers. The Big Bang spawned a massive real estate boom and bust whose consequences took years to clean up (shades of the subprime crisis). As a result, Tokyo never rose above second-tier financial-center status.

There is a lesson here for Chinese policymakers seeking to transform Shanghai into an international financial center and the renminbi into an international currency. Tread cautiously when deregulating your financial markets. Be careful for what you wish for, and be even more careful how you attempt to make that wish a reality.

BANCOR TO THE WORLD

This lack of alternatives meant that the post–World War II international monetary system was dollar based. The problem for other countries, starting with Britain, was how to limit the ability of the United States to manipulate that system to its advantage.

The war had brought Great Britain to the brink of extinction as an independent nation and substantially reduced its economic and financial power. It was clear already before the conclusion of hostilities whose economy would be strong and whose would be weak. If they were going to shape the postwar international monetary system, British officials realized, they would have to rely on the power of ideas rather than the power of their economy.

So they turned again, in 1941, to their leading idea man, Maynard Keynes. Within weeks Keynes had come up with a scheme for a global central bank that he dubbed the Clearing Union. Each country would receive a line of credit denominated in bookkeeping units known as "bancor." Governments could use those credits to purchase imports. Countries would be prevented from running balance-of-payments deficits indefinitely by the fact that their credits with the Clearing Union were limited. But they would also be discouraged from running chronic balance-of-payments surpluses by provisions requiring them to turn over a portion of any bancor and foreign currencies they earned to the Clearing Union.

While the Keynes Plan referred generically to countries running balance-of-payments surpluses, there was no doubt whom specifically it had in mind. Everyone realized that Keynes's charges and penalties were targeted at the United States.

American negotiators, led by Harry Dexter White, were smart enough to understand this strategy. The son of immigrant parents—his surname was an Anglicization of Weit—White had risen from modest working-class origins in Boston to the undergraduate program at Stanford, from which he graduated with distinction, and then the Ph.D. program and an assistant professorship at Harvard. In 1934, after an unhappy stint at Lawrence College in Wisconsin, he was hired as an economic analyst at the U.S. Treasury. From there he rose to assistant to the secretary.

White necessarily possessed considerable strength of intellect to rise so far so fast. His Treasury superiors described him as a man of "extraordinary energy and quick intelligence."[14] Keynes acknowledged this capacity in his typical deprecating way, referring to White as "one of the few constructive brains in the Treasury."[15] White was as strong willed—some would say stubborn—as Keynes, if less charming. He was also as well schooled in international monetary matters, having written his dissertation on the French franc between 1880 and 1913, and was more than capable of dealing with Keynes's more technical arguments.[16]

White's own plan for monetary reform, on which he began working after Pearl Harbor, substituted for Keynes's automatic taxes only the vague possibility of sanctions against a country running chronic external surpluses.[17] Keynes had proposed that countries be provided credit lines at the Clearing Union totaling $26 billion—the equivalent today would be $16 trillion, greater than the value of all goods and services produced in the United States. The Americans feared, not without reason, that the financial resources of the Clearing Union would all be used to purchase U.S. goods, forcing America to effectively give them away. White therefore reduced Keynes's $26 billion to $5 billion.[18]

Most importantly, the White Plan did away with bancor, proposing instead that the Stabilization Fund (White's name for the Clearing Union) lend national currencies deposited by governments.[19] The United States would provide the single largest share of the Fund's resources, reflecting its weight in the world economy.

These differences were then hashed out in bilateral negotiations. More accurate would be to say that the two sides eventually agreed to something closely resembling the American proposal, reflecting America's leverage and Britain's lack thereof. When American negotiators, in order to bring the export lobby on board, insisted that the Articles of Agreement of the new institution, now called the International Monetary Fund, include the expectation that countries would remove restrictions on the use of their currencies for import and export transactions within 5 years, Britain had no choice but to agree. When the Americans insisted on eliminating Keynes's tax on countries running chronic balance-of-payments surpluses and on doing away with bancor, again it had no choice. The main U.S. concession was to raise the total resources of the Fund from $5 billion to $8.5 billion, still far below Keynes's opening bid of $26 billion. The assent of the other allies and neutrals was obtained in July 1944 at the conclusion of an exhausting two-week conference in the leafy resort town of Bretton Woods, New Hampshire.[20]

MARSHALLING SUPPORT

But still unclear was how, given the limited availability of credits, countries would obtain the dollars needed to finance imports from the United States. At the end of World War II, Europe and Japan desperately needed imported food and fuel for social stability. They needed capital goods for economic reconstruction. For the time being, the United States provided them through the United Nations Relief and Reconstruction Administration and the 1946 Anglo-American loan. But these bridging measures were of limited duration.[21] And no one knew what would happen when they expired. American policymakers fancied that, with reconstruction and the peacetime reconversion of wartime armaments factories, Europe and Japan would immediately regain the capacity to earn the dollars needed to purchase imports. But in practice, reconversion took time. And exporting manufactures required first importing the capital equipment and other inputs required to produce them. The exports couldn't come first.

The implications were alarming for Europe and Japan and more broadly for the international system. Countries short of cash might resort to exchange controls and clearing arrangements like those exploited by Germany in the 1930s. If they did, the open trading system that was a U.S. priority would be placed at risk. And from government control of imports, it might be a small step to government control of the economy.

With the intensification of the Cold War, this risk became too great for U.S. policymakers to bear. They responded with the Marshall Plan for Europe and the Dodge Plan for Japan, the first named for the World War II general appointed secretary of state in 1947, the second for the less imposing but no less influential chairman of Detroit Bank who served as special U.S. ambassador to Japan starting in 1948.

The Marshall Plan absorbed 10 percent of the federal budget in its first year. It was an extraordinary act of generosity, and Marshall was just the man to shepherd it through the Congress. The secretary was an exemplary citizen-soldier. His father had fought in the Civil War as a member of the Augusta, Kentucky, Home Guard, and the young Marshall had spent virtually his entire adult life in the military. By 1947 he had become a trusted public figure. He exuded the self-discipline and analytical rigor of a consummate military man. As army chief of staff from 1939 to 1945, Marshall never minced words about the need for personal sacrifice when testifying before Congress. Now, in 1947, he was characteristically blunt about the need for sacrifice to keep Europe in the Western camp.

Dodge, no kin of the automotive family of the same name, was a banker who had worked in Frankfurt and Berlin as financial advisor to the U.S. military government of Generals Dwight Eisenhower and Lucius Clay. Moving to Japan, he briskly applied the lessons he had learned in Germany.

The Marshall and Dodge Plans provided dollars to finance the imported inputs needed to get exports going again, averting the danger that countries would be forced to resort to barter. In this sense the Marshall and Dodge Plans saved the Bretton Woods System and, by implication, the international role of the dollar. Not without reason, some observers have referred to the post–World War II international monetary system not as Bretton Woods but as the "Marshall-Dodge fixed-rate dollar standard."[22]

To accumulate reserves, countries must run trade surpluses—something that Europe and Japan were in no position to do in the second half of the 1940s—or else the reserve currency country must lend and invest abroad. After hesitating, the United States provided other countries with dollars through the Marshall and Dodge Plans. China today, like the United States in the 1940s, is running trade surpluses but also seeking to encourage wider international use of its currency. For other countries to get their hands on renminbi, China will therefore have to lend and invest abroad. That this lending and investment is something we are now beginning to see is an indication that Chinese officials know what's up.

Hedgehog's Dilemma

The defeated powers Germany and Japan were the most successful at exporting and acquiring dollars. Denied foreign policy ambitions, they focused on growing their economies. Britain still had its empire. France had Algeria, which many Frenchmen regarded as an integral part of the French nation. Both countries had overseas commitments creating budgetary burdens. Both complained of the difficulty of acquiring the dollars needed to purchase foreign goods.

In the 1940s it had been possible to argue that the immensity of U.S. economic power, combined with the severity of postwar economic problems in other countries, made it impossible for them to obtain dollars without American help. Come the 1950s, however, Germany had shown that by investing and cutting costs it was possible to restart the export engine and accumulate all the dollars that might be required. This was something at which France also eventually succeeded by devaluing the franc, balancing its budget, and extricating itself from Algeria. It was something at which Britain only finally succeeded in the 1980s with the advent of Margaret Thatcher.

The point is that, sick men like Britain notwithstanding, by the end of the 1950s the dollar shortage was over. This was not an entirely happy development. The Bretton Woods arrangements had assumed that the dollar was as good as gold. The fact that the stock of foreign-held dollars was now poised to exceed U.S. gold holdings thus posed a threat to the system. It exposed the United States to the equivalent of a bank run if foreign holders all rushed to exchange their dollar claims for gold at the U.S. Treasury's teller's window, known colloquially as the "gold window." American monetary liabilities to foreigners first exceeded U.S. gold reserves in 1960.[23] It was no coincidence that the first serious episode of speculation against the dollar was in the second half of that year.

These problems should not have come as a surprise. There was an obvious flaw in a system whose operation rested on the commitment of the United States to provide two reserve assets, gold and dollars, both at a fixed price, but where the supply of one was elastic while the other was not. The Belgian-born economist Robert Triffin had warned of this problem in 1947 in a study for the Federal Reserve Board.[24] The short, round-faced Triffin was a hedgehog rather than a fox. He knew this one big thing and wrote of it virtually to the exclusion of all else, as an economist at the Organization of European Cooperation and Development (the forerunner of today's OECD) and then as professor at Yale University. He did this so single-mindedly that his name became synonymous with the problem.

The Triffin Dilemma was that if the United States refused to provide dollars to other countries, trade would stagnate and growth would be stifled. But if the United States did provide an unlimited supply of dollars, lubricating growth and trade, confidence in its commitment to convert them into gold would be eroded. Eventually there would be a run on U.S. gold stocks, destroying the country's ability to maintain the $35 gold price. Or the United States might preemptively abandon its obligation to pay out gold at a fixed price. Either way the gold-dollar system was doomed. Triffin's solution was to create an artificial unit along the lines of Keynes's bancor that governments would be obliged to accept in international transactions. But, as of the early 1960s, he had few takers.

There is an evident analogy with the situation linking the United States and emerging markets like China and India in the early twenty-first century. The rapidly growing catch-up economies, Europe and Japan in the 1960s, emerging markets today, found themselves accumulating dollars almost despite themselves. Then as now they worried whether those dollars would hold their value. Then as now their worries created the danger of a disorderly scramble out of dollars that might destabilize financial markets.

The main difference today is that there are alternatives to the dollar in the form of the euro and, prospectively, other currencies. This creates at least the possibility of a smooth transition as foreign central banks and governments gradually diversify their reserves. If central banks and governments want to hold more euros, the European Central Bank can supply them.[25] Since the euro and the dollar float against one another, this shift can be accompanied by a gradual adjustment in the relative price of the two currencies. The dollar can decline against the euro without threatening the stability of financial markets and the international system.

INTO THE DEEP END OF THE POOL

Not so in the 1960s. With other countries lacking deep and liquid financial markets open to the rest of the world, gold was the only alternative to the dollar. And newly mined gold was in short supply.[26]

If countries worked together, however, they might buy time. If countries holding dollars agreed not to convert them into gold, the system might be preserved while a permanent solution was sought. But there was an obvious incentive to convert one's dollars into gold while others were exercising restraint. And since everyone was aware of this possibility, there was a temptation to cheat.

In 1961 the United States sought to address the problem by proposing an arrangement, the Gold Pool, in which other countries agreed to hold onto their dollars and reimburse the United States for half of its gold losses.[27] Charles Coombs, vice president of the New York Fed, negotiated it on behalf of the administration. The Gold Pool was a blatantly asymmetric arrangement in which all the transfers went one way. It was an indication of the extent to which the structure of the system had other countries over a barrel.

The Gold Pool was a happy arrangement so long as there was no need to activate it. And through 1964 there was no need owing to large amounts of Soviet and South African gold flowing onto the market.[28] But starting in 1965, supplies fell off. The members of the pool now had to sell gold to prevent its dollar price from rising on the London market. They had to reimburse the

United States for half its losses. What had been a commitment in theory now had actual implications in practice. Italy began offsetting its contribution to the Gold Pool's sales in London by converting dollars into gold in the United States. France, never a friend of the dollar, dropped out of the pool in early 1967, a fact disclosed by Paul Fabra, a financial journalist for *Le Monde*, in what was presumably a strategic leak by de Gaulle's government.

All this heightened the urgency of a permanent solution. French leaders, more than a little anachronistically, advocated returning to a system in which gold alone was used to settle accounts. In doing so they drew inspiration from the impassioned writings of Jacques Rueff, a long-standing champion of the gold standard. Rueff had worked at the Bank of France in the 1930s, rising to the rank of deputy governor before being dismissed under the Vichy government's anti-Semitic laws. He had firsthand knowledge of the gold standard's operation, although how he could have seen France's unhappy experience then as something to be emulated now is another matter. One explanation is that, as a follower of the Austrian economist Ludwig von Mises, Rueff was an ardent opponent of government interference with the market and viewed the gold standard as a guarantee that governments would not tamper with the monetary system. Another is that he was phobic about inflation, having lived through France's high inflation in the 1920s. Indeed, the young Rueff had advised the prime minister, Raymond Poincaré, on how to bring that inflation under control. His advice of budget cuts and one last devaluation did the trick.

As an opponent of economic planning, Rueff had been banished to the wilderness following World War II. But when de Gaulle returned to power and the problem became how to rein in inflation, the General called on Rueff to draft a stabilization plan. Once more he recommended budget cuts and one last devaluation, and once more the strategy worked. As a result of this triumph, Rueff acquired de Gaulle ear. He also acquired the public's, which he bent by publishing some eighty-five articles on monetary matters in the course of the 1960s. When de Gaulle attacked the dollar at a press conference in early 1965, castigating the Bretton Woods System as "abusive and dangerous" and arguing that the world should return to a gold-based system, he was channeling Rueff. It did not hurt that Rueff's arguments resonated with de Gaulle's insistence that France should not take a back seat to any country, monetarily or otherwise.

But here, in fact, French leaders were engaging in the same kind of wishful thinking to which American policymakers succumbed in 1946. It was not clear, given limited gold production, where under a gold-based system the world would obtain the reserves needed to support an expanding volume of trade and investment. Rueff suggested raising the price of gold, but this ignored the danger that doing so once might create expectations that governments would do so again, encouraging gold hoarding and other destabilizing consequences. Raising the price of gold would reward countries—such as, not entirely coincidentally, France—that had done the most to undermine the system by converting their dollars. Raising the gold price would also create a windfall for the Soviet Union and South Africa. Predictably, *Pravda* applauded de Gaulle's comments attacking the dollar.

The French position reflected a peculiar reading of history that ignored the fact that a pure gold-based system had not existed for the better part of a century, neither under the pre–World War I gold standard nor its interwar successor. Under both arrangements central banks had found it necessary to supplement their gold reserves with foreign bonds and bank deposits, including, it should be noted, French bonds and deposits. The French proposal may not have been realistic, but it nonetheless stood in the way of reaching agreement on an alternative.

Germany, not much more realistically, simply sought to preserve the existing system. Anxious to enhance its image as a loyal member of the Western alliance, it prioritized cooperation with the United States. Some German officials were less than enamored of the Americans. Karl Schiller, the moody professor who became economics minister in 1966, objected to the United States exploiting its security leverage and urged following de Gaulle's example of selling dollars. For most German politicians, however, the security argument for cooperating dominated. Then there was the fact that Bundesbank was a large holder of dollars as a result of Germany's chronic surpluses. For the German central bank then, like the Chinese central bank now, any international monetary initiative that downgraded the role and reduced the value of the dollar would have had costly financial consequences.

British policymakers generalized from the decline of sterling; they saw the dollar as next in line. As early as 1962 they proposed supplementing and ultimately replacing national currencies as reserves with a synthetic unit along the lines of Keynes's bancor. This new unit, they suggested, could be introduced by exchanging it for national currencies already in the possession of central banks. This might have the ancillary benefit, from the British point of view, of removing the overhang of sterling in official hands and eliminating the possibility that it might all be sold off in a sudden panic on news of economic problems. But a financially weak Britain was in no position to drive the debate.

THE VINEYARDS OF INTERNATIONAL FINANCE

The outcome thus hinged on the U.S. position. The problem was that there was no U.S. position. Lacking other ideas, American officials simply restated their commitment to the $35 gold price. They resorted to scattershot tactics to strengthen the U.S. trade accounts. They instituted a Buy American policy for the Defense Department and tied U.S. foreign aid to purchases of American goods. They imposed a tax on foreign interest income and arm-twisted U.S. firms not to invest abroad. The difficulty with these expedients, aside from the fact that they distorted international markets, was that preventing the United States from running current account deficits and investing abroad also prevented other countries from acquiring reserves. It just shifted the world from one horn of the Triffin Dilemma to the other.

Thus, the only real alternative to abandoning the system was to take up Britain's call for "paper gold." Already in 1960, in advance of his inauguration, President-Elect Kennedy had appointed a task force to study the dollar problem. Professor Triffin was a member of this task force and did not hesitate to inject his proposals for a synthetic reserve unit.

But Douglas Dillon, the hardheaded ex-banker who served as Kennedy's treasury secretary, had little patience for Triffin's ideas. Dillon was former chairman of the investment bank Dillon, Read and son of the firm's founder, Clarence Dillon. He had moved from banking to diplomacy and from there to policy by virtue of having been a major contributor to Eisenhower's 1952 presidential campaign.

Eisenhower had first appointed Dillon ambassador to France, a position for which he was qualified mainly by the fact that his family owned the Haut-Brion vineyard. The French were less reassured by this investment in *terroir* than they were disturbed by Dillon's lack of fluency in their language. Subsequently

Dillon served as undersecretary of economic affairs and of state under Eisenhower, where he distinguished himself. Contrary to the silver-spoon presumption (by the time his stint in Paris ended in 1957, his rudimentary French had become quite good), he was a quick learner and a stickler for detail. So Kennedy plucked him from Eisenhower's cabinet to reassure the markets and make good on a commitment to appoint a bipartisan cabinet.[29] The two men had much in common: both were Harvard graduates, both had been naval officers during World War II, and both were sons of nouveau riche Wall Street wheeler-dealers.[30] Dillon assured the president-elect that if he disagreed on an important matter of policy he would resign without causing a row. Kennedy was fully aware that Dillon had been a large contributor to the Nixon campaign. The choice thus spoke volumes about the need for a treasury secretary with investment banking experience and the gravitas to calm the markets.

Under Dillon, U.S. dollar policy had three straightforward elements. First, foreign governments should pay more of the costs of U.S. troops stationed in Europe. Second, the United States should use taxes and regulation more aggressively to support its currency. Third, the Europeans would be arm-twisted not to sell their dollars for gold. As for Triffin's ambitious academic schemes, the nicest thing Dillon had to say was that they "weren't very practical."

With exceptional amounts of Soviet and South African gold flowing onto the market in 1963–1964, this approach sufficed for a holding action. But starting in late 1964 and especially after de Gaulle's press conference in 1965, confidence began to ebb. Ten industrial countries (dubbing themselves, not very creatively, the Group of Ten) formed a committee to weigh proposals for reforming the system. There was a consensus on the need for change, but not much else. The French proposed issuing paper claims that governments would treat as equivalent to gold. This was essentially an effort to achieve the French objective of raising the price of gold, but through the back door. The maneuver would take place outside the IMF, which the French saw as dominated by the Anglo-Saxons. Other countries proposed instead working through the IMF by expanding the ability of countries to borrow from the Fund and in that way satisfying their need for additional reserves.

But in the absence of agreement, there was an inability to act. The report of the Group of Ten, published in the summer of 1965, concluded only that there existed "a range of views" on what to do.

WHITE HORSE WITH BLACK STRIPES

In April 1965 treasury secretary Dillon was succeeded by his undersecretary, Henry Fowler. The son of an engineer on the Norfolk & Western Railway, the folksy Fowler fashioned himself a country lawyer, taken to drinking root beer at sit-downs with the president. Unlike Dillon, he spoke no foreign language and had little experience in international finance. He did not initially enjoy the respect of his foreign counterparts. On an international swing designed to introduce him to the Europeans, the French finance minister, Valéry Giscard d'Estaing, pointedly failed to meet him at Orly Airport.

But Fowler quickly acquired definite views. He was skeptical that the gold-dollar system could be maintained. To Giscard and then the other Europeans, he indicated a willingness to discuss international monetary reform. The resulting discussions proceeded on two tracks: one via yet another Group of Ten study group, this one under Otmar Emminger, the no-nonsense vice president of the Bundesbank, the other in the Executive Board of the IMF. Fowler signaled his willingness to contemplate the creation a new reserve asset. France, finding that its proposal for an increase in the gold price received no support from Germany or other European countries, reluctantly agreed.

In August 1967 finance ministers finally recommended that the IMF be authorized to issue bookkeeping claims called Special Drawing Rights (SDRs for short) to supplement gold and dollar reserves. The term "special drawing rights," substituted for "reserve drawing rights" at the insistence of the French, supposedly indicated that the new unit was a loan, not a currency. Since it was subject to repayment, the French reassured themselves, it would not be inflationary. Experts like Emminger dismissed the distinction. "What difference does it make?" he asked. "Is a zebra a white horse with black stripes or a black horse with white stripes?"

The SDR was linked to gold at a value equal to one U.S. dollar.[31] The new unit would be allocated to IMF members in proportion to their existing rights to borrow from the Fund. Governments would be obliged to accept these bookkeeping claims from other governments and in transactions with the IMF itself. Through the periodic issuance of SDRs, the IMF could now provide countries with the additional reserves they needed to support their expanding trade and payments without adding to the overhang of dollars. Secretary Fowler, for whom the agreement was a personal triumph, hailed it as "the most ambitious and significant effort in the area of international monetary affairs since Bretton Woods."

There were just two problems. First, SDRs were not very useful, since they were acceptable in transactions only with other governments and the IMF itself. Governments could not use them in transactions with private parties. Second, members holding 85 percent of voting power in the IMF had to agree before any SDRs were issued. France insisted on this provision to protect against what it saw as the danger of excessive liquidity creation. It assumed that with the Europeans voting as a bloc and possessing more than 15 percent of votes in the Fund, they could avert this danger. And different countries for different reasons hesitated to support issuance on a significant scale. France wanted to ensure that issuing SDRs, in relieving the pressure on the dollar, did not also relieve the pressure on the United States to cut its external deficit. Germany worried about the inflationary consequences. Developing countries argued that SDRs should be allocated to countries with the most need, namely themselves. As a result, the amendment to the Articles of Agreement under which SDRs could be created was only formally agreed to in May 1968, and the SDR facility was only finally activated in January 1970. It was too little, too late.

DOMINOS

It was too late because Britain's chronic balance-of-payments problems had already come to a head. The August 1967 agreement to create the SDR was followed just three months later by a sharp devaluation of the pound. Britain's troubles resulted from wage increases and the Arab-Israeli War, which led to the closure of the Suez Canal, disrupting international trade and raising the price of oil—and not incidentally leading oil-exporting countries in the Middle East to move funds out of sterling, given that Britain made no secret of its support for Israel. Occurring against the backdrop of a chronically uncompetitive industrial sector in Britain, these events made devaluation unavoidable.

The decision was announced on a cold and foggy Saturday when the markets were closed. Most Britons learned of it courtesy of the BBC, which, enjoying its broadcasting monopoly, was recycling *Midnight Lace*, a stale Doris Day thriller, which it interrupted to announce the less than thrilling news of a 14 percent reduction in the currency's value. "I am quite shocked," Sir Patrick Hennessy, chairman of Ford Motor Company's British operations, told the press. "I have personally told my business friends abroad that it would not happen."[32]

Sterling now mattered less than in 1931, but it still mattered enough for its devaluation to raise questions about the dollar. Another de Gaulle press conference in which the General alluded to the possibility that sterling's devaluation might topple the dollar did not help. The price of gold shot up.

Obliged as they were to drive it back down, the remaining members of the Gold Pool sold $1 billion of gold in November and another $1 billion in December. By March U.S. gold losses were running half a billion dollars *a day*. One Swiss bank reportedly had to strengthen its vault to contain all the privately held gold that was flooding in.

Out of options, on Thursday, March 14, U.S. Treasury officials telephoned their British counterparts, requesting that they shut the London gold market. Sterling may no longer have been a first-class international currency, but one legacy of its earlier status was that London was still the main place where gold was traded. Closing the market required a proclamation by the queen. Although it was almost midnight, Prime Minister Harold Wilson rushed to Buckingham Palace, where he obtained the consent of Queen Elizabeth to close the market.

The United States then called an emergency meeting of Belgium, Britain, Germany, Italy, and the Netherlands, the remaining members of the Gold Pool. France should not have been offended, since it had already terminated its participation in the arrangement. But de Gaulle was characteristically piqued; he pointedly kept the Paris Bourse open while the London gold market was closed.

After two days of tense negotiations, U.S. and European officials agreed to a scheme devised by Italian central bank governor Guido Carli for a "two tier" gold market. Carli's opinions carried weight; more than two decades earlier, at the precocious age of thirty, he had represented Italy at the Bretton Woods Conference. From there he went on to serve on the Executive Board of the IMF and, in Italy, at the foreign trade ministry, treasury, and central bank. He was widely respected for his candle power. His characteristically clever scheme divided transactions into a market tier on which the price of gold was free to fluctuate and an official tier where central banks would transact with one another at the official $35 price. Central banks were now relieved of having to devote real resources to the futile quest to keep the market price of gold from rising. At the same time, the dollar's link to gold at the official $35 price, and therefore the entire Bretton Woods apparatus, remained in place.

President Johnson, echoing the comments of his treasury secretary the previous year, hailed the provisions of the two-tier gold market as "the most significant reforms of the international monetary system since Bretton Woods."[33] Not everyone was impressed. Leonid Brezhnev gleefully saw the decision as signaling "the beginning of the devaluation of the United States dollar" and "the possibility of a profound crisis of the capitalist system."

Others, while not sharing Brezhnev's sense of schadenfreude, similarly questioned the viability of the arrangement. They understood that governments would be tempted to buy gold from the United States at $35 an ounce and sell it for a higher price on the market. The only thing restraining them was fear of the unknown. If there was a run on U.S. gold reserves, rupturing the link between gold and the dollar, no one knew what kind of U.S. monetary policy would follow. No one could anticipate the implications for the international system.

Fear of the unknown was then trumped by fear of the known. With the election of Richard Nixon to the presidency in 1968, U.S. policies became increasingly unilateral and inflationary. Nixon saw no reason to cooperate with other countries. Rather, he sought to manipulate the system to maximal U.S. advantage and to free American foreign policy from financial constraints. Instead of negotiating, he adopted "bullying tactics" to get other countries to hold dollars.[34]

Nixon selected former Texas governor John Connally to play "bullyboy on the manicured playing fields of international finance" (Connally's words). Nixon reached across party lines when appointing Connally as treasury secretary, just as Kennedy had reached across party lines when appointing Dillon. That Connally was longtime sidekick and onetime campaign manager of Nixon's predecessor LBJ made the appointment startling. It came into focus when it was learned that Connally, while nominally stumping for Hubert Humphrey in the 1968 presidential campaign, had helped to identify oil and gas titans who might contribute to the Republican candidate.

The appointment reflected the president's fascination with Connally, who cut the kind of dashing figure to which Nixon himself could never aspire. The former Texas governor was tall and handsome, with wavy white hair. Having been a thespian in school, he could be smooth and articulate. Like any actor, he was a publicity hound. He saw the treasury as a platform from which he could advance his presidential aspirations.

Better even a global than a national stage. Although international finance was not his strong suit—the oil depletion allowance was more like it—in May 1971 Connally turned down a request to testify before Congressman Wilbur Mills's powerful House Ways and Means Committee in favor of a speech to an international monetary conference in Munich because he thought he could earn political points by attacking the Europeans on their own turf. "Considerations of friendship," he warned them, were no longer enough for the United States to carry Europe's water. The dollar problem would have to be solved by European countries assuming more of the U.S. defense burden and opening further to U.S. exports. If they didn't, Connally continued, they would be subject to whatever policies the U.S. chose to enact.

Nixon's foreign policy adviser Henry Kissinger warned privately that Connally's scare tactics might backfire. And as Kissinger had predicted, at the Bank for International Settlements in June, European central bankers objected to both the tone and the content of Connally's speech. When news of the clash leaked to the market, the ongoing drain of gold from the Treasury accelerated. On August 13 Britain, seeking to move before it was too late, asked the United States to convert some of its dollars into gold. This was the last straw; left no alternative, the United States suspended the conversion of dollars into gold, blaming "international speculators." To make this look like an assertion of strength, Nixon dressed it up as a New Economic Program complete with tax cuts and a 90-day wage and price freeze. There was also a temporary 10 percent surcharge on imports designed to ensure that "American products will not be at a disadvantage because of unfair exchange rates." In other words, the surcharge was intended to ensure, now that exchange rates were going to be adjusted, that they would be adjusted to U.S. advantage.

This abrupt, unilateral action was "hardly designed to win friends, or even to influence people, abroad," in the words of the investment advisor Peter Bernstein.[35] The 10 percent surcharge, in particular, won the United

States no friends. But it placed other countries over a barrel. At the next meeting of finance ministers, Connally demanded to know what concessions the Europeans were prepared to offer in return for the United States dropping the surcharge and then, theatrically cupping his hand to his ear, observed, "I don't hear any suggestions."

The tactic was effective. With the stick of the surcharge, the United States was able to obtain, at a conference at the Smithsonian Institution in December, a new set of exchange rates that amounted to a significant devaluation of the dollar. The result was packaged as a revaluation of foreign currencies in a not very effective sop to U.S. prestige. One-upping his predecessor's rhetoric in 1968, Nixon called it "the most significant monetary achievement in the history of the world."[36]

But while the exchange rates were now different, the system was otherwise the same. Other currencies were still pegged to the dollar, the only difference now being that the U.S. Treasury no longer stood ready to convert dollars into gold for foreign central banks and governments. Nothing prevented the United States from running whatever policies it chose, a prospect that understandably alarmed countries pegging to its currency.

The danger materialized soon enough. Nixon blamed his defeat in the 1960 presidential election on the Federal Reserve's tight monetary policy, which had depressed the economy. With the 1972 election approaching, he pressured the Fed under Arthur Burns to pump up the money supply. "Err toward inflation," Nixon instructed him in a meeting at the White House.[37]

Burns was not accustomed to unsolicited advice. Formerly a very senior Columbia University professor where he had tutored, among other students, Alan Greenspan, he was convinced of appropriateness of the prevailing policy.[38] But Nixon was not done. He hinted at legislation that would have allowed him to pack the Federal Reserve Board as FDR had attempted to pack the Supreme Court, and had Charles Colson, subsequently of Watergate fame, plant stories with United Press International about Burns lobbying for a pay increase.[39] Burns in fact had only suggested that future Fed chairmen receive higher salaries so that they would be on an even footing with their European counterparts. But this was not the way the story was spun. So Burns goosed the money supply. Inflation accelerated. Pressure on the dollar intensified.

Clearly, something had to be done. So another committee was formed. The Committee of Twenty (with one finance minister or central banker for each of the twenty country groupings represented on the board of the International Monetary Fund) sought to reconcile the desire for exchange rate stability with the need for currencies to move against the dollar. Its proposal for an oxymoronic system of "fixed but adjustable rates" went nowhere. In the spring of 1973, in the midst of its work, another run on the dollar commenced, and the new set of exchange rates so laboriously agreed to at the Smithsonian collapsed.

The Committee of Twenty blithely continued work for another year before abandoning its deliberations. An interesting aspect of that work was the Report of the Technical Group on Indicators, which described how a specific set of indicators (the change in international reserves and the trade deficit or surplus) might be used to introduce "symmetry into the adjustment process." This was code for the need to compel adjustment by chronic surplus countries, in this case Germany. The discussion paralleled the present debate over whether some kind of international mechanism should be created to compel China to appreciate its currency. It is thus worth recalling that that earlier discussion went nowhere.

QUELLE SURPRISE

None of this—not the devaluation, not the import surcharge, and not the inflation—enhanced the stature of the dollar. "The dollar is regarded all over the world as a sick currency," read Leonard Silk's lede in an article in the *New York Times*, which appeared, not without irony, on July 4, 1973. "Once upon a very recent time," *Time* wrote, "only a banana republic would devalue its money twice within 14 months." Parallels were drawn with sterling's decline as an international currency. "For someone who spent the 1960s in England," wrote the academic Emma Rothschild in the *New York Times*, "the decline of the dollar is like coming home." Other currencies that were revalued in 1971–1973 were seen as increasingly serious rivals. There were widespread predictions of the dollar's demise as the dominant unit in international transactions. The conventional wisdom, in other words, sounds remarkably familiar to modern ears.

It was anticipated that rivalry for reserve currency status would grow increasingly intense. With the shift to flexible exchange rates in 1973, it was thought that countries would need fewer reserves. Now that exchange rates were flexible, a shock to the balance of payments could be met by letting currencies adjust. No longer would central banks have to hold the currencies of others in order to intervene in the foreign exchange market.

What followed was therefore a surprise—two surprises, actually. The first one was that there was no decline in the demand for reserves. A series of studies found that countries when shifting to flexible exchange rates held the same or even more reserves. The explanation was simple: a floating exchange rate did not mean a freely floating exchange rate. Countries intervened when they concluded that the exchange rate had strayed too far from its fundamental value, and they came to this conclusion not infrequently. Their intervention required reserves—even more reserves given the continued expansion of trade and capital flows.

The second surprise was that there was no shift away from the dollar. Volatility there was in the share of dollars in foreign exchange reserves in the 1970s, but no secular decline. The dollar's share of total identified international reserves remained close to 80 percent in 1977, as the United States pumped out dollars and the members of the Organization of Petroleum Exporting Countries (OPEC), having jacked up oil prices, parked their earnings in New York.[40]

STRONG DOLLAR POLICY

It was not the collapse of the dollar peg in the early 1970s so much as the subsequent inflation and mounting unease over the conduct of American monetary policy that precipitated movement away from the dollar. Consumer price inflation rose in every year of the Carter presidency, which did not make holding dollars attractive. Fears of U.S. intentions were fanned by statements by Treasury Secretary Michael Blumenthal in the summer of 1977 that the dollar was overstrong, the implication being that the secretary favored depreciation.

When Blumenthal's "open mouth policy" caused the dollar to sag, the Arabs began muttering about using another currency when setting oil prices. The chastened secretary flew off to the Middle East to reassure them. The Europeans, seeing their currencies rise and their exporters squirm, reacted with fury. Blumenthal, the *Frankfurter Allgemeine Zeitung* wrote, was playing a "selfish, risky game that shows little responsibility toward the world economy." With

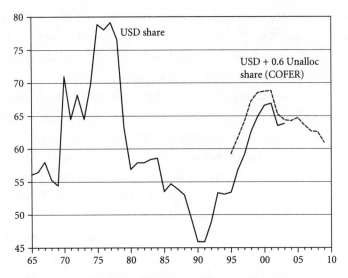

Figure 3.1. U.S. Dollar Share of Reserves.
Sources: IMF Annual Reports, IMF unpublished data, and Currency Composition of Official Foreign Exchange Reserves (COFER) data, December 30, 2009, version.

the situation threatening to spiral out of control, Blumenthal reversed course and announced that he believed in a strong dollar. It would be a long time before a U.S. treasury secretary would again be sufficiently courageous—or reckless—to say otherwise.

Arthur Burns, still Fed chairman, had been among those who blew a fuse over what he perceived as Blumenthal's attempt to debase the currency, leading Blumenthal in turn to lobby against Burns's reappointment. In this he was too successful: Burns was succeeded in March 1978 by G. William Miller, a slight, likeable Oklahoman whose command of the nuances of monetary policy was less than complete. Miller, the son of a storekeeper, had grown up in a town so small that it had no jail; as he described it, prisoners were simply chained to a log. He was given to telling bad jokes and laughing so hard that he botched the punchline. But he was also a force of nature: he had graduated from the Coast Guard Academy and the law school of the University of California, Berkeley and built a medium-sized textile manufacturer, Textron, into a giant conglomerate that produced Homelite chain saws, Speidel watchbands, and the Bell UH-1 helicopters, or Hueys, that were the workhorses of the Vietnam War.

Miller was a passionate advocate of equal employment for minorities, which may explain his single-minded pursuit of full employment. Basically he thought that the Fed should pursue employment growth to the exclusion of other goals. He denied that monetary policy could be effective in restraining inflation. Fighting inflation was first and foremost the responsibility, he insisted, of other branches of government. In the spring of 1979, with inflation continuing to accelerate, economists as ideologically diverse as the conservative consultant Alan Greenspan and the liberal Brookings Institution fellow Arthur Okun called for tighter money. Miller resisted, fearing that raising rates would squelch employment growth. Blumenthal and Charles Schultze, the head of Carter's Council of Economic Advisors, their efforts at private persuasion having failed, were driven to leaking their complaints about Miller's inaction to the press, in turn driving the president to ask them to desist.

Predictably, the dollar resumed its decline. Foreign currencies became so expensive that U.S. troops stationed in Europe had trouble making ends meet. NATO chief Alexander Haig reported that sympathetic West Germans were giving his soldiers care packages of food and cigarettes.

Complaints mounted about U.S. policy and the losses to which it exposed foreign holders of dollars. OPEC again discussed the possibility of pricing oil in another unit. Saudi Arabia and other members of the cartel made noises about moving their reserves into other currencies. Since doing so might weaken the dollar, their noises raised concerns that other countries might move preemptively in order to avoid ending up holding the bag, making talk of a dollar crash self-fulfilling.

Consideration was therefore given in late 1978 to creating a Substitution Account at the IMF through which dollar reserves could be exchanged for SDRs in an orderly fashion. The idea foundered on the question of who would take the losses if the dollar depreciated. If the answer was the IMF, then establishing the account was tantamount to transferring the risk of losses from some IMF members to others—from those holding lots of dollars to those holding few. If the answer was the United States, which would be asked to guarantee the holdings of the account (as the UK had been asked to guarantee the reserves of the sterling area after its 1967 devaluation), then the United States would incur very significant additional obligations. And this clearly was not something that the United States was willing to do.

Support for a Substitution Account evaporated in any case when Paul Volcker replaced Miller at the Fed in August 1979 and his tight-money policies caused the dollar to strengthen.[41] As Nixon's undersecretary of the treasury for international monetary affairs, Volcker had already been involved two devaluations of the dollar, in 1971 when the Bretton Woods System collapsed, and in 1973 when the Smithsonian Agreement came apart. In 1973, as the Treasury's most conspicuous secret agent, he had flown 31,000 miles in five days, shuttling between Tokyo, Bonn and other capitals in a vain effort to salvage the agreement.[42] Given his 6-foot, 7-inch frame, the German press immediately identified him on the streets of Bonn and exposed his supposedly secret mission. Volcker had no desire to oversee another unsuccessful currency adjustment. Having been in and out of the Federal Reserve System since 1952, he was Miller's opposite not just physically but in his knowledge of domestic and international finance. As president of the Federal Reserve Bank of New York and therefore a member of the Federal Open Market Committee, he had already voted twice, in defiance of Miller, for raising interest rates.

For Carter, desperate now to support the dollar and restrain inflation, Volcker was the man. On cue, the Federal Open Market Committee under Tall Paul raised interest rates.[43] The dollar recovered, causing talk of a Substitution Account to wither. But the proposal had already hit the rocks over the question of who would bear the exchange risk. The United States, in particular, was unwilling to see discussions continue, fearing pressure for it to guarantee the value of the dollars held in such an account. This is important to recall now that the idea of a Substitution Account through which countries like China might exchange their dollars for SDRs is again in the air.

The Dollar Endures

Yet there was no migration away from the dollar. OPEC talked about pricing oil in a basket of currencies but did nothing. Nor was there active movement by central banks and governments into other currencies.[44] Only Iran, where the revolution and hostage crisis created high tension with the United States, significantly altered the composition of its reserves.[45] In 1977–1980, when there was the most talk about the dollar losing its exorbitant privilege, the main thing accounting for its declining share of global reserves was that other currencies became more valuable as the dollar depreciated, not that central banks sold what they held. The share of dollars then stabilized after Volcker took over at the Fed and the currency strengthened.[46]

The dollar's continued dominance surprised many observers then, but it is hardly surprising now. The United States was still the world's largest economy. It was still the leading trading nation. It still had the deepest financial markets. The deutschmark, its main rival, was the currency of an economy only a fraction its size. Germany was not a big supplier of the financial securities that were attractive to central banks and other foreign investors in any case, because its government budget was balanced and its financial system was bank based. Since the early 1970s the German authorities had required prior approval for sales of domestic fixed-income securities to nonresidents. They had raised reserve requirements on foreign-owned bank deposits to discourage capital inflows that might fuel inflation. When in 1979 Iran threatened to convert its dollar reserves into deutschmarks, the Bundesbank warned it off, fearing that capital inflows would swell the money supply and stoke inflation. It made clear that it would do whatever it took to discourage central banks and governments from accumulating deutschmarks. The United States, as a larger economy, could provide the international reserves required by other countries "without having its economic policy damaged by the fluctuations of capital flows," the Bundesbankers observed.[47]

None of this made the deutschmark attractive for international use. The share of foreign exchange reserves in deutschmarks hovered below 15 percent all through the 1980s.

Nor were there other options. The UK, with its history of inflation and subpar growth, was in the early stages of a Thatcher experiment whose ultimate success remained uncertain. France suffered from slow growth, high unemployment, and financial problems that it sought to bottle up by tightening controls on international capital flows, further diminishing international use of its currency.[48]

The new player was Japan, whose share in global reserves had risen in the 1970s. That Japan was now an important trading nation and that everyone expected the yen to strengthen made it an obvious currency to add. But Japanese bond markets were small. The yen accounted for only 8 percent of total global reserves at its peak, which came in 1991. From there, Japan descended into an economic and financial funk, and the importance of the yen as a reserve and international currency descended with it.

The More Things Change

When the IMF economist George Tavlas surveyed this landscape in 1998, he noted that, notwithstanding talk of a tripolar yen-deutschmark-dollar world, the dollar still dominated international transactions.[49] Petroleum prices were set in dollars. Other commodity prices were quoted in dollars. Two-thirds of all international bank loans were denominated in dollars. 40 percent of international bond issues marketed to foreign investors were in dollars.[50] Dollars still accounted for more than 60 percent of total identified official holdings of foreign exchange. The dollar's dominance remained an established fact.

This period was also when there was talk of a "new economy" and of whether America's surging stock market signaled the advent of a cluster of high-tech innovations on which the country was singularly well suited to capitalize. The idea that the United States was set to outperform a rigid Europe and a depressed and deflated Japan bred confidence that the dollar would remain the dominant international currency. And new economy or not, the dollar's dominance was supported by a lack of alternatives. The greenback was the predominant international currency, if for no other reason than by default.

But the time for celebration would be brief. For already movement was afoot to create what would constitute, for the first time in fully seven decades, a serious rival.

CHAPTER 4

RIVALRY

The dollar's difficulties would hardly matter if foreigners had nowhere to go. Were they stuck for lack of an alternative, as they were stuck after the breakdown of Bretton Woods, doubts about its prospects would be just that: doubts. But since 1999, there has existed another currency, the euro, with the potential to become a major rival. The euro area is not without its problems, as recent events have underscored, but then neither is the United States. If the euro emerges from its crisis with its institutions strengthened, it could yet represent a serious alternative to the dollar in the international sphere.

This alternative did not arrive overnight. The creation of the euro was the culmination of a process that was literally centuries long. George of Poděbrad, the fifteenth-century king of Bohemia, suggested a European federation with a single currency to finance a European army to fight the Turks. Napoleon argued for a single currency issued under French auspices to promote the integration of the continent.[1] (French confidence that once a single currency was created France would come to control it is another enduring theme of Europe's monetary history.) European currencies had been effectively interchangeable under the gold standard that prevailed until 1914.[2] Although World War I interrupted the operation of the gold standard, it also led the Count Richard Coudenhove-Kalergi to create the Pan-European Union, which worked to cultivate support for a European federation and a European currency. In the 1950s and 1960s Jacques Rueff, whom we met in chapter 3, argued for a single European currency linked to gold as an alternative to the dollar—one that again presumably would operate under French direction.

World War II, as the pivotal event in Europe's twentieth-century history, had profound implications for the process. Virtually all the figures playing important roles in the negotiations leading to monetary union had their outlooks shaped by their experiences during the war. They saw European integration as preventing a recurrence of equally tragic events. With the German Federal Republic's economic resurgence in the 1950s, they saw locking Germany into Europe as even more important. While the locking mechanism put in place in 1958, the European Economic Community (EEC), stopped well short of economic and political federation, it excited talk of deeper integration and, inevitably, of a single European currency.[3] And just when memories of those earlier events began to fade, German reunification brought them back to life. Absent this history, it is impossible to imagine that the French would have taken the momentous step of giving up the franc, the symbol of their grandeur, or that Germans would have given up their beloved deutschmarks.

This history also reminds us that the euro is fundamentally a political project. This is its weakness, since it explains how it was that the euro was created before all the economic prerequisites needed for its smooth operation were in place. But it is also its strength, since it explains why the member states now feel compelled to complete them—and why the euro is likely to emerge from its crisis stronger than before.

But it is equally unlikely that that the transition to the euro would have occurred as it did absent the problems created by the dollar. Whenever doubts arose about the dollar and funds flowed out of the United States, they did not flow equally into all European markets. Instead they flowed mainly into Germany, the home of Europe's most redoubtable currency. The deutschmark rose against the French franc, confronting German exporters with a loss of competitiveness and French policymakers with a loss of face. Given the inordinate size of U.S. financial markets, the result was, in the words of Otmar Emminger, the Bundesbanker whom we met in chapter 3, like "being in a boat—or a bed—with an elephant."

The instability of the dollar thus encouraged Europeans to contemplate a single currency to insulate themselves from these disruptions. Indirectly, then, the dollar's troubles led to the creation of an alternative, the euro, with the capacity to rival it on the world stage.

Other motives fused with the quest for insulation from destabilizing monetary impulses, just as several motives lay behind the creation of the Federal Reserve. At the start of the 1990s there was Germany's need to gain French assent to German reunification, for which it could offer monetary union as a quid pro quo. Subsequently there was the wish in reunified Germany for a more assertive foreign policy, which could be pursued only in the context of a more deeply integrated European Union. In France there was the desire to wrest monetary control from a German central bank that dictated policy Europe-wide. The French, in the Gaullist tradition, also wanted a European currency that could rival the dollar. They valued monetary power for the same reasons they valued military power. They sought less dependence on the United States monetarily as well as militarily. The euro was their monetary *force de frappe*.

The end of the Cold War played into their hands. France had always sought a European deterrent and a defense alliance independent of the United States. But so long as Soviet troops lurked in the woods around Berlin, West Germany depended on the American defense umbrella. It was the "obedient ally."[4] When the United States asked it to support the dollar, it did. And when Paris offered schemes for creating a European alternative, Bonn hesitated. This changed with the end of the Cold War and the collapse of the Soviet Union. It is a reminder of how exceptional was the half century after 1945 when the dollar reigned supreme.

Until the 1970s, the Bretton Woods System provided Europe the currency stability it required. Stabilizing European currencies against the dollar stabilized them against one another. Completing the Common Market, as Europe did in 1968, would have been harder in the face of currency swings. Importers and exporters would have seen their business disrupted. Governments would have found it more difficult to remove trade barriers and establish a common external tariff.

They would have also found it harder to extend the side payments needed to buy off agrarian opposition to the Common Market. Europe's less productive farmers saw a common market in agricultural products as a threat. Their lobby was too powerful to ignore, and their opposition could have torpedoed the European project. When they demanded officially administered prices, governments acquiesced. But this was not something that a single government could provide on its own. If France attempted to set grain prices above the levels prevailing elsewhere in the Common Market, it would have been flooded with grain from other members. Hence the Common Agricultural Policy under which the members agreed to harmonize their agricultural support prices. But since the French Government set them in francs while the German Government set them in deutschmarks, and other members of the Community likewise set them in their own currencies, disorderly exchange-rate fluctuations would have wreaked havoc with the system. Again, Bretton Woods came to the rescue. It is thus predictable that the first significant steps in the direction of a common European currency coincided with the death throes of Bretton Woods.

EARLY SOUNDINGS

Less predictable was that the initiative came from German chancellor Willy Brandt. Brandt, the child of a single mother who worked as a shop clerk, was raised by his maternal grandfather, a truck driver and ardent socialist. He took to his grandfather's politics, joining the Socialist Youth and Socialist Workers Party. When not politicking, Brandt worked as a shipping agent. With the Nazis' rise to power, Germany became inhospitable to a young socialist, and Brandt used his maritime connections to escape to Norway. In 1938, when the German authorities revoked his citizenship, he applied for Norwegian nationality. Brandt thus returned to Berlin in 1946 untainted and did not long resist the lure of politics. In 1949 he went to work for the mayor of West Berlin. In 1957 he himself was elected mayor, the position that was his springboard into national politics. He served as chairman of the Social Democratic Party from 1964, as foreign minister in the Grand Coalition of Christian Democrats and Social Democrats from 1966, and as chancellor from 1969.

Brandt was less concerned with monetary matters than with regularizing relations with the Soviet bloc. He had felt betrayed by the United States when it did nothing to counter the erection of the Berlin Wall in 1961. Germany's future, he concluded, would be decided by Germans themselves, and a key aspect of that would be improving relations with the Eastern bloc and the USSR. Brandt's great achievement as chancellor was to negotiate nonaggression pacts with

Poland and the Soviet Union and to establish diplomatic relations between East and West Germany.

Economics, by comparison, was not his thing. But as foreign minister in 1968, Brandt had a ringside seat when dollar troubles fanned tensions in Europe. Fears that the United States might devalue caused a tidal wave of capital to flow toward Germany. The inflow pushed the deutschmark up. This raised additional questions about the franc, whose health was already in doubt, what with widespread street protests ("the events of May") and the de Gaulle Government on its last legs. The General may have been past his prime, but he resisted the pressure to devalue, regarding it as an embarrassing admission of defeat—more so now given his penchant for lecturing the Americans about the weakness of the dollar. De Gaulle dismissed as "the worst absurdity" the idea that he might be forced to devalue. If the problem was to be solved, he insisted, the solution should come from Germany.

But the German Government, in the persons of economics minister Karl Schiller and finance minister Franz Josef Strauss, was adamant about not revaluing, fearing the damage to German exports. Schiller and Strauss staked their reputations on maintaining the prevailing exchange rate to the dollar. At a fractious summit of industrial countries in Bonn in November 1968, the decision was taken not to decide. De Gaulle imposed exchange controls, buying time but doing nothing to solve the problem.

The logjam was broken only after Georges Pompidou took over from de Gaulle in mid-1969. Pompidou was more pragmatic than his predecessor and, though nominally also a Gaullist, could blame the need to devalue on the General. He moved in August, deftly devaluing while much of France, not just politicians and financiers but also journalists, was on vacation.

In the interim, however, capital inflows had fanned fears of inflation in Germany. This became the central issue in the September 1969 election that brought to power the coalition of Social Democrats and Free Democrats under Brandt. Not having staked its reputation on the preservation of the prevailing exchange rate, the new Brandt Government was free to revalue as one of its first acts. German exporters were not pleased, but then not everyone could be. They blamed the French for forcing them to take this painful medicine. The Franco-German alliance at the heart of Europe showed signs of coming apart at the seams.

Brandt saw this rupture at firsthand. He now moved to repair it. His chosen instrument was a monetary agreement designed to prevent more currency problems.

But in advancing his plan, Brandt had to overcome several pockets of resistance. The Bundesbank, which saw itself as the guardian of price stability, viewed cooperation with France as threatening its ability to fight inflation. The Foreign Office warned that closer cooperation in Europe might weaken the commitment to transatlantic monetary cooperation.[5] The notion that Germany should play the role of obedient ally was still very much alive. But with the election of President Nixon in November 1968 and his administration's increasingly unilateral policies, the case for cooperating with the Americans became harder to make. The argument for deepening the Community became stronger.

Nor was the Frenchman in the street necessarily enthusiastic about giving up the franc. Devaluation was an embarrassment, but national sovereignty, of which the franc was a potent symbol, was a valued ideal. That said, stability-minded politicians like Valéry Giscard d'Estaing, minister of economy and finance from 1962 to 1966 under de Gaulle and from 1969 to 1974 under Pompidou, saw cooperation with Germany as freeing French monetary policy from domestic politics. They saw it as a way of importing Germany's stability culture. Giscard also saw a common European currency as essential for safeguarding the Common Agricultural Policy, from which French farmers derived substantial benefit, and as constituting a full-fledged rival to the dollar.[6]

Pompidou possessed characteristic French confidence that if Brandt's initiative did eventually result in a single European currency, France would control it. The status quo as he saw it had France caught between an irresponsible and increasingly powerful Germany on the one hand and an equally irresponsible and still powerful United States on the other. In asserting at the December 1969 summit of European countries where Brandt offered his monetary integration proposal that the Community should take "control of its own destiny," Pompidou was really alluding to the need for France to regain control of its own destiny, and its monetary destiny in particular.[7]

Whether this peculiar coalition could reach agreement on a common currency was very much in doubt. And when in doubt, appoint a committee. Out of the summit thus came a committee of officials under the chairmanship of Luxembourg's prime minister, Pierre Werner. While Luxembourg was not an obvious choice, Werner had experience as a banker. He had attended the Bretton Woods Conference in 1944. He had an impeccable reputation, having supported the Resistance during Germany's wartime occupation. He was an effective politician and keen advocate of European integration.

The report of the Werner Committee, issued in October 1970, saw irrevocably locking exchange rates as essential for preservation of the Common Market and as insulating Europe from destabilizing monetary impulses from the United States. It proposed a Europe-wide system of central banks similar to the Federal Reserve System. It emphasized the need to coordinate the national budgets of the countries cohabiting in the monetary union. And it pointed to the desirability of a system of intergovernmental transfers to aid weak countries, analogous to the federal tax and transfer system through which funds are redistributed in the United States.

These were ambitious recommendations guaranteed to excite a negative reaction from committed nationalists, who the authors of the Werner Report went to considerable lengths to disarm. Rather than insisting on replacing national currencies with a new European unit, which subsequent experience would show was essential to the viability of this enterprise, they suggested that national currencies could be retained for their symbolic value. They evaded such questions as how the European system of central banks would operate, who would make decisions, and what the relationship would be between the monetary authorities and politicians. And rather than suggesting a quick move to monetary union, they recommended a three-stage transition over 10 years.

The fact that the Werner Report avoided the issue of exactly how and by whom Europe's common monetary policy would be made was a fatal weakness. It allowed the president of the Bundesbank, Karl Klasen, to tap into German fears that the common monetary policy would be dictated by French-speaking politicians and become an engine of inflation. At the same time it excited fears in France that decision making might be removed from politics and frustrate the efforts of the French to regain control of their monetary destiny. Although European economics and finance ministers endorsed the Werner Report in March 1971, they took no concrete action to implement it. The report's one enduring legacy was the idea of an extended three-stage transition, at the end of which exchange rates would be irrevocably locked.

ANIMAL CRACKERS

But as monetary shocks continued to radiate outward from the United States, it became urgent to do something. In the first four months of 1971, investors again grew worried about the prospect of dollar devaluation and shifted funds to Germany. On May 10, overwhelmed with capital inflows, the Bundesbank stopped intervening to stabilize the deutschmark, allowing it to rise against the dollar.[8] The Netherlands, with its close economic links to Germany, followed suit.

Not so France, which investors did not view with the same confidence and which was not on the receiving end of capital flows. The French reaction was one of irritation. Germany had acted unilaterally, and the appreciation of the deutschmark had again falsely implicated the franc. Pompidou informed the other member states that France would not participate in the meetings of the Committee of Central Bank Governors until the situation was regularized— that is, until Germany and the Netherlands restored their fixed parities.

Fence mending had barely begun when on August 15 Nixon suspended the conversion of dollars into gold.[9] This again unsettled investors, causing the franc and deutschmark to diverge further. France was forced into action. Presidents Nixon and Pompidou met halfway, on Terceira in the Portuguese Azores. Pompidou got the upper hand by flying in on the Concorde. The Congress had just rejected Nixon's proposal to build a supersonic transport, making the Concorde a not very subtle statement of French superiority.

The two presidents also met halfway in terms of policy. Nixon wanted a large dollar depreciation to goose the U.S. economy, but Pompidou feared that this step would saddle Europe with a large loss of competitiveness. France lacked financial leverage, but Pompidou, ex-banker and onetime schoolteacher, could expound at length on exchange rates, a subject for which the American president had little patience. One can imagine the exasperated Nixon impatiently tapping his foot while listening to Pompidou's endless exposition of currency relationships.

In the end the two presidents agreed that the dollar should be devalued by precisely 7.9 percent, somewhat less than the United States had hoped. Nixon looked exhausted and flubbed his lines at the concluding press conference. He had stayed up most the night between the two days of talks listening to the

National Football League game between the Washington Redskins and the Los Angeles Rams on Armed Forces Radio. Pompidou, on the other hand, was in fine fettle. Following the press conference he retired to the Hotel Angra, the only hotel in town, for an aperitif and more bantering with reporters.[10]

Other countries were brought on board at a meeting in the Castle Building at the Smithsonian Institution on December 17 and 18. Their agreement hinged on the willingness of Germany to revalue against the dollar by more than Nixon and Pompidou's 7.9 percent so that other countries, with weaker economies, could revalue by less. After a difficult phone call to Brandt back in Bonn, the economics minister, Schiller, agreed to revalue the deutschmark by 14 percent. This was the last act of the obedient ally.

Defending the Bretton Woods parities had been expensive. Germany and the Netherlands had bought dollars hand over fist prior to floating their currencies, so they took large losses with the dollar's devaluation. Failing to see any real change in U.S. policy, they were understandably reluctant to be backed into this corner again. At the Smithsonian they therefore insisted that the Bretton Woods provision permitting currencies to move by only plus or minus 1 percent be replaced by more permissive plus or minus 2.25 percent bands.[11]

This more flexible arrangement, while relieving the pressure to buy dollars, created other problems. If the deutschmark rose by a full 2.25 percent while the dollar fell the corresponding amount, and the franc did the opposite, the deutschmark/franc rate would move by 9 percent, disrupting the Common Agricultural Policy and creating problems for German manufacturers. This danger materialized in 1972 when Arthur Burns responded to the pressure from Nixon to cut interest rates.[12] Lower U.S. rates caused the dollar to weaken and capital to again flow toward Germany. Something had to be done. In March 1972 it was: the European countries agreed to hold their bilateral exchange rates to narrower margins. Not for the first time, erratic U.S. policies pushed Europe into monetary cooperation.

The new system was a deutschmark-centered arrangement under which the six EEC member states, three candidates for membership—Denmark, Ireland, and the UK—and Norway participated.[13] (In the case of the latter it may have helped that Chancellor Brandt spoke Norwegian.) The participating countries effectively created for their currencies narrow fluctuation bands inside the Smithsonian's wider bands. Their arrangement was infelicitously dubbed the

Snake in the Tunnel, the visual metaphor being a European snake wriggling in the Smithsonian tunnel. When the Smithsonian tunnel collapsed and the dollar began floating in 1973, the Snake in the Tunnel became the Snake in the Lake. The highly open economies Belgium and Luxembourg preferring even narrower fluctuation bands, theirs was the Worm wiggling in the stomach of the Snake.

But simply asserting the desire to hold exchange rates within narrow bands does not make it so. Monetary and fiscal policies must be adapted. When speculators bet against a currency, central banks must support it, and support must come from strong- and weak-currency countries alike. But while Europe spoke the language of cooperation, none of these preconditions was in place when the Snake was established. Countries simply continued on their merry fiscal and monetary ways. Denmark and the UK were driven out of the arrangement almost immediately.[14] When in early 1973 the United States decided to devalue by another 10 percent, there was further pressure on weak European currencies, forcing Italy to withdraw.

Changing the Guard

By March 1973 it had become clear that the United States was about to abandon all pretense of stabilizing the dollar. Edward Heath, whose signal achievement as prime minister had been to bring the UK into the European Economic Community, traveled to Bonn for discussions of the issue. Given sterling's recent ejection from the Snake, Heath asked for German help in solving the currency problem, help that he characterized as "a joint European response." Presumably he had in mind that Germany would deploy its dollar reserves to support the pound.

Brandt's response was to ask that Heath first commit to stabilizing sterling against the other European currencies by reentering the Snake. This brought the two sides to an impasse. Heath and his advisors were unwilling to make an exchange rate commitment of the sort that had repeatedly collapsed in the past, bringing down British governments with it, without a promise of unlimited German support.[15] But Brandt and his finance minister, Helmut Schmidt, were unwilling to extend unlimited support to sterling for fear that doing so would only validate inflationary British policies. This was not the last time that this particular standoff would occur.

Once the dollar began floating in March 1973, the remaining members of the Snake agreed to float jointly against it. In the absence of an agreement on reserve pooling and more generally on the stance of policy, the system was German led. The Bundesbank set the level of interest rates, and other central banks followed. But with the Bundesbank pulling one way and governments pulling the other, the tension could be acute. In 1973, when commodity price inflation rose, the Bundesbank tightened. France, reluctant to go along, suffered capital outflows, forcing it to withdraw from the Snake in 1974. It returned in 1975 but again withdrew in 1976. In each instance France blamed Germany for failing to adapt its policy to broader European needs, in other words, to France's needs. The Germans accused the French of inadequate discipline.

All this was disheartening to the champions of European integration, who had seen the Snake as a step toward monetary union. Helmut Schmidt, the former finance minister who succeeded to the chancellorship late in 1974 when one of Brandt's close personal advisors was unmasked as an East German spy, was a committed Europeanist. Schmidt also had extensive grounding in economics, having earned a degree in the subject and, on leaving university, working in the department of economic policy of the city-state of Hamburg. He now saw agreement to stabilize currencies as a route to deeper European integration. He also saw it as a way of playing down Germany's economic and financial dominance, which raised hackles elsewhere in Europe. Schmidt could sell an exchange rate agreement to German exporters as protecting them from further losses of competitiveness due to deutschmark appreciation. The question was whether he could sell it to the Bundesbank.

Schmidt's French counterpart, Valéry Giscard d'Estaing, took over as French head of state following Pompidou's sudden death from lymphoma in 1974. Giscard was a modernizer. On election night he had scandalized the political establishment by saluting his opponent, the socialist François Mitterrand, in English as well as French. He instructed male guests to his inauguration to wear ordinary business suits rather than the traditional striped pants, and on arriving at the Elysée Palace reviewed a functioning army unit as opposed to the silver-helmeted Republican Guard.

He now sought to inject a similar pragmatism into monetary affairs. Giscard had already overseen, in one capacity or another, three embarrassing devaluations of the franc. He viewed an agreement on exchange rates as a way for France to achieve stability while also having more say in European monetary affairs. Having been born in Germany—his father served as an administrator when France occupied the Rhineland after World War I— but grown up in France, Giscard had heard about Franco-German conflict and hyperinflation over the dinner table. Like Schmidt, he was committed, intellectually and emotionally, to European integration. For once, Europe's monetary fate was in the hands of two men who were both committed Europeanists and, as former ministers of finance, economically well informed.

Death by Committee

The question was when to move. Roy Jenkins, the controversial British politician who in 1977 became president of the European Commission, the EEC's proto-executive branch, provided an opening. James Callaghan's Labour Government had banished Jenkins to Brussels over his advocacy of European integration, which did not sit well with Labour backbenchers, and a lavish lifestyle unbecoming of a socialist. There Jenkins fell under the spell of Robert Triffin, the Belgian international monetary economist who was employed by the Commission as a consultant.[16] In a speech at the European University Institute in Florence in late 1977, Jenkins advocated relaunching negotiations for European Monetary Union. Echoing the Werner Report, he proposed enlarging the budget of the European Economic Community to provide assistance to countries, presumably including his own, that would find it hard to adapt to a rigorous German-style monetary policy.

Although Jenkins's ideas received a frosty reception in London, they provided an opening for Schmidt and Giscard.[17] This being another period of dollar weakness, capital flows from the United States to Germany again pushed the deutschmark up and eroded Germany's export competitiveness. For Schmidt this was a "dollar calamity."[18] Between mid-January and mid-February 1978 the Bundesbank spent DM 1.7 billion in foreign exchange markets to limit the currency's appreciation. But the effort was fruitless. France, Italy, and the UK having all left the Snake, there was no larger group of European currencies to share the pressure. The deutschmark felt it full bore.

European governments responded at their April 1978 meeting in Copenhagen by—who would have guessed—forming a committee. Over the next couple of months its members met five times without much progress.

By June Giscard and Schmidt had had enough. They delegated responsibility for drawing up the plan to Horst Schulmann of the Federal Chancellor's Office and Bernard Clappier, who was governor of the Bank of France but acted as the French president's personal representative. Downing Street was invited to join so that the initiative could be a joint effort of the three big European countries. When it became clear that they would be unable to deflect Schulmann and Clappier from their ambitious plans, the British simply stopped attending their meetings.

Schulmann and Clappier proceeded unhindered not just by the English but by their own finance ministers, who were kept in the dark about their deliberations, as was Otmar Emminger, now Clappier's counterpart at the Bundesbank. Their blueprint was unveiled in July 1978 as a joint Giscard-Schmidt initiative. There would be a new set of 2.25 percent exchange rate bands modeled on the Snake.[19] To ensure that this was not another German-dominated system, bands would be defined relative to a basket of European currencies. A trigger mechanism would force strong-currency countries to relax monetary conditions and weak-currency countries to tighten. Central banks would be obliged to intervene to keep currencies in the grid. After 2 years a European Monetary Fund would be established to administer the pooled reserves of the members. At an unspecified future date, there would be a transition to monetary union.

An agreement acquired new urgency for the German Government later in July, when the Carter administration pressed it to expand demand and reduce the German trade surplus. For an inflation-adverse country, this pressure was not welcome. Schmidt was already not particularly fond of Carter, whose folksy informality did not sit well with a chancellor not accustomed to being addressed by his first name. He grew even less fond of him now.

Schmidt and Giscard's proposals were not exactly to the taste of the British Government, although, having met Clappier and Schulmann's ambitions by boycotting their meetings, it should not have been surprised by the result. The train having left the station, the British now set their sights on a deferral from the obligation to participate. Schmidt and Giscard were happy to agree if doing so was the price of proceeding.

Nor were the proposals to the liking of the Bundesbank. A trigger mechanism forcing the Bundesbank to expand would limit its ability to fight inflation. Obliging it to intervene in support of weak currencies could make it complicit in the reckless policies of other countries. Pooling reserves would threaten its independence as enshrined in the Bundesbank Law. Emminger, no fan of the plan that had been sprung on him, launched a last-ditch counterattack. But Schmidt was a passionate believer in European integration, having fought on the eastern front during World War II and been a prisoner of war of the British army for three months in 1945. He responded, in the first ever in-person visit by a head of the West German state to the famously independent central bank, with an emotional speech to the Bundesbank Council. Schmidt invoked Auschwitz and the war and characterized the new agreement as the capstone of postwar reconciliation.

Council members could hardly remain unmoved. What they could do was demand concessions. They insisted that the trigger mechanism be dropped. They tolerated no more discussion of reserve pooling. They countenanced no discussion of substituting a basket of currencies for the deutschmark as the pivot of the system. They insisted on no more talk of monetary union. They demanded an opt-out from unlimited intervention obligations.[20]

The Government conceded the key points. Economics minister Otto von Lambsdorff confirmed as much to the Bundestag: "The Bundesbank has the responsibility to intervene and the option not to intervene if it is its opinion that it is not able to do so."[21]

It is unlikely that this saddened Chancellor Schmidt. He could resist France's more radical proposals, telling the French that while he favored them personally, the Bundesbank prevented him from acting.

THE UNSTABLE EMS

The European Monetary System (EMS) thus came into operation without a trigger mechanism or unequivocal intervention obligations. Its operational component, the Exchange Rate Mechanism, or ERM, resembled the Snake more than its founders were prepared to acknowledge. The main difference was that when problems of competitiveness built up, countries now adjusted their currencies within the mechanism rather than abandoning it. The first such "realignment," as these adjustments were cosmetically known, was in September 1979, barely six months after the start of the system, when other currencies were devalued by 2 percent against the deutschmark.[22] The next 4 years then saw five more realignments, the most dramatic of which, in 1981, 1982, and 1983, involved further devaluations of the French franc.

This was a problem for François Mitterrand, who finally defeated Giscard for the presidency in 1981. Mitterrand was nominally a Socialist and a Europeanist, though principled stands were not his strong suit. Born in 1916 into a rural Catholic family in a village not far from the town of Cognac, the young François was drafted into the French army with the outbreak of World War II and immediately sent to the Maginot Line, where he was wounded by German artillery shrapnel and taken prisoner in June 1940. He spoke later of having befriended in prison a circle of Communists who started him on his intellectual journey to the left. But after escaping from prison camp on a third attempt and slipping through the Jura Mountains into Vichy-controlled southern France, Mitterrand found employment as a civil servant in the collaborationist Vichy government. He then joined the Resistance in 1943, for whom he organized war prisoners' groups to agitate against the Nazi occupation. Similar contradictions would characterize his later life. Aloof and cerebral, Mitterrand's motives were hard to decipher for even his close advisors. As president he regularly changed direction when doing so was expedient.

On winning the presidency in 1981 on his third attempt (which he likened to his third successful attempt at escaping the German prison camp), Mitterrand vowed to "break with capitalism." He nationalized the banks and five large industrial companies. He ramped up social spending, raised the minimum wage, and shortened the workweek. Demand boomed and inflation soared. The franc predictably came under pressure.

Two realignments followed, in October 1981 and June 1982. But negotiating realignments was difficult: rates against not just the deutschmark but the entire group of European currencies had to be agreed. The process was embarrassing for a left-wing Government concerned to establish its economic bona fides.

But with the French authorities pushing hard on the economic accelerator, capital continued to flow out even after two devaluations. By early 1983 the situation had again deteriorated markedly. In March Mitterrand toyed with the idea of withdrawing from the EMS to save further embarrassment. But while doing so would have saved him from having to engage in currency negotiations with Germany, it would not have saved the franc. Nor would it have saved Mitterrand from being tarred with the devaluationist brush. It might not even have allowed the French Government to continue its expansionary policies, since it would have removed the franc's one real source of credibility.

These points were driven home by Jacques Delors, the banker and economist who served as Mitterrand's minister of economy and finance. Delors's wartime experience—as a youth in southern France he had lived under German occupation, and his best friend had been deported to Auschwitz for carrying messages for the Resistance—predisposed him toward European integration. His family background encouraged him to see monetary integration as a means to that end. Delors's father had worked as a messenger for the Bank of France. After World War II, the son followed in the father's footsteps, joining the central bank at the tender age of nineteen.

Despite stints as a trade union official, employee of the state planning commission, and member of the European Parliament, Delors never quite lost the visage of an austere, technocratic central banker. Although nominally a Socialist, he was on the very moderate left and less convinced than many of his colleagues of the ability of the state to outguess the market. He was also more pro-European than many of his Socialist colleagues and worried that the Government's program of aggressive demand stimulus, by threatening the stability of the franc, might threaten the European project. In his position as Mitterrand's minister of economy and finance, Delors became known as the "Apostle of Rigor."

The Apostle now sounded the alarm. Withdrawing from the Exchange Rate Mechanism, he warned, would shatter France's ambition of charting the course of European integration. Not one to stand on socialist principle, Mitterrand accepted Delors's advice, cutting back on spending while undertaking one last devaluation within the ERM to encourage external demand.

This last step required German cooperation. But Germany hesitated. Its economy was just beginning to emerge from its early-1980s recession, and revaluing the deutschmark would not be helpful.

This put the ball squarely in the court of Helmut Kohl, the conservative Christian Democrat who had assumed the chancellorship in 1982. Kohl was a different kind of West German leader. He was the first chancellor of the Federal Republic not to speak English. He was the first one too young to actually fight in World War II or, like Brandt, to have to flee, though the experience of the war had a powerful impact on his attitude toward Europe.[23] While his girth, gregariousness, and modest background—his father had been a low-level government functionary, and the young Helmut had supplemented his allowance by raising rabbits—caused him to be regularly underestimated, he ended up as the longest-serving chancellor in West German history. With time Kohl became known for exceptional persistence—something that would not have surprised his wife, whom he wooed with more than 2,000 love letters. Among the things in which he persisted was the pursuit of European integration.

Kohl may not have known much economics, but he knew enough to understand that giving in to pressure to revalue could choke off a recovery that was just getting its feet. But as a committed Europeanist he did not want to be responsible for the collapse of the Community's newly constructed monetary system. And having grown up in the Rhineland—Palatinate, close on the French border, Kohl was instinctively sympathetic to France.

Mitterrand, like Kohl, may not have understood economics, but he understood Germany and appreciated that threatening to withdraw from the EMS could get its attention. Over the third weekend in March, at a meeting in Bonn, Delors repeated the threat. Not one normally given to theatrics, he "threatened, raged and [threw] temper tantrums" in a performance worthy of John Connally. "What am I supposed to do with arrogant and uncomprehending people?" he asked in a dismissive reference to German reluctance to revalue.[24] Shocked by the histrionics, the Germans caved. Kohl instructed his finance minister, Gerhard Stoltenberg, to revalue the deutschmark against the other EMS currencies, limiting the need for the franc to move downward against the group and saving face for France.

Having achieved the improvement in external competitiveness needed to encourage exports, Paris could now proceed with spending cuts without risking a massive recession. Unemployment rose but not by enough to jeopardize the Socialist Government. And as the budget moved toward balance, the franc stabilized. The EMS entered a quiet period in which there were realignments but no crises. Having put this early episode of monetary brinkmanship behind it, Europe could get back to business.

One Market, One Money

The outcome enhanced the stature of Mitterrand, Kohl, and Delors, three men who would play key roles in the next phase in European integration. Delors acquired the Government's budget portfolio to go with his responsibilities for economy and finance. He then became president of the European Commission with French and German backing. The Kohl Government may have been shocked by Delors's 1983 histrionics, but it appreciated that it had been he who convinced Mitterrand of the overriding importance of monetary stability.

Delors then launched the Single Market in 1986 and relaunched the monetary union project in 1988. The Single Market, a Europe-wide market in goods, capital, and labor, was his effort to reinvigorate an integration process that had stalled out in the early 1980s. Monetary union he saw as the "jewel in the crown" of Europe. In long-standing French tradition he saw the goal of creating a European reserve currency alongside the dollar as one of the important results of this process. He succeeded in getting into the Single Market Act a commitment to monetary unification but not a deadline—the act referred only to the "progressive realization" of monetary union.

To French leaders, this promised that one day they would be able to wrest back control of Europe's monetary steering wheel. Another bout of franc weakness in the mid-1980s heightened their enthusiasm. The French blamed their difficulties on the decline of the dollar starting in late 1985, which caused the deutschmark to strengthen through no fault of France's own. This reinforced the argument for freeing France from the tyranny of a dollar-centered international system.

The Kohl Government was all for the Single Market, since German exporters could always use better market access, but its attitude toward monetary union was more guarded. The chancellor was personally supportive, but he cautioned Mitterrand that Germans would be reluctant to give up their precious deutschmarks without getting something exceptional in return. Kohl may have been alluding to the kind of deep political integration that would allow Europe, and thus Germany, to assert itself on the foreign policy stage. Or he could have been looking forward to the possibility, one day, of German reunification.

In his support for the Single Market but reluctance to commit to monetary union, Kohl had an ally in the British prime minister, Margaret Thatcher, who saw the Single Market as a lever for rolling back regulation but monetary union as a Gallic dirigiste conspiracy. Over the opposition of some of her top advisors, she kept sterling out of the ERM.

But neither Kohl nor Thatcher was capable of stopping the crafty Delors. In turning now from the Single Market to monetary union, Delors had the support of Paris, whose discomfort with the status quo grew stronger the longer it was forced the follow Germany's monetary dictates. The same was true of Europe's other weak-currency countries, Italy for example.

Delors then received support from the most unlikely of sources, the German Foreign Office. In February 1988 foreign minister Hans-Dietrich Genscher penned a memorandum sketching the case for a European central bank. The German foreign ministry had traditionally privileged the defense alliance with the United States. Genscher's memo was an indication that the growing weakness of the Soviet Union had caused priorities to shift. Genscher himself was a committed Europeanist. He saw the creation of a European central bank as the next logical step in the direction of political integration and as liberating German foreign policy from its historical shackles. He emphasized also that putting a European central bank in charge of a single currency would reduce Europe's dependence on the dollar, an argument sure to appeal to the French.

Those in charge of economic policy, such as the finance minister, Stoltenberg, and the Bundesbank president, Karl Otto Pöhl, were aghast. But with a formidable international coalition arrayed against them, they were unable to block the formation of an expert committee under Delors to draw up plans.

LONG AND WINDING ROAD

The decision to form the Delors Committee was taken in the spring of 1988. Its report, published a year later, described a three-step transition to monetary union not unlike that of the Werner Report 20 years before.

But, in contrast to its predecessor, the Delors Report emphasized the importance of giving the new monetary institution a price stability mandate. It was explicit about the need for a European central bank and for pooling the reserves of the participating countries. In a bow to Thatcherite skepticism, it did not insist on the need for political integration to *accompany* monetary integration, although Delors for one hoped that political integration would *follow*. It did not endorse a substantially larger EEC budget, a union-wide system of taxes and transfers, or other compromises of national fiscal prerogatives, such proposals having led to the demise of the Werner Report. While these concessions were politically expedient, they would, with time, create serious problems for the monetary union. And those problems would turn out to be important for limiting the ability of the euro to rival the dollar.[25]

The key provision was central bank independence, on which Germany insisted but to which France, where the central bank was traditionally subservient to the state, had long been opposed.[26] Mitterrand had already moved some way from the traditional French position as a result of the monetary difficulties of the 1980s. Having been convinced by Delors of the benefits to France of the discipline of the Exchange Rate Mechanism, he appreciated the advantages of insulating monetary policy from politics. Members of the Delors Committee channeling the German view secured agreement on the need for a significant degree of economic convergence prior to the transition to monetary union and therefore on the setting of preconditions for countries to participate. Delors opposed these last provisions, worrying that preconditions might cause the wrong country (read: France) to be excluded, but was forced to concede in the face of the German veto.

With these compromises, the Delors Committee could finalize its report, which was endorsed by European governments at their summit in June 1989. Not everyone was convinced. Opinion in the corridors of the Bundesbank ranged from skeptical to downright hostile. President Pöhl and his colleagues were confident that they would prevail. They knew that a government that proposed that Germans give up their rock-solid deutschmarks for a European money would be committing political hari-kari.

At this point, the process almost certainly would have stalled out again. What prevented this was, with hindsight, blindingly obvious: the end of the Cold War. The decision of European governments to negotiate a legally binding agreement on monetary union was taken in December 1989, little more than a month after the fall of the Berlin Wall and Kohl's announcement of a ten-point plan for German reunification. Now that Germany's land area, population, and economic capacity were set to expand at a stroke, it became even more urgent to lock it into Europe. Deepening the European Union, a process in which monetary unification was the next step, was the logical way of doing just that. This was the case Mitterrand made to a skeptical Margaret Thatcher when the two met at Chequers shortly before the fall of the Wall.[27]

German economic and monetary reunification formally required the assent of the four post–World War II occupying powers: the United States, France, Britain, and the Soviet Union. A crumbling Soviet Union was in no position to resist. Its leverage was limited to negotiating an agreement that East German property seized by the Soviets during their occupation would not be repatriated to its former owners. And once Moscow acquiesced, France could not stand in the way. But the uncertainty lasted long enough for Mitterrand to threaten Genscher that he might ally with Thatcher and Gorbachev to make reunification as difficult as possible. This was enough for Paris to secure from Bonn agreement to proceed to the next step, an intergovernmental conference on European Monetary Union in 1990.

Proceed they did. The Bundesbank was allowed to draft the statute of the European Central Bank. Predictably, it emphasized independence, insulation from political interference, and a mandate for price stability. With reunification now a fait accompli, the German position hardened. The new central bank should be structured federally, like the Bundesbank. Its ability to finance government budget deficits should be limited, like the Bundesbank's. Countries should first bring down their inflation, budget deficits, and debts in order to participate. Budget deficits would have to be limited to 3 percent of national income, government debts to 60 percent. Exchange rates would have to be held stable. All these provisions went straight into the draft treaty agreed to at the summit in the Dutch city of Maastricht in 1991.

At Maastricht President Mitterrand secured only one concession, but a vital one. It was that the new regime would start at the latest in 1999.

Fault Lines

No sooner did European leaders take this momentous step than the ground shifted beneath them. A magnitude 7 earthquake struck the Exchange Rate Mechanism. There had been no currency realignments in more than 5 years.

Those of optimistic temperament could claim that national policies had been successfully reconciled to the imperatives of exchange rate stability. Italy had moved from the wide band allowed the system's weak sisters to the conventional 2.25 percent band. The UK had entered the ERM in 1990, Mrs. Thatcher having finally bought the argument that doing so was a painless way of bringing down inflation.[28] Having demonstrated its ability to live with stable exchange rates, Europe was ready for monetary union.

But there was another interpretation. It was not the absence of a need but the absence of an ability that dictated no more realignments. The act creating the Single Market had mandated removing controls on capital flows as part of building an integrated market not just in merchandise but in financial capital. The directive mandating the liberalization of capital flows entered into force on July 1, 1990.[29] With nothing now to restrain capital movements, there was no breathing space for organizing realignments. If markets got wind that a government was prepared to realign downward, there could be a surge of capital out of the currency as investors rushed to sell before its value fell. If they were right, they would reap enormous gains. And if they were wrong and the currency didn't move, they lost nothing. The Hungarian-American investor George Soros alone mobilized billions of dollars, most of it borrowed, to bet against the pound in 1992.

So governments could no longer contemplate realigning for fear of exciting adverse speculation. When imbalances built up, there now was no way of venting them. Inflation-prone Southern European countries made progress after 1987 in bringing their inflation rates down. But the effects of inflation were cumulative. Inflation rates still just marginally higher than Germany's, if allowed to persist, could cumulate into a serious loss of competitiveness. By the early 1990s this had become a major problem for countries like Italy.

In Britain, the problem was different, but the result was the same. When the country entered the ERM in 1990, sterling was unusually strong against the deutschmark. The Bundesbank had restrained the normal temptation to raise interest rates while the Federal Republic was still digesting the former East Germany. And the British economy was at the peak of the business cycle, disguising the weakness of the country's industrial sector. Once the Bundesbank began raising rates in November 1990—and it now raised them aggressively to make up for lost time—the high sterling exchange rate began to bite.

The situation being delicately balanced, even a small shock could upset the apple cart. That shock came from, of all places, tiny Denmark. Unlike most of its neighbors, Denmark put the Maastricht Treaty to a public referendum. On June 2, 1992, voters rejected the treaty by the narrow margin of 50.7 to 49.3 percent. They were to ratify it later in a second referendum, but no matter; for now the prospects for monetary union grew dim. And if there might be no monetary union, the incentive for governments to keep their exchange rates stable so as to qualify for participation was reduced.

Understanding this logic, speculators pounced, attacking the lira and pound. The standard defense was to raise interest rates, making it more expensive for speculators to borrow money to bet against a currency. But the Italian Government was burdened with heavy debts, which grew heavier at higher interest rates.[30] In the UK, home mortgages were tied to the level of interest rates; homeowners howled when rates were hiked. In Sweden, not yet an EU member but having tied the krona to the ERM, the problem was a weak banking system. Across Europe, unemployment was high. All this created doubts about whether governments were prepared to stay the course.

On July 16, the Bundesbank raised the discount rate again—its tenth successive increase—citing capital inflows that again caused its money supply targets to overshoot. The rate reached its highest level since 1931. The Bundesbankers may not have been purposely ratcheting up the pressure on questionable candidates for monetary union, but if this was a consequence of their actions, then it is hard to imagine that they regretted it. The new British Government of John Major pressed the German Government not to raise rates. In July Major wrote Chancellor Kohl, urging restraint. But the German Government didn't make monetary policy—the Bundesbank did. And it didn't respond well to pressure.

By August, sterling and the lira had fallen as far as permitted by ERM rules. There was then one last attempt, at an emergency meeting in the English resort town of Bath, to organize a response. This would have married devaluation of the weak ERM currencies to a cut in German interest rates. But the finance ministers were unable to agree on who should devalue by how much. Britain and France feared association with Italy and discouraged talk of collective realignment. Britain's chancellor, Norman Lamont, badly badgered his German counterparts, causing them to stiffen their necks—and their interest rates.

In the second week of September the magnitude of George Soros's bet against sterling was conveniently leaked to the press. Then on the evening of September 15 the German financial newspaper *Handelsblatt* released excerpts from an interview with Bundesbank president Helmut Schlesinger in which he blandly observed that "further devaluations cannot be excluded."[31] With markets in New York still open, the pressure on weak European currencies became excruciating. A desperate Bank of England raised its key interest rate from 10 to 12 percent the following morning and announced the intention of raising it further. But this failed to calm investors, who understood that the impact on variable-rate mortgages and unemployment would drain away public support. The authorities couldn't afford to keep rates high for long. Investors could afford to wait them out.

Seeing the writing on the wall, Lamont canceled the second promised increase in interest rates. Shortly before midnight, the Monetary Committee of the European Community accepted Britain's request to take its currency out of the ERM and did the same for Italy. Some of the Community's poorer economies, such as Spain, having been exempted from the relevant provisions of the capital markets directive, still had capital controls in place, so while they, too, were forced to devalue, they were able to stay in the ERM.

Speculators now trained their sights on the franc, the last major European currency not yet devalued against the deutschmark. When the Maastricht Treaty barely squeaked to victory in the referendum in France on September 20, investors began to wonder whether the French authorities were prepared to take hard measures to defend the franc. Not without reason: with unemployment high, Paris preferred to see the problem resolved by lower interest rates in Germany rather than higher rates in France. The French Government pushed the German Government in the hope that the latter would push the Bundesbank.

They key meeting, between French treasury secretary Jean-Claude Trichet (the same Jean-Claude Trichet later to head the European Central Bank) and a phalanx of senior German officials, took place on the sidelines of the IMF–World Bank annual meetings in Washington, D.C., on September 22. Trichet told Bundesbank president Schlesinger, much as Schmidt had told Emminger in 1978, that the German central bank's obduracy jeopardized five decades of Franco-German cooperation. Once again, invoking the legacy of

World War II was enough to make the Bundesbankers blink. They agreed to a joint statement of support for the franc-deutschmark parity and to additional credits for the Bank of France. The Bundesbank then moved to cut German money market rates. With this the tension subsided.[32]

At least it subsided temporarily. The Portuguese and Spanish were forced to devalue again in November and once more the following May; evidently the escudo and peseta were not as sacrosanct as the franc. With other countries gaining competitiveness at its expense, before long the pressure on France was back. And with unemployment rising, investors again openly questioned whether the French had the stomach to raise interest rates to defend the franc. June 1993 saw a new prime minister, Edouard Balladur, and a new finance minister, Edmond Alphandéry. The leadership change was yet another reason for uncertainty, prompting additional capital outflows.

The situation quickly grew desperate. In late June Alphandéry requested an urgent meeting with his German counterpart, Theo Waigel. Waigel, unwilling to be cornered, cited other pressing business. When the Bundesbank Council again declined to cut its discount rate, massive sales of francs ensued. In the last week of July alone, the Bank of France spent $32 billion buying francs but failed to calm the markets. At an emergency meeting the following weekend, finance ministers and central bank governors bowed to the inevitable, agreeing to widen ERM bands from 2.25 to 15 percent. Currencies were now sufficiently free to move that they no longer offered speculators one-way bets.

LUXEMBOURG'S REVENGE

But whether this more permissive ERM still offered a path to monetary union was uncertain. Britain and France blamed the crisis on the Bundesbank's high interest rates. Germany, in their view, had failed to appropriately repay them for agreeing to reunification. The Germans saw the French and British as having been laid low by their own indiscipline. The dispute reopened old sores. It reopened the question of whether such very different countries could comfortably share a currency.

Given all this recrimination, the fact that over the next 6 years nine European countries successfully completed the transition to monetary union takes some explaining. Explanation starts with the simple fact that recessions do not last forever. Having endured a recession in the early 1990s, after 1993 Europe enjoyed an expansion, buoyed by depreciated currencies that boosted export competitiveness. Everything was easier with economic growth. In particular, reducing budget deficits as required for admission to the monetary union was easier.

And just as a weak dollar had contributed to Europe's earlier financial difficulties, a strong dollar now relieved them. Under the influence of treasury secretary Robert Rubin, the Clinton administration restrained the growth of government spending. America's fiscal position strengthened, and confidence in its currency returned. The dollar rose, further enhancing Europe's competitiveness. This meant faster growth and lighter fiscal burdens. It meant strong growth in 1997, the year when governments seeking to the join the monetary union were required to reduce their budget deficits to 3 percent of GDP. It meant that Italy, which had been driven out of the Exchange Rate Mechanism in 1992, found it possible to reenter. There is no little irony in the fact that a strong dollar helped make possible the transition to the euro, given that a weak dollar had regularly provided impetus for Europe to move in this direction.

For monetary union to happen, Europe still had to capitalize on these circumstances. Fortunately, the political context was favorable. In Germany, Helmut Kohl, with his strong personal commitment to political integration, remained in office; he was voted out only in September 1998, by which time preparations for the transition to the euro were complete. In France, the desire to escape a status quo where Germany controlled European monetary conditions had been strengthened by the embarrassments of 1992–1993. Moreover, with German unification, the need to lock Germany peacefully into Europe was seen as more pressing than ever, and monetary unification was the most powerful mechanism available for doing so. From the start, monetary union had been a political project. And in the end, politics, for better or worse, carried the day.

In Germany, as always, there was the specter of inflation, which the Bundesbank raised at every turn. Securing the support of the central bankers, or even their acquiescence, required extending them concessions, some symbolic, some real. Kohl secured his partners' agreement that the European Monetary Institute, the forerunner of the European Central Bank, would be located in Frankfurt, the home of the German central bank. Assuming that this meant that the ECB would also be situated there, Frankfurt would have a leg up in the competition to become Europe's financial center. Waigel negotiated a Stability Pact under which governments were obliged to limit their budget deficits to 3 percent of GDP after adopting the euro. Germany secured agreement on calling the new currency the euro rather than the more French-inflected ecu. It secured the appointment as founding president of the ECB Wim Duisenberg of the Netherlands, a country that for decades had followed strictly Germanic monetary policies. It got Otmar Issing, a hard-core monetarist and member of the Bundesbank directorate, as the new central bank's chief economist.

With France and Germany now on board, the only question was who would come along for the ride. In the scenario regarded as most likely, the answer was a handful of Germany's stability-minded neighbors, epitomized by the Netherlands. Other countries might join but only once they had demonstrated the discipline needed to limit their deficits and bring down their debts. But in another scenario, other less stability-minded countries like Italy, Portugal, and Spain would participate from the start. There was the danger that they would run deficits and press the ECB for more accommodative monetary policies if in. But there was also the danger that they would regularly depreciate their currencies and steal a competitive advantage on German, French, and Dutch exporters if out.

The decision ultimately turned on little Luxembourg. With its low debt and stable policies, its credentials were impeccable. But Luxembourg was already in a monetary union with Belgium; Belgian francs circulated in both countries. This would have made it awkward to leave Belgium out. But if Belgium, with its high ratio of public debt to GDP, was in, then it would be impossible to invoke the Maastricht Treaty's public debt ceiling to keep the others out. In this way the monetary union started off in 1999 with nine members, including not just Belgium but also Ireland, Italy, Portugal, and Spain. Greece, though a problem case, was not that different from the Iberians, so it was then admitted in 2001. This decision to go for a large monetary union was fateful. It saddled the euro area with a set of heavily indebted members with deep structural problems. This was something that would eventually come back to haunt it and handicap efforts to obtain for the currency a more prominent international role.

Had Britain, home to Europe's leading financial center, also joined, things might have been different. But unlike Italy, Britain had only a brief flirtation with the EMS. Tony Blair could credit his victory in the 1997 general election to the damage done to the Conservative Government of John Major by the 1992 crisis and sterling's ignominious ejection from the Exchange Rate Mechanism. Blair was understandably reluctant to repeat the experiment. That after 1992 Britain followed stable policies reassured other European countries about the consequences of its remaining outside. A euro that was the currency of not just nine European economies but also the UK and the City of London would have been an even more formidable rival to the dollar. But it was not to be.

Even without London's help, however, Europe's new currency posed an intriguing alternative to the dollar. And, before long, the search for alternatives would become more than just a matter of intrigue.

CHAPTER 5

CRISIS

Stability is the sine qua non of a currency that is widely used in international transactions. Whether they rely on it as a means of payment, unit of account or store of value, a currency's stability is the first thing to which exporters, importers, and investors all look. Nothing, it follows, can more seriously damage the regard in which a currency is held than a full-blown financial crisis—that of course being precisely what the United States experienced in 2008–2009.

It is entirely natural, therefore, that in the wake of the crisis questions should have been asked about the dollar's international role. The assertion that the United States had a comparative advantage as an originator of high-quality financial assets came to be dismissed as a joke. The belief that the complex financial instruments retailed by U.S. institutions were as reliable as treasury bonds was shown to be false. The immensely large budgetary costs of digging the economy out of the hole created by the crisis raised suspicions that the Fed might seek to inflate away the debt, especially that part held by foreigners. All this pointed to the possibility that the crisis was a turning point. It could prompt a large-scale migration away from the dollar on the part of importers, exporters, and foreign investors alike. And the existence now of alternatives such as the euro seemed to suggest that the possibility was more than hypothetical.

But there were also those who suggested that all this dollar doom and gloom was overdone. Each time the crisis reached new heights—first in July 2007 with Bear Stearns's liquidation of two in-house hedge funds, then with the collapse of Bear in March 2008, and finally with the bankruptcy of the investment firm Lehman Brothers the following September—the dollar strengthened against the euro and other currencies. The dollar was still the ultimate safe haven for frightened investors around the world. And if it could survive these events with its international role intact, it could survive anything. Or so its defenders insisted.

Making sense of their arguments and determining whether they are right require understanding not just the impact of the crisis but also the role of the dollar's exorbitant privilege in bringing it about.

Roots of the Crisis

At the root of the crisis lay financial irregularities unchecked by adequate regulation. Banks outsourced the origination of mortgage contracts to specialized brokers. Often these individuals had little professional training, there being no meaningful federal or in some cases even state licensing requirements. In many states, brokers had no fiduciary responsibility to their so-called clients, the homeowners they sometimes all but dragooned into signing contracts. This meant that the broker bore no legal responsibility if a homeowner somehow, just somehow, misunderstood the terms and ended up unable to pay. And the broker suffered no financial consequences, having been paid his fee and passed the mortgage along to the bank that was in effect his real employer.

Banks then packaged batches of these contracts into residential-mortgage-backed securities or passed them on to other banks and special-purpose vehicles able to do so. The resulting securities were then sold not just to other banks but to pension funds, mutual funds, and other investors. There being a limited market for bonds backed by some of these securities, they were then repackaged as collateralized debt obligations (CDOs). The holders of these even more complex instruments had different claims on the income streams associated with the underlying mortgage-backed securities. The typical CDO was separated into a senior tranche, holders of which got paid first out of the income on the underlying mortgage-backed securities; a mezzanine tranche, holders of which got paid second; and the disarmingly named "equity" tranche, holders of which got paid last if at all. The next step was then CDOs squared, CDOs made out of other CDOs. Next were CDOs cubed.

This, argued the investment banks that earned generous fees for slicing, dicing, and repackaging the mortgage-backed securities in question, was all a way of more efficiently separating out risks and shifting them to those with the right risk-bearing ability. The reality, we now know, was different. This complex process was in fact a way of disguising risks rather than simply assembling them into more efficient bundles. It ended up shifting risks from those with more risk tolerance to others with less risk tolerance—to, say, the Missouri State Employees' Retirement System and the Teachers Retirement System of Texas—who often had little idea of the attributes of the assets they were buying.[1] But all this is wisdom after the fact. At the time, the riskiness of these instruments was inadequately appreciated by the wider investment community. It was not something that the originating investment banks were inclined to advertise. Nor were they obliged to do so since they did their work in the absence of meaningful regulatory oversight.

It was also a business model that would not have been viable without help from confederates, starting with the rating agencies. Pension funds and mutual funds, whose covenants limited the amount of risk they were permitted to take on, needed investment-grade ratings from Standard & Poor's and Moody's to purchase CDOs.[2] The rating agencies rated the CDOs, but they also advised their originators how to structure them so that the senior tranche would win an AAA rating. For this latter activity they earned handsome fees. It is easy to imagine how their employees would have felt pressure to confer the expected rating. The rating agencies deny that they were subject to conflicts of interest. One wonders.

But the originator still might find few willing buyers of the speculative equity tranche. Not infrequently the originating bank ended up having to hold it on its own balance sheet. This was a constraint on expanding the business. A solution was then found in the form of insurance to further "enhance" the securities. For a fee, the risk of default could be transferred to another entity. Suitably insured, some portion of the equity tranche could then be sold off to other investors. The mechanism for obtaining this insurance, once obscure, was the now notorious contract known as a credit default swap. And the leading underwriter of these insurance contracts was the thinly capitalized American International Group (AIG). Exactly what those responsible for decision making at AIG were thinking will forever be a mystery. Be this as it may, they, too, took their decisions in the absence of meaningful regulatory oversight.[3]

Savvy investors, starting with the investment banks themselves, understood that holding the equity tranche was risky. There would be losses if the housing market turned down. The credit default swap providing the insurance might not be worth the paper it was written on if the provider, or counterparty, got into trouble. Investment banks presumably did not anticipate the size of the hole that CDOs could blow in their balance sheets. But they probably did anticipate earning low returns on this part of their portfolios. Their response was to attempt to boost the return on capital by expanding their balance sheets. In other words, they used more borrowed money—in some cases, *much* more borrowed money—to maintain the now customary profit margin. From this flowed the explosive growth of leverage—the ratio of borrowed funds to own capital—of bank and nonbank financial institutions.

This was not a phenomenon limited to the investment banks at the center of the crisis. Other financial institutions not so deeply invested in residential-mortgage-backed securities, CDOs, and other "sophisticated" financial instruments also levered up. Behind this was the growth of a wholesale money market on which financial institutions could borrow large sums for periods as short as overnight. There was also the willingness of regulators to look the other way. In particular, investment banks, which once gambled only their partners' money but now gambled the money of others, and their conduits and special-purpose vehicles remained largely outside the regulatory net.

ASLEEP AT THE SWITCH

But even commercial banks were permitted to take on more leverage. Standard regulatory practice dictated requiring a commercial bank to hold core capital— its shareholders' own funds—equal to 8 percent of the bank's investments as a cushion against losses. Now the regulators, in their wisdom, allowed them to substitute less liquid instruments for shareholders' common equity. Commercial banks were permitted to substitute so-called hybrid instruments and junior debt, the holders of which get paid just before equity holders but after other claimants. These not so liquid instruments were known as "Tier 2 capital" to distinguish them from the funds of bank shareholders, so-called Tier 1 capital. Under the Basel Accord, the agreement on capital adequacy negotiated by the Basel Committee on Banking Supervision (the committee of national regulators that meets at the Bank for International Settlements, the bankers' bank in Basel), banks were permitted to hold as little as 2 percent common equity as a share of risk-weighted assets.

As a result, commercial banks had less capital to cushion themselves against losses. They had fewer reserves out of which to pay their debts if things went wrong. Again, the regulators averted their eyes. Even worse, they bought into the idea that the banks were now capable of more efficiently managing their risks, justifying the substitution of cheaper and less liquid forms of capital. Internal models of the riskiness of banks' activities and, where they were too small or "backward" to possess them, commercial credit ratings were used to place assets into different categories, inelegantly called "buckets," according to their risk.

The distinction between Tier 1 and Tier 2 capital was incorporated into the Basel Accord on capital adequacy signed onto by the so-called financially advanced countries in 1988. This is a first hint, then, that the trends in question had been under way for some time and were not limited to the United States. In fact, many of those trends, from excessive leverage to the tendency for regulators to buy into the arguments of the regulated, infected the banks and financial systems of other countries, from Germany to the United Kingdom. For European banks, the American model of minimizing capital and using high levels of leverage was something to be emulated, not scorned. Ultimately, common global tendencies produced a common global crisis.

This securitization machine, itself almost as complex as the securities it spit out, had a voracious appetite for fuel. With leverage rising, portfolios expanding, and investors stretching for yield, it required extensive inputs of high-yielding securities. This need in turn encouraged the creation of more CDOs and residential-mortgage-backed securities, which in turn encouraged the origination of more mortgages. Banks loosened their credit and documentation standards. Mortgage brokers moved down the credit-quality spectrum in search of borrowers. It was an elaborate dance, although not one in which all participants were fully in touch with their partners.

To be sure, the rapid growth of subprime mortgages involved more than just this financial legerdemain. But the originate-and-distribute model, and the perverse incentives it created, was an important factor in what started out as the now quaintly sounding "subprime crisis" and developed into the most serious global credit crisis in 80 years. And as for what enabled all involved to act on those incentives, the answer is simple: inadequate regulation.

Once the dominos were lined up, just one had to be toppled to bring them all tumbling down. The first domino was the residential property market, which peaked in 2006. The second, starting in 2007, was losses for specialized investment funds invested in complex securities backed by subprime mortgages.[4] As CDO prices fell, investors received collateral calls and were forced to sell other securities. Declines in the prices of those securities then forced still other investors to sell. Before long, a full-fledged fire-sale was under way.

Suddenly aware of the risks, banks drew in their horns. In precisely those parts of the financial system where leverage was greatest, deleveraging now occurred with a vengeance. And precisely those financial institutions like Bear Stearns that had funded themselves most aggressively on the wholesale market now found themselves with collateral calls they could not meet.

Faced with extraordinary uncertainty, spenders stopped spending, plunging the economy into a tailspin and causing banks to be hit by problems on previously sound loans and investments. Regulators, finally roused from their slumbers, responded unpredictably when deciding whom to save (AIG) and whom to sacrifice (Lehman Brothers). By the final months of 2008, the situation had degenerated into a full-blown financial crisis and set the stage for the deepest recession since World War II.

DIGGING DEEPER

So far, so good. But this account begs as many questions as it answers. It begs the question of who permitted the development of an immensely large and dangerous market in complex securities. It begs the question of why banks were allowed to use their own models to gauge the riskiness of their investments and determine, essentially for their own convenience, the size of the capital cushion to be held against them. And it begs the question of how it was that the regulators remained asleep at the wheel.

The key players in the run-up to the crisis firmly positioned themselves as believers in letting markets work. In particular, they were believers in letting derivatives markets work on the grounds that they were efficient mechanisms for redistributing risk. Larry Summers, the Harvard professor who served as undersecretary, deputy secretary, and secretary of the treasury in the Clinton years, was convinced, in his incarnation as an official, that derivatives "serve an important purpose in allocating risk by letting each person take as much of whatever kind of risk he wants," as his views were described by Robert Rubin, his political mentor and predecessor as treasury secretary.[5] Summers himself put it more technically but no less unequivocally. "By helping participants manage their risk exposures better and lower their financing costs, derivatives facilitate domestic and international commerce and support a more efficient allocation of capital across the economy. They can also improve the functioning of financial markets themselves by potentially raising liquidity and narrowing the bid-asked spreads in the underlying cash markets. Thus, OTC [over-the-counter] derivatives directly and indirectly support higher investment and growth in living standards in the United States and around the world."[6] Summers the academic had been more skeptical about the efficiency of markets, but that kind of iconoclasm did not transfer easily to the policy domain.[7]

Rubin himself was more circumspect, having managed the fixed-income division at Goldman Sachs, which traded mortgage-backed securities, fixed-income futures, options, and other derivatives. The fixed-income division under Rubin had experienced problems in 1986 as a result of traders not anticipating "unlikely market conditions."[8] Rubin's traders had placed big bets on the assumption that the prevailing level of interest rates would remain broadly unchanged. When rates dropped unexpectedly, the division took losses of $100 million, a large amount of money at the time.

With his awareness of the tendency for traders to be incapable of imagining the worst, one would have expected Rubin to have been an even stronger proponent of regulating derivatives markets. His autobiography suggests that, with benefit of hindsight, he agrees.[9] But hindsight is 20/20. At the time—specifically, in 1998—Rubin, together with Summers and Federal Reserve chairman Alan Greenspan, opposed measures to regulate derivatives trading.

Specifically, they opposed such measures when they were proposed by Brooksley Born, head of the Commodity Futures Trading Commission (CFTC). Born was a formidable opponent. As an undergraduate at Stanford University in the early 1960s, her desire to become a doctor rather than a nurse had been frustrated by a guidance counselor who insisted that this was no occupation for a woman. Born went to Stanford Law School instead, where she was one of only four women in her graduating class, and from there to a leading Washington, D.C., law firm, where she developed its derivatives practice before being appointed to the CFTC in 1995. All this suggests that Born had considerable strength of will. She was not strong enough, however, to prevail over "the Committee to Save the World," as Rubin, Greenspan, and Summers were dubbed by *Time Magazine* for their actions following the collapse of the mega hedge fund Long-Term Capital Management in August 1998.

What Born actually proposed was relatively modest: a "concept paper" identifying the risks posed by the growth of unregulated financial derivatives and sketching a framework for regulating them. This was still enough to provoke a furious reaction from Greenspan, Rubin, and Summers, whose saw it as the camel's nose under the tent. The three opposed CFTC regulation that would have forced derivatives traders to engage in greater disclosure and hold a larger capital cushion against losses, as suggested in Born's concept paper when it finally appeared. They supported only the creation of a clearinghouse to net transactions in derivatives, something that would have helped to mitigate the problems that arose in 2008 as a result of AIG's immensely complex party-to-party transactions.[10] Even then they supported just a voluntary clearinghouse, not a mandatory one. And a clearinghouse was not something for which dealers like Goldman Sachs that made a profit on each and every derivatives trade were particularly interested in volunteering their support.[11]

Subsequent treasury secretaries Paul O'Neill and John Snow, coming from business rather than finance, were in no position to rock the boat. Nor were they inclined to do so as long as things were going well. Henry Paulson, also coming as he did from Goldman Sachs, was a bird of a different stripe, but that hardly made him an advocate of hardheaded regulation.

Alan Greenspan, chairman of an institution with considerable responsibility for supervising and regulating financial institutions, was fundamentally a believer that markets knew best. For one normally inclined toward oracular statements, Greenspan put it with uncharacteristic bluntness in testimony to the House Committee on Banking and Financial Services: "Regulation of derivatives transactions that are privately negotiated by professionals is unnecessary."[12] Greenspan opposed regulation of the derivatives market when it was considered by the Congress in 1994. He opposed stricter oversight of derivatives by the CFTC in 1998. In 2003 he told the Senate Banking Committee that it would be a mistake to more extensively regulate derivatives markets. "What we have found over the years in the marketplace," he asserted, "is that derivatives have been an extraordinarily useful vehicle to transfer risk from those who shouldn't be taking it to those who are willing to and are capable of doing so." By October 2008, of course, he was singing a different tune, warning the U.S. House Oversight and Government Reform Committee against relying on "the self-interest of lending institutions" and acknowledging the need for regulation of derivatives markets.[13]

Greenspan's successor, Ben Bernanke, as a student of the Great Depression, might have been expected to hold different views. But it was hard, intellectually and politically, to abandon the score handed down by the maestro, especially when the investment community was enjoying such healthy returns. Bernanke also may have had a tendency to overlook the vulnerability of the "shadow banking system," that is, the hedge funds, conduits, and special-purpose vehicles where so many CDOs and so much housing-related risk were held, since no shadow banking system had existed in the 1930s. Other regulatory agencies, meanwhile, saw their budgets and human resources cut by a President George W. Bush who may not have been a financial sophisticate but knew one thing: regulation was the problem, not the solution.

HERD BEHAVIOR

Yet this blame game, which became understandably popular in the wake of the crisis, assigns too large a role to individuals, even individuals in positions of power. What informed decisions in the run-up to the crisis was not the personal ideology of a few powerful individuals but a powerful collective psychology. A central tenet was the belief that it had become possible, using modern mathematical tools, to more effectively price and manage risk. Elegant mathematical formulae like the Black-Scholes model could be used to determine prices for options and other derivatives. Subject to the simplifying assumptions needed to render the model tractable, it was possible to give a numerical estimate of the maximum loss that would be incurred on an investment in the course of the next day with, say, 99 percent probability. Subject to yet more assumptions about, say, the correlations of returns on different investments, it was possible to characterize the distribution of returns on a bank's investment portfolio. The maximum loss that might be incurred on that portfolio was soon given its own name, Value at Risk (VaR).

These techniques were not without value. Black-Scholes could be used to detect instances where the price of a complex derivative diverged significantly from the value of its components. It offered profits for those prepared to engage in arbitrage, for example buying the underpriced components while selling, or shorting, the overpriced composite. It provided a business model for entities like the hedge fund Long-Term Capital Management (LTCM), founded by the serial financial entrepreneur John Meriwether and his merry band of Nobel laureates in 1994. Similarly, the practice inaugurated by J.P. Morgan chief executive officer Dennis Weatherstone after the 1987 Wall Street crash, that he should have a "4:15 Report" summarizing the risk of the bank's investment portfolio on his desk each day within 15 minutes of the market close, was a fundamentally sensible request for a CEO. This was the practice that evolved into VaR, with J.P. Morgan being the institution that developed the methodology and published it, also in 1994.[14]

The problem was the tendency to push these processes too far. LTCM initially made handsome profits from its arbitrage transactions. Typically they involved buying and selling similar securities, for example U.S. treasury bonds of the same maturity issued on slightly different dates, as a way of exploiting small differences in the prices at which they traded.[15] But the more money LTCM took in from investors and the more traders adopted its techniques, the smaller those arbitrage opportunities became. The very success of the model and the drive to maintain profitability encouraged Meriwether and his LTCM partners to use more and more borrowed money to exploit smaller and smaller opportunities. The pseudoscientific nature of the undertaking created excessive confidence about the outcome. When the unlikely happened—Russia defaulted on its foreign bonds in August 1998, and asset prices moved unexpectedly—LTCM was pushed to the verge of bankruptcy, nearly toppling the U.S. financial system.

This should have been a warning shot across the bow of those using mathematical methods in the elusive quest to master risk. But the failure of LTCM was dismissed as an anomaly; big countries like Russia, it was said, do not default every day. If LTCM had overreached, this reflected the overweening ambition and supreme self-confidence of the principals, who included the

Nobel laureate Myron Scholes of Black-Scholes fame, and not any intrinsic limitations of their techniques. Complex mathematical formulae thus came to be
used even more widely to price even more complex securities. The fact that
every quant now had a powerful microcomputer on his desk encouraged the
building of ever more complex models, which of course fed the salaries of the
quants, the only ones capable of manipulating the models. Banks built more
elaborate models of Value at Risk, supported by specialized practitioners—J.P.
Morgan having spun off the methodology and its practitioners into an independent company with the confidence-inspiring name RiskMetrics Group in
1998—whose incomes depended on how widely the practice was adopted. The
methodology was taught in business schools, giving it scholarly legitimization,
and prescribed by newly minted risk-management consultants.

The fact that the models were based on simplifying assumptions, necessarily in order to render them tractable, meant that in the hands of careful
practitioners they were never used as more than a starting point for thinking
about risks. Careful practitioners similarly understood that the model was fit-
ted to a relatively short series of observations of the prices of certain assets.
Information on the prices of complex mortgage-related securities spanned only
the period when home prices had gone up, for example, and consequently contained little information about what might happen if prices came down. The
problem was that there were few incentives to be a careful practitioner.

In this way the starting point became the end point. What started as a
daily dose of self-discipline for a single CEO was applied more widely and
mechanically. Banks, confident that they had reduced their risks to a single
number, became confident of their ability to shoulder more. Regulators, convinced by the regulated of the reliability of the methodology, allowed VaR to be
used as an input into setting capital requirements. The Securities and Exchange
Commission, when requiring financial institutions to provide their shareholders more information about the risks they were taking, accepted VaR as a
logical summary measure. And banks, seeing how VaR affected the amount of
costly capital they had to hold, had an incentive to tweak their portfolios—and
the methodology—to produce more favorable estimates of Value at Risk. The
sense that risk, having been mathematicized, had been mastered grew pervasive. False confidence encouraged institutions to take on more risk. It encouraged the regulators let them. So long as things turned out as expected, more

risk meant more profits. Many people were generously compensated for going along. No one was generously compensated for exercising "undue" caution.

The timing is important here. When disaster struck in 2008, VaR was still less than 15 years old. The microcomputer revolution was still recent; LTCM had been famous for spending lavishly on state-of-the-art workstations, which were thought to give it a leg up on its competitors by allowing it to solve more complicated equations faster. Periods of rapid financial innovation are seedbeds for crisis. They are periods when there has not been sufficient time for innovations to be fully road tested. And with financial practice changing rapidly, it is especially hard for the regulators to keep up. In particular, it is hard for them to keep up with claims by the regulated that they have become more adept at managing risks.

No More Cozy Living

A further ingredient in this toxic brew was the intensification of competition. The Glass-Steagall Act separating commercial and investment banking and limiting the investment activities of deposit-taking banks was revoked by the Gramm-Leach-Bliley Act of 1999. Commercial banks, now able to more efficiently manage risk, could be entrusted to take on a wider range of investment activities, or so the authors of the bill believed. Defenders of Gramm-Leach-Bliley object that commercial banks were not at the center of the subprime crisis. It was not they but investment banks that originated CDOs and ended up stuck with the risky equity tranche. It was not they but investment banks and broker-dealers like Bear Stearns that were so dangerously leveraged.

But to argue this point is to miss the big picture. As commercial banks branched into new activities, they disturbed the investment bankers' cozy lives. Seeing their rents competed away, investment banks responded by moving into riskier activities and using more borrowed money in the scramble to survive. It is no coincidence that Bear Stearns, which once upon a time had earned a comfy living charging fixed commissions for stock trades but now saw this business eroded by deregulation and technological innovation (the emergence of discount brokers like Charles Schwab, for example) took the most dangerous gambles involving the highest levels of leverage.

Competitive pressure was further ratcheted up by financial globalization. The changes in technology and practice fostering the belief that banks could manage more risk and use more leverage while requiring less regulation were not limited to the United States. The same logic implying that financial institutions could master more lines of business and invest in a wider class of assets suggested that they could do business in more places. The European Union, as part of its Single Market program, removed all restrictions on the ability of banks to do business in other European countries. More generally, the period saw a sharp intensification of cross-border competition.

And, again, institutions feeling the chill winds of competition took on more risk in the effort to maintain customary profit margins. The British building society Northern Rock levered up its bets by supplementing the deposits of retail customers with money borrowed from other banks. Icelandic banks offered suspiciously high-interest online savings accounts to British, Dutch, and German households to finance risky bets. Sleepy German savings banks took on some of the worst performing U.S.-originated-and-distributed CDOs. Leverage was even higher among European financial institutions than in the United States. Either false confidence was higher, or the intensification of competitive pressure was greater, or both. In Europe, too, regulators averted their eyes.

Gambling to survive—doubling up one's bets—is not the only conceivable response to an existential threat. The alternative is to hunker down. Hunkering down in this case would have meant shrinking the enterprise. But compensation schemes provided no incentive to respond in this way. Successful bets meant big paydays. If those bets put the firm in an untenable position tomorrow, well, that was someone else's problem. The need for corporate boards and, failing that, government agencies to regulate compensation to better tie it to the long-term performance of the enterprise is now widely understood. But this was not something on which regulators insisted, or even mentioned, before it was too late.

LIQUID ACCELERANT

If flawed regulation was the spark, then central bank policy was the accelerant. Financial excesses would not have spread so quickly to such destructive effect had the Fed not poured fuel on the fire.

Ironically, the very success of the Fed in stabilizing the economy and, thereby, financial markets may have been a factor in the buildup of risk. The period after Paul Volcker's conquest of inflation saw a reduction in economic volatility that came to be known as "the Great Moderation." Whether good policy or good luck was mainly responsible is contested, but it is hard to imagine that the improvement in policy since the G. William Miller years played absolutely no role.[16] The same naive belief that the Fed had tamed the business cycle had underlain talk of a "New Era" of stability in the 1920s and fueled an earlier Wall Street boom. A less volatile economy, it had been argued then and was argued again now, meant less volatile financial markets. Institutional investors, indeed investors of all kinds, felt more confident about taking on risk. As Donald Kohn, vice chairman of the Federal Reserve Board, put it in 2008, not long after things went south, "In a broader sense, perhaps the underlying cause of the current crisis was complacency. With the onset of the 'Great Moderation' back in the mid-1980s, households and firms in the United States and elsewhere have enjoyed a long period of reduced output volatility and low and stable inflation. These calm conditions may have led many private agents to become less prudent and to underestimate the risks associated with their actions."[17] The very success of the Fed at becoming more transparent about its intentions and reducing uncertainty about the future may have been a prime factor in the development of this complacency.

Even if one is skeptical that policy was responsible for the decline in economic volatility and, through this channel, for complacency on the part of investors, there was always the belief that the Fed under Greenspan would intervene to put a floor under asset prices in order to prevent a destabilizing crash. Virtually the first act of Chairman Greenspan had been to cut rates following the 1987 Wall Street crash. The Fed cut again following the LTCM debacle in 1998. By this time "Greenspan put"—the idea that the Greenspan Fed was ready to effectively guarantee a minimum level of asset prices—had become part of the financial lexicon.

But the idea crystallized when the Fed cut rates to 1 percent following the collapse of the tech bubble and Greenspan spoke in 2002 on the subject of asset prices and monetary policy.[18] The chairman argued that asset bubbles are hard to identify while they are developing, making it impractical to direct monetary policy against them. He went on to suggest that there is no such difficulty of detecting bubbles after the fact and that the role for monetary policy is to limit the destabilizing consequences. Investors came to believe, rightly or wrongly, that because the Fed would intervene it was no longer necessary to worry about the slim possibility, the so-called tail risk, of asset prices collapsing. The danger of large losses being less, the temptation to take on risk was more. And there was nothing to restrain the risk takers, what with the Federal Open Market Committee and the regulators, including the Fed itself, in denial about their ability to detect bubbles, much less to limit their growth.

TAYLOR RULES

The final grounds on which to implicate the Fed is that monetary policy was significantly looser in 2002–2005 than it would have been had the Fed followed the same script as in the previous 15 years. From the end of the Volcker deflation in the mid-1980s through the bursting of the tech bubble in 2000, Fed policy was well captured by the "Taylor Rule." Named after the Stanford economist John Taylor, who had identified it in 1992, the Taylor Rule was a stylized relationship linking the central bank's main policy lever, the interest rate at which banks lend to one another, known as the federal funds rate, to its principal policy objectives: inflation and the level of idle resources.[19] The Taylor Rule had done a good job of capturing the Fed's reaction to changes in inflationary pressures and business cycles from the mid-1980s through the end of the 1990s. It continued to track policy after the turn of the century. When the tech bubble burst in 2000, causing unemployment to rise and inflation to subside, the Taylor Rule pointed to the need to cut rates. Over the course of 2001, the federal funds rate was cut from 6.25 percent to 1.75 percent, in line with its predictions.

But once the economy bottomed out late in 2002, causing the gap between actual and potential output to stop widening, the Taylor Rule suggested raising rates. Instead the Fed reduced the funds rate still further until it reached a low of 1 percent in mid-2003. There the policy rate remained for a year, at the end of which it was fully 3 percentage points below the levels suggested by the rule.

This was when Greenspan and his colleagues grew concerned that the economy was slipping into a Japanese-style deflation from which it might be difficult, even impossible, to extricate it. (Actually, the word "deflation" was too alarming to use in public. Greenspan referred instead in congressional testimony to "an unwelcome further fall inflation.") Given the Fed's awareness that monetary policy affects the price level and economy with a lag, it sought to make policy with the future in mind. In other words, it was expected deflation rather than actual deflation, something that was not in fact visible, that dictated its actions.[20]

With benefit of hindsight we can say that the Fed overestimated the risk of deflation from early 2002 through mid-2004. It extrapolated too mechanically from the deflation that followed the bursting of Japan's financial bubble in the late 1980s.[21] Chairman Greenspan's self-named "risk management approach" to monetary policy dictated erring on the side of averting the risk of a Japanese-style deflationary crisis.[22] In the event, this policy erred in the direction of fueling an even greater boom and bust down the road.

This story of lax monetary policy fueling the mother of all credit booms has its critics, notably Federal Reserve officials past and present. They object that the Fed controls only short-term interest rates, not the long-term rates that matter for investment. But while long-term rates may be what matter for firms contemplating investments in factories, this is not equally the case of individuals deciding whether to buy a home. Insofar as rates on fixed-rate mortgages did not fall enough, households desperate to join the homeownership society could opt for adjustable mortgages, the initial rates on which, linked to one-year interest rates, were temporarily low.[23] Lenders seeking to attract additional business by offering teaser rates on which interest payments were below market rates for the first few payment periods were better able to finance the tease. And with a boom in the demand for housing, there was then a boom in housing starts.[24]

STRETCHING FOR YIELD

But while the run-up in asset prices in 2003–2006 centered on residential real estate, it was a broader phenomenon. For monetary policy to have been important, it would have to had to fuel leverage and risk taking not just by home buyers and builders but by investors in other assets. Monetary policy operating on short-term rates could have done so in a number of ways. First, lower nominal interest rates encouraged institutions to take on more risk in order to match previous returns. Some investors use previous returns as a gauge of managers' performance. If returns go down, they blame the managers. To retain clients, the manager is forced to make riskier investments and use more leverage.

Second, some financial firms, such as pension funds and insurance companies, are required to pay out fixed nominal amounts to their investors.[25] A pension fund operating a defined benefit plan, for example, is obliged to make a specified monthly payment to its contributors. If market interest rates go down by more than the company expected when signing the pension contract, the yield on safe securities may not be enough for it to meet its obligations. A bank that has offered certificates of deposit and whose other liabilities bear fixed interest rates may likewise find itself squeezed. In both cases portfolio managers, to meet the institution's obligations, will have to move into riskier investments or take on more leverage.

Third, lower interest rates cheapen wholesale funding—they reduce the cost of borrowing chunks of money from other institutional investors. Lower money market rates thus encourage financial intermediaries to borrow more and expand their balance sheets. This behavior will be particularly visible among broker-dealers who rely on the wholesale money market for their funding.[26] Predictably, broker-dealers like Bear Stearns were among the most highly leveraged of all financial institutions in the run-up to the crisis. They then fell the hardest.

Finally, if lower interest rates and more ample liquidity boost stock prices, including the stocks of financial institutions themselves, banks will want to increase their lending. Higher share prices mean that banks have more capital—the funds that their owners have subscribed to fund the operations of the institution are worth more. If the bank doesn't expand its lending, some of this capital will be sitting idle. If the firm is not fully utilizing its lending capacity, it will be leaving money on the table. This forgone opportunity is something it will seek to correct. Low interest rates that translate into higher equity prices will thus trigger a lending boom.

Under these circumstances, equities and land will become more valuable, encouraging financial institutions to lend against them. Banks will give more loans to borrowers with lower credit scores, since if bad behavior recurs they can always seize and liquidate their collateral. If something causes the value of that collateral to fall, all bets are off. But that is a problem for the future. It was not something about which lenders, caught up in the moment, especially worried.

Low interest rates thus encouraged investors to assume more risk and use more leverage. Although the level of interest rates was not the only factor at work, it fanned the flames. Similarly, Federal Reserve policy was not the only thing keeping interest rates low. Not just short- but also long-term rates, which are not directly under the Fed's control, were unusually low around the middle of the decade. Even when the Fed allowed the funds rate to rise in 2004, rates on bonds and fixed-rate mortgages remained anomalously low. This was the bond market "conundrum" on which Chairman Greenspan commented in a much-noted February 2005 speech. These low long-term rates may have been yet another manifestation of the Fed's success at becoming more transparent and limiting perceived uncertainty about the future. The reduction in uncertainty gave investors the confidence to bid up bond prices.[27]

ENTER THE DOLLAR

But another, potentially more important culprit, fingered by Fed chairmen Greenspan and Bernanke once the low level of long-term rates came to be seen as less boon than problem, was foreign central bank purchases of U.S. government bonds and the securities of the quasi-governmental agencies Freddie Mac and Fannie Mae (so-called agency securities). And behind those foreign purchases lay the status of the dollar as the world's reserve currency.

Some of the facts are incontrovertible. Central banks made extensive purchases of U.S. treasury and agency securities. In 2008–2009 they became the dominant foreign purchasers as private investors, increasingly concerned about the stability of the dollar, drew back. Central banks were motivated by the lessons they drew from the Asian financial crisis of 1997–1998, namely that capital flows are volatile and the only guaranteed protection against an abrupt reversal is to stockpile dollars so that short-term foreign liabilities, not just of the government but of the private sector as well, can be paid off. Korea, one of the countries most traumatized by the crisis, boosted its reserves, mainly of dollars, from 5 to 25 percent of GDP. Others followed, accumulating U.S. treasury and agency securities hand over fist. It must have been true that the prices of these dollar assets were higher, and the interest rates they bore were lower, than in the absence of this additional demand. And as the return on relatively safe assets fell, other investors "stretched for yield" by shifting into riskier securities.

But beyond these points, agreement does not extend. Bernanke referred to a "global savings glut" when explaining why foreign capital had been flowing into U.S. debt securities.[28] This terminology was unfortunate in that global savings and the savings of emerging Asian economies, China in particular, which were among the principal buyers of U.S. securities, had been trending downward for 7 years. Emerging Asian savings, after having averaged nearly 33 percent of GDP in the last 4 years of the 1990s, fell to 31 percent in the first half of the 2000s, the so-called savings-glut years.[29] But investment rates in emerging Asia fell even more, first because of the crisis-induced recession in 1998 and then as Asian governments abandoned the practice of running their economies under high pressure of demand. With Asia's saving having risen relative to its investment, its excess funds had nowhere to flow but abroad. There being no shortage of U.S. debt securities, the U.S. treasury and agency market became the logical destination.

China was its own story, of course. China is not accurately characterized as having engaged in lower levels of investment. But its savings rates soared even higher as Chinese households socked away funds to provision for education, health expenses, and other contingencies. Enterprise managers, under no pressure to pay out dividends, retained earnings for capacity expansion at home and acquisitions abroad. All that additional savings had to go somewhere; in practice it could only go overseas. Capital outflows from China ballooned from one-tenth of 1 percent of global GDP in 2002 to nearly 1 percent of global GDP in 2007. On this basis it is argued that China's financial underdevelopment contributed to the buildup of systemic risks.[30]

TANGO LESSONS

But it takes two to tango. High levels of Chinese saving were matched by low levels of U.S. saving. Household savings rates in the United States fell from 7 percent in the early 1990s to near zero in 2005–2007. At the time it was argued that this drop reflected the robust health of the economy and a Great Moderation that justified higher asset prices. Higher asset prices that included higher real estate prices made U.S. households, whose most important investments were their homes, feel wealthier. And on this basis they saved less.[31] We now know that this vision of a permanent increase in wealth was an illusion, albeit one on which too many households that extracted equity from their homes based their decisions.

In the absence of this behavior—that is, with more U.S. savings—flows of capital toward the country would have been less. Still, there is little question that developments in the rest of the world, whether they are characterized as a savings glut or an investment strike and whether they are located primarily in emerging Asia or more broadly, contributed to the flow of capital into U.S. debt markets. They also had a self-reinforcing character. Capital inflows contributed to the rise in U.S. asset prices, which made the country appear more creditworthy, encouraging foreign investors to lend it more, much as a bank lends more against more valuable collateral.

There is also the question of whether all this dollar accumulation by central banks really reflected the demand for insurance. Some central banks

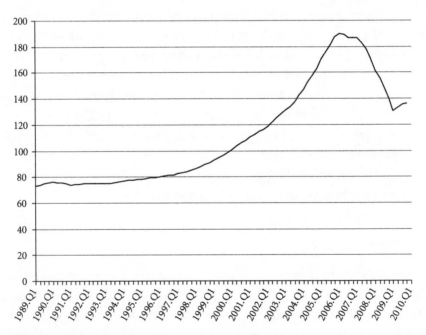

Figure 5.1. S&P/Case-Shiller U.S. National Home Price Index.
Source: Standard & Poor's.

accumulated reserves not as insurance against a sudden reversal in the direction of capital flows but as an inadvertent by-product of policies of export-led growth. Emerging-market central banks, most notoriously the People's Bank of China, bought foreign currencies to prevent their exchange rates from rising. This encouraged the exports of manufactures that were the engine of economic development and the vehicle for transferring workers to the modern industrial sector.

Views of the relative importance of these motives tended to shift over time. Early observers emphasized worries about financial volatility on the part of Asian policymakers as the main factor motivating the accumulation of reserves. Subsequently some of the very same commentators emphasized the reluctance of governments to allow their exchange rates to rise and risk disrupting the process of export-led growth.[32]

Whatever the motivation, the result was an enormous accumulation of reserves. But why dollar reserves? Europe is as important as the United States in providing a market for Asian exports. In principle, Asian central banks and governments could have intervened to prevent their currencies from rising against the euro. They could have acquired euros—and British pounds and Swiss francs—instead of dollars.

Privilege Once More

The fundamental explanation for the decision to target the dollar was its status as the leading international currency. With other countries still shadowing the dollar, doing likewise produced stable exchange rates not just vis-à-vis the United States but more generally. For countries engaged in intra-Asian trade in parts and components, this indirect way of stabilizing exchange rates was of considerable benefit. With the largest share of world trade invoiced and settled in dollars, stabilizing local currencies vis-à-vis the dollar was particularly convenient for exporters. And pegging to the dollar encouraged the practice of accumulating dollar reserves.

Then there is the fact that the market in U.S. debt securities was so liquid. The costs of buying and selling them were low. Central banks and governments could make purchases and, when necessary, sales without moving prices. And those markets were so liquid precisely because of the participation of so many foreign central banks and governments. This was the dollar's exorbitant privilege as the once and still reserve and international currency.

The issue is how much impact all this foreign finance had on U.S. interest rates. Were foreign purchases mainly responsible for Greenspan's bond market conundrum? While foreign capital inflows were large, U.S. debt markets were larger. As late as the end of 2006, a majority (55 percent) of U.S. government bonds and an even larger fraction (85 percent) of the securities issued by the quasi-governmental agencies Freddie Mac and Fannie Mae were held by domestic investors. That said, foreign and especially Asian central bank purchases became increasingly important as the period progressed. One study finds that yields on 10-year bonds were at least half a percentage point (50 basis points) lower in 2005 than if there had there been no additional foreign purchases since the beginning of 2004.[33] Another suggests that that 10-year bond yields were 70 basis points lower as a result of foreign capital inflows.[34] Still another suggests that the increase in U.S. treasuries held by foreigners depressed yields by 90 basis points.[35]

Given the notorious inability of economists to agree, this is a remarkable degree of consensus. It suggests that foreign purchases of U.S. debt securities were largely, even wholly, responsible for Greenspan's conundrum. This was the dollar's exorbitant privilege in yet another guise.

But would long-term interest rates a half or even full percentage point higher have made all that much difference for the course of the crisis? The perverse financial practices and lax regulation that were at its root still would have been there. Mortgage brokers still would have had no fiduciary responsibility to the households with which they did business. Financial institutions still would have repackaged mortgage-backed securities into complex derivatives. Standard & Poor's and Moody's still would have advised originators on how to structure CDOs before proceeding to rate them. The belief that the economy and financial markets had become less volatile still would have encouraged risk taking.

But not to the same extent. With mortgage finance more expensive, the housing market would not have overheated so dramatically. There would not have been as much lending on the security of overvalued collateral. Borrowed money would have been more expensive. Leverage would have been less. When the process unwound, it would have unwound less violently.

APRÈS LE DELUGE

In the event, the violence with which it unwound was unprecedented. Investors took deep losses on the financial derivatives that had been the signature of the boom. Foreign central banks halted their acquisition of U.S. agency securities when the troubles of Freddie and Fannie became apparent. The happy belief that capital, whether private or public, flowed toward the United States because of the country's singular capacity to originate and distribute high-quality financial assets dissolved in the face of these events. The slogan "They sell us high-quality merchandise, we sell them high-quality financial assets" was replaced by "They sell us toxic toys, we sell them toxic securities."

There was no sign, however, of foreign investors and, specifically, foreign central banks withdrawing from the U.S. treasury market. Foreign purchases continued unabated, although there was some tendency now for central banks to buy shorter term treasuries. But with the deep recession caused by the crisis and the massive budget deficits that followed, questions were increasingly asked about the sustainability of the Treasury's debt. With a majority of U.S. government debt now held by foreigners, the temptation to inflate it away was greater. Foreign investors could see the writing on the wall. Questions were increasingly asked about whether foreigners would retain their healthy appetite for U.S. treasury securities—and, if not, what their growing distaste might imply for the dollar.

There was growing dissatisfaction as well with an international monetary system that gave the United States access to cheap foreign finance that it deployed in such counterproductive ways. It was entirely reasonable that central banks should want to accumulate reserves as a buffer against volatile capital flows. But it was unreasonable that the only way of doing so was by shoveling financial capital into the United States and fueling the excesses that drove the global financial system to the brink. America, it followed, was no longer to be entrusted with its exorbitant privilege. A privilege abused was not a privilege that others would willingly extend. On how a new international monetary system should be structured there was little agreement. The one point on which the critics agreed was that it should entail a more limited role for the dollar.

On all these grounds, pessimism reined about the dollar's future as a store of value, means of payment, and unit of account and, by implication, about its international role. The dollar was doomed. The dollar was in terminal decline. Without official foreign demand to prop it up, the dollar exchange rate would collapse, eroding America's living standards and geopolitical leverage.

The only question being: were these pessimistic forecasts right?

CHAPTER 6

MONOPOLY NO MORE

In the wake of the crisis, doubts are pervasive about whether the dollar will retain its international role. Recent events have not exactly enhanced the reputation of the United States as a supplier of high-quality financial assets. It would not be surprising if demonstrations of the dysfunctionality of American financial markets soured investors on U.S. debt securities. Meanwhile, a budget-deficit-prone U.S. government will be pumping out debt as far as the eye can see. It will be tempted to resort to inflation to work down the burden. That temptation will be even greater now that a majority of its marketable debt is held by foreigners.

Foreign investors, the Cassandras darkly warn, will not sit still for this. They will seek to protect themselves by curtailing their dollar holdings. The end result, the worriers caution, could be a mass migration to other currencies.

If developments in the United States raise doubts about the dollar's international role, developments abroad deepen them. The post–World War II recovery of Western Europe and Japan and now the emergence of China, India, and Brazil have reduced the economic dominance of the United States. It is not obvious why the dollar, the currency of an economy that no longer accounts for a majority of the world's industrial production, should be used to invoice and settle a majority of the world's international transactions. Nor is it clear why the dollar should still constitute a majority of the reserves of central banks and governments. As the world economy becomes more multipolar, its

121

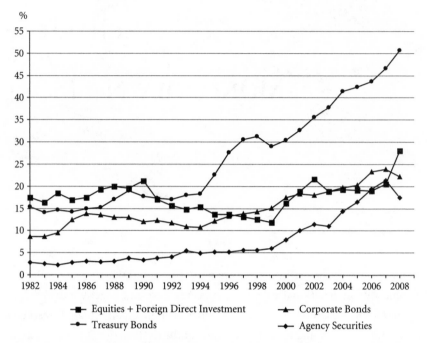

Figure 6.1. Foreign Holdings of U.S. Securities as a Percentage of Total U.S. Amount Outstanding. *Source*: Federal Reserve Board Flow of Funds Accounts of the United States.

monetary system, logic suggests, should similarly become more multipolar. This reasoning implies at a minimum that the dollar will have to share its international role.

Moreover, what is true of the economic logic for a dollar-based international monetary and financial system is true also of its political logic. When after World War II the United States stationed large numbers of troops in Europe and Asia, our allies there saw supporting the greenback as an appropriate quid pro quo. Today, in contrast, China, our largest foreign creditor, is not a close ally. In many parts of the world, the American security umbrella is neither as essential as it once was nor, indeed, as welcome. It is not obvious that the best way for foreign countries to ensure their security is by propping up the dollar. All this makes them increasingly critical of America's exorbitant privilege.

AN INCONVENIENT TRUTH

There is only one problem with these arguments. It is that there has been little actual diminution of the dollar's role in international transactions. There has been no discernible movement away from the dollar as a currency in which to invoice trade and settle transactions. One recent study for Canada, a country with especially detailed data, shows that nearly 75 percent of all imports *from countries other than the United States* continue to be invoiced and settled in U.S. dollars.[1] The dollar similarly remains the dominant currency in the foreign exchange market. The most recent Bank for International Settlements survey showed that the dollar was used in 85 percent of foreign exchange transactions worldwide, down only marginally from 88 percent in 2004.[2] Some 45 percent of international debt securities are denominated in dollars.[3] OPEC continues to price its petroleum in dollars.

While U.S. nemeses like Iran and Venezuela regularly offer proposals for pricing oil in another currency, there is no agreement about what constitutes an attractive alternative. The famous instance was in November 2007 when, at a closed-door session in Riyadh, a camera was inadvertently left on, broadcasting into a nearby press room a quarrel between the Iranian and Saudi foreign ministers over whether OPEC should move away from dollar pricing. In October 2009 a sensational if undocumented press report had the Gulf States conspiring with China, Russia, Japan, and France—now there's an odd coalition—to shift the pricing of oil away from dollars.[4] But so far all this has been a tempest in a teapot.

Data on the currency composition of central banks' foreign reserves are incomplete, since not all countries report. China, importantly, is among the nonreporters. But data from the IMF, the best source on the subject, show the share of dollars in total identified official foreign exchange holdings as of the first quarter of 2010 as 61 percent, down only marginally from 66 percent in 2002–2003.[5] If one goes back further, to the first half of 1990s, the dollar's share in total identified official holdings of foreign exchange was actually lower than recently. *Plus ça change.*

Although the IMF's statistics are not perfect, other sources point in the same direction. For example, surveys of financial institutions conducted by the U.S. Treasury suggest that foreign central banks continued to accumulate

Billions of U.S. dollars

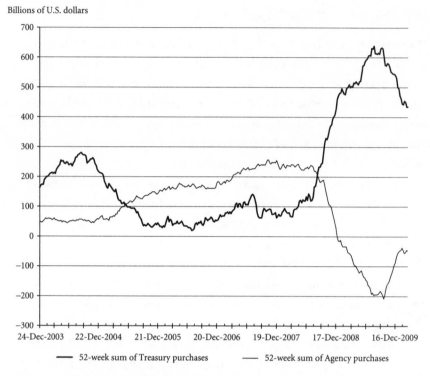

—— 52-week sum of Treasury purchases   —— 52-week sum of Agency purchases

Figure 6.2. 52-Week Change in Custodial Holdings on Behalf of Foreigners.
Source: Federal Reserve Board.

treasury bonds following the outbreak of the crisis—if anything at an accelerating pace.[6] There was a sharp fall in foreign central bank accumulation of
"agency securities"—the securities of the quasi-governmental mortgage
agencies Freddie Mac and Fannie Mae—but not of U.S. treasuries.

Still the One

What explains the gap between rhetoric and reality? Above all the simple fact
that, jeremiads about American declinism notwithstanding, the United States
remains the largest economy in the world. It has the world's largest financial
markets. This may not be true forever, but remains true now.

Moreover, the dollar has the advantage of incumbency. Consider an
exporter deciding in what currency to quote the prices of his exports. Exporters
want to limit fluctuations in their prices relative to those of competing goods in

order to avoid confusing their customers. If other exporters are invoicing and settling their transactions in dollars, each individual exporter has an incentive to do likewise.[7] And to continue doing so.

And what is true of trade is true of other international transactions. That so many exports are priced and settled in dollars makes the dollar the dominant currency in foreign exchange markets, since exporters from other countries, when they want to pay their suppliers, workers, and shareholders, must first convert the proceeds back to their home currency. It makes the dollar the dominant unit in currency forward and futures markets, since exporters will want to use those markets to ensure against unexpected exchange rate movements while the transaction is still under way. Since it pays for exporters of financial services, like exporters of merchandise, to avoid confusing their customers, they, too, will price their products in the same currency as their competitors. Thus, the fact that international bonds were denominated in dollars in the past creates a tendency for them to be denominated in dollars in the present.

For many central banks, it similarly makes sense to stabilize their exchange rates against the dollar even though the United States no longer accounts for a majority of their foreign trade and financial transactions—if for no other reason than that other countries stabilize their exchange rates against the dollar. Because other countries peg to the dollar, doing likewise stabilizes a country's exchange rate not just against the United States but more broadly. Beyond that, there is a reluctance to shift away from dollar pegs, since they are the established basis for monetary policy, and a change may sow uncertainty.

Central banks will want to hold reserves in the same currency in which the country denominates its foreign debt and invoices its foreign trade, since they use those reserves to smooth debt and trade flows. They will want to hold reserves in the currency of the country to which they peg, since they use them to intervene in foreign exchange markets.

Although central banks naturally welcome returns on their investments, they also seek to limit the riskiness of their reserve portfolios. Importantly, the currency to which they peg will be the most stable in terms of its domestic purchasing power (that is, in its command over domestic goods and services). And the identity of the predominant anchor currency is no mystery. As of mid-2009, fifty-four countries pegged to the U.S. dollar, compared to just twenty-seven to the euro, the runner-up.[8]

Calculations of what combination of dollars and other currencies are attractive to central bank reserve managers assume for convenience equally liquid markets in bonds and deposits denominated in different currencies.[9] This assumption may be unrealistic, but relaxing it only works in the dollar's favor. Central banks value liquidity in their reserve instruments so that they can use them in market intervention. If a financial instrument is not readily convertible into cash, then it is not readily used in market operations.

It therefore matters greatly that the market in U.S. treasury bonds and bills has unrivaled liquidity whether measured by turnover or transactions costs. The U.S. treasury market is, quite simply, the most liquid financial market in the world. This reflects the scale of the U.S. economy and its financial development. But the status quo is self-reinforcing. Because the U.S. market is so liquid, foreign investors undertake transactions and concentrate their holdings there. The fact that they undertake their transactions and concentrate their holdings there in turn lends it additional liquidity.

Thus, in the same way that incumbency is an advantage in the competition to be an international financial center, it is an advantage in the competition for reserve-currency status. Incumbency is not everything. And its advantages may be weakening; the costs of comparing prices in different currencies and switching between them are declining with the development of modern information technologies. But as any politician will tell you, the advantages of incumbency are not to be dismissed. They are one reason that, questions about its reelection prospects notwithstanding, the dollar is unlikely to be voted out of office just yet.

SMALL POTATOES

Yet another factor favoring a continuing role for the dollar is that all the other candidates for international currency status have serious shortcomings of their own. The UK and Switzerland are simply too small for the pound sterling and Swiss franc to be more than subsidiary reserve and international currencies. Both lack the size to provide debt instruments on the scale required by the global financial system. The UK is barely a sixth the economic size of the United States. Switzerland is barely a thirtieth. Given the importance of market size for liquidity, the share of their currencies in global reserves is even less. Sterling accounts for less than 4 percent of identified global reserves, the Swiss franc for less than 1 percent.

The same is even truer of still smaller economies. When Russia's central bank announced in 2009 that it was diversifying its reserves to include Canadian dollars (nicknamed "loonies"), those anticipating the death of the U.S. dollar gleefully took note. But the announcement caused nary a ripple in the U.S. dollar exchange rate. Canadian government bond markets are simply too small to make a dent in global reserve portfolios or for Russia's decision to buy loonies to have a discernible impact on the greenback.

Japan is a larger economy, but its government long discouraged international use of the yen on the grounds that this would undermine Japan's ability to maintain a competitive exchange rate and would otherwise complicate its conduct of industrial policy.[10] This reluctance to internationalize the yen may now be a thing of the past. Japanese officials are anxious to see their currency play a larger role, especially in Asia. But past policy continues to shape market liquidity. And a decade of no growth and zero interest rates have made holding reserves in yen unattractive. The yen accounts for barely 3 percent of total identified official holdings of foreign exchange.[11] Going forward, Japan's aging population and antipathy to immigration do not favor a rapidly expanding global role for its economy or its currency.

WHOM TO CALL

This leaves the euro, notwithstanding its recent difficulties, as the most serious rival to the dollar for now.[12] The euro area possesses the requisite scale. Its exports are nearly double those of the United States.[13] Germany is a major exporter of capital goods to emerging Asia. Euro-area companies operate branch plants in countries to their east, countries that are increasingly linked into Western Europe's production networks and supply chains. Euro-area banks own and operate many of Eastern Europe's banks. This makes the euro a logical currency in which to invoice and settle transactions for importers and exporters in economies adjoining the euro area as well as other parts of the world.

If a first-class international currency needs a first-class central bank, then this, too, is something the euro possesses. The ECB has shown itself to be extraordinarily serious about the maintenance of price stability. Although it was roundly criticized for its exceptional purchases of government bonds in the spring of 2010, it continues to take its price-stability mandate seriously. It shows absolutely no inclination to embark on reckless inflationary polices.

At the same time the ECB understands its responsibility as an emergency lender. In 2008, at the height of the crisis, it extended emergency loans to countries whose banks and firms had borrowed in euros. It provided other central banks with euros in exchange for their currencies. Such swaps are the signature of a central bank that recognizes its currency's international role. Henry Kissinger's quip, "You don't know who to call when you want to telephone Europe," no longer applies to monetary policy. You call the ECB.

And appropriately for an aspiring supplier of reserve assets, the euro area also possesses an ample stock of government debt securities. Its bond markets are accessible to foreign investors, controls on capital flows being a thing of the past.

It is important to recall these positive attributes, especially at times when the euro becomes currency traders' punching bag. Recall, for example, that the euro area served as a safe harbor in the 2008 crisis. That episode demonstrated that the European Central Bank, as the issuer of a recognized international currency, has more capacity to provide emergency liquidity than, say, the National Bank of Denmark or the Swedish Riksbank, the central banks of countries still outside the euro area. The ECB provides emergency assistance in euros, a unit that is widely used in cross-border transactions and to which risk-averse investors flee in a crisis. And in times of crisis, these attributes make the euro area a safe place to be.

The ECB's intervention was most critical in the period following the failure of Lehman Brothers, when it cut interest rates and flooded financial markets with liquidity. In contrast, the National Bank of Denmark, still the steward of a national currency, had to raise interest rates in response to deleveraging by foreign investors that led to a sharp fall in the value of the krone. Even had the Danish central bank disregarded the implications for the exchange rate and flooded financial markets with krone, this would have been no help to Danish firms and banks with obligations in euros. At the height of the crisis the National Bank had to negotiate emergency swap lines with the ECB, which provided it with the euros needed to relieve the pressure on those firms and banks.

But those arrangements were ad hoc. Whether they will be repeated is uncertain. The only guarantee of access to the ECB's liquidity facilities is by adopting the euro. The governor of the Danish central bank, Nils Bernstein, acknowledged as much in an interview in the *Irish Independent*: "The crisis has shown that we can manage economically outside the euro, but it has also demonstrated that there are big advantages during a crisis to be inside and much more protected against turmoil and to have access to the euro system's facilities."[14] The euro area's difficulties in 2010 will undoubtedly cause candidates for membership to think twice before coming in. But as they cast their minds back to 2008, they will recall that it is not particularly attractive to stay out either. Estonia, by choosing to adopt the euro at the beginning of 2011, has already voted with its feet.

The obvious exception is Britain, where the crisis tarnished the reputation of a pro-EU Labour Government and led to its replacement by a euroskeptical opposition. Given London's position as an international financial center and sterling's history as a reserve currency, Britain's joining the euro area would make the biggest difference to the euro's status as an international currency. But this is not something that is going to happen anytime soon, given the sour aftertaste from Britain's earlier flirtation with the Exchange Rate Mechanism.[15]

This leaves growing the members' own economies as the best way of creating a larger platform for the euro.[16] But Southern European countries, grappling with a difficult process of fiscal consolidation, now face an extended period of slow growth. More generally, the capacity to grow is not one of Europe's strengths. The continent has inflexible product and labor markets. Firms are reluctant to hire because they are unable to fire. Start-ups are slow to ramp up because of obstacles to ramping down. They hesitate to scale up until they are confident that they can continue to employ those they take on.

Some will say that these problems are overstated. But even if these other criticisms of Europe's economic prowess are contestable, there is no question that the continent is challenged demographically. Its population is aging. Its net reproduction rate, the number of daughters per woman who survive to average reproduction age, is only 0.75, well below the value of unity required for a stable population. Immigration from Turkey and North Africa could make up the difference, but few in Europe relish this prospect. Most Europeans oppose admitting Turkey to the EU, which would be the obvious way of solving Europe's demographic problem. What is true for Japan is true for Europe: a stagnant population will mean a stagnant economy. This stasis will not translate into a larger platform for the euro or make it more attractive as an international currency.

A CURRENCY WITHOUT A STATE

The euro, as the currency of an economic zone that exports more than the United States, has well-developed financial markets, and is supported by a world-class central bank, is in many respects the obvious alternative to the dollar. While currently it is fashionable to couch all discussions of the euro in doom and gloom, the fact is that the euro accounts for 37 percent of all foreign exchange market turnover. It accounts for 31 percent of all international bond issues. It represents 28 percent of the foreign exchange reserves whose currency composition is divulged by central banks.[17] It is second only to the dollar on all these dimensions of "international currenciness," although it remains a considerable way behind the leader.

So why hasn't its progress been faster? There is the novelty of a unit that came into existence barely a decade ago. There is the fact that Europe's bond markets are not larger and more liquid.[18]

But most fundamentally, the problem is that the euro is a currency without a state. It is the first major currency not backed by a major government, there being no euro-area government, only the national governments of the participating countries.[19] The European Commission is the proto-executive not of the euro area but of the European Union, which encompasses also the UK, Sweden, Denmark, and other EU countries that have not adopted the euro. The Commission has limited power to help governments with financial problems or to force them to take steps that they do not deem in their national interest. The manifest inability of the Commission to enforce the Stability and Growth Pact, which is intended to limit budget deficits, is a prime case in point.

This absence of a euro-area government is the main factor preventing the euro from matching the dollar in international importance. When Europe develops economic and financial problems, managing them requires cooperation among its national governments, which is far from assured. When a government develops budgetary problems so serious that it is impossible to resolve them without international assistance, providing it is something on which European countries as a group must agree. Their leaders have to negotiate a burden-sharing agreement, and then a host of national parliaments have to ratify it. The possibility that they won't do so quickly, or at all, raises fears of unpredictable financial fallout. This in turn creates reluctance on the part of central banks in other parts of the world to put their eggs in the euro basket.

The Greek crisis illustrates the point. How Athens developed a "big fat Greek deficit" in excess of 13 percent of national income is a story in itself, one that unfolded over a period of years. Be that as it may, in early 2010 investors awoke to the fact that Greece's financial position was untenable. They demand-ed that the Greek government reduce its budget deficit by fully a tenth of national income in 3 years, a Herculean task, or else they would go on strike.

Greek prime minister George Papandreou made a valiant attempt to nar-row the deficit. But public-sector workers, unconvinced that they should bear the burden of austerity, resisted accepting big pay cuts. Households and companies similarly resisted heavy increases in taxes.[20] While there were good reasons why the government and Greek society had to go back to living within their means, the adjustments required met with considerable political opposition. But absent those adjustments the markets refused to advance the Greek government the funds it needed to service its debt and finance its other operations. The country was stuck between a rock and a hard place.

The only solution, barring a restructuring of the public debt that, for better or worse, no one was prepared to contemplate, was to stretch out the adjustment. But an extended adjustment might be possible only if other European countries advanced Greece a loan, conditional on Athens laying out a credible plan for balancing its budget. Here the absence of a powerful executive at the level of the euro area came to the fore. There was no European government with the capac-ity to lend, only the German, French, and other national governments.[21] German officials, with regional elections coming, catered not to Europe's interests but to German voters. And German voters were angry as heck about having to bail out their profligate Greek neighbors.

All this encouraged political grandstanding. German chancellor Angela Merkel made aggressive remarks about refusing to participate in a bailout for consumption by her domestic constituents while at the same time providing private reassurances to Papandreou. Papandreou, seeking a better deal, threatened to shun his European partners for the IMF, causing embarrassment in Paris and other European capitals. Investors began to worry that Greece would be forced to default on its debt, damaging French and German banks stuffed full of Greek bonds. The absence of a convincing resolution of the Greek problem caused investors to develop similar doubts about Portugal, Spain, and other Southern European countries. This led to panicked sales of their bonds, raising questions about the solvency of the European banks that had invested in those bonds themselves. Catastrophe was averted only when national leaders, meeting in Brussels, agreed to a $1 trillion fund to guarantee national debts and the ECB agreed to emergency purchases of government bonds. Obviously, this brinkmanship hardly reassured foreign central banks and others contemplating whether to use euros in their international transactions.

Everyone understands what is needed to address the problem. Europe needs stronger oversight of national budgets to prevent governments from getting into this pickle in the first place. It needs closer coordination of fiscal and other policies to prevent competitive positions from getting out of whack. And it needs no more emergency agreements at two o'clock in the morning. Instead it needs a proper emergency financing mechanism—a euro area crisis management institution run by a committee of technocrats answerable to the European Parliament and the member states. They would have a pool of resources that could be loaned to countries with strong policies experiencing financial problems through no fault of their own.[22] They would have the power to extend emergency financial assistance, either unilaterally or in conjunction with the IMF, and conditioned on the recipient's implementation of adjustment measures.[23] They could purchase euro-zone government bonds in the event of disruptions to sovereign bond markets—and prevent the ECB from being pushed into doing so. When such assistance was not enough, they would step in to restructure the debts of the insolvent country. They would impose a "haircut" on the bondholders (writing down the value of their claims to a fraction of their face value) and giving them a menu of new bonds to choose from.[24] A permanent mechanism of this sort would help to deal with Europe's immediate difficulties but, more important, it would be in place to address future problems.

All this would involve significant additional delegation of national prerogatives to a European institution, which is why there was more talk than actual movement in this direction. Yet, three months into the Greek crisis, German finance minister Wolfgang Schäuble had come around to view that Europe needed this kind of mechanism. The European commissioner for economic and financial affairs, Olli Rehn, proposed requiring governments to clear their budgets with the Commission before submitting them to their national parliaments. He proposed extending Commission oversight to sensitive national arrangements that had previously been regarded as off-limits, such as the parliamentary procedures used to negotiate the budget, which might pose an obstacle to sensible outcomes, and the structure of national wage-bargaining arrangements, where these interfered with the maintenance of competitiveness. The European Central Bank issued a document endorsing both strengthened surveillance of national policies and the creation of a euro-area crisis management institution.[25] Even more significantly, in late June the European Council, made up of EU heads of state or government, agreed.

But it remained unclear whether European governments were prepared to move ahead with such changes. Would German voters agree to have their taxes go to fund the operations of a euro-area crisis management institution? Would the EU get serious about budgetary rules with teeth? Would the members of the monetary union allow the European Commission to interfere with delicate national prerogatives such as the procedures and conventions used to negotiate the budget and bargain over wages?

The answer, in each case, is unclear. And so long as Europe lacks the political will to create an emergency financing mechanism and, more generally, to put in place the other policies needed to complete its monetary union, the euro's economic attractions as an alternative to the dollar will remain limited.

POWER OUTAGE

Historically, the leading international currency has always been issued by the leading international power. Nothing threatens that country's existence. One reason the dollar dominated after World War II was that Fortress America was secure. As the English political economist Susan Strange put it in Cold War days, "It is just possible to imagine a future scenario in which West Germany is overrun by an exuberant Red Army while Fortress America remains inviolate across the Atlantic, but it is impossible to imagine the converse: a West German state surviving while the United States is overrun or the North American continent laid waste by nuclear attack. As long as this basic political asymmetry persists, there is no chance whatever of the Deutsche mark being the pivot of the international monetary system."[26] Foreign central banks and other investors want to know that their money is safe. And safety has more dimensions than just the financial.

The leading power also has the strategic and military capacity to shape international relations and institutions to support its currency. After World War II the United States could insist that its allies support the dollar, and countries like Germany had no choice but to comply. The unmatched power of the United States permitted it to shape international institutions, at the Bretton Woods Conference and after, to support the dollar's exorbitant privilege. Europe, in contrast, lacks a common foreign policy. It doesn't even have a position on how to reform the International Monetary Fund and the international financial system to reduce their dependence on the dollar.

With time, Europe will move to a common position on reform of the international monetary system in ways that enhance the position of the euro. It will develop a common position on IMF reform. But these innovations won't spring full-blown from Europe's brow tomorrow or the day after. The continent will move gradually, if in spurts, toward deeper integration, as it always has. And because institutional reform will be slow, the euro's rise as an international currency will be slow.

The one place where the euro is likely to gain market share rapidly is on the euro area's own fringes. The euro is already the dominant currency for trade settlements and invoicing in non-euro-area EU countries. The EU is also seeking to develop stronger ties to the non-EU countries to its south and east. It has put in place a "Union for the Mediterranean" to deepen its links with non-EU countries bordering that sea. It relies on Russia for its energy supplies, which means that Russia in turn relies on it for revenues.

As countries in its neighborhood deepen their links with the EU, they will rely more on the euro. Thus, in 2009 Russia announced that it was raising the weight of the euro in the basket of currencies used to guide its exchange rate policy, reflecting the growing importance of the euro area in its foreign trade and payments. And as the euro becomes more important to Russia as a guide for policy, its central bank will want to hold a larger share of euro-denominated reserves.

Still, this is a recipe for a regional reserve currency, not a dominant global unit. For the euro to rival the dollar as a global currency, one of two things would have to happen. Attitudes toward sovereignty would have to change. Europe would have to move toward deeper political integration; it would have to issue euro-area bonds and create government bond markets with the liquidity of the U.S. treasury market. Or the United States would have to badly bungle its economic policies, sowing distrust of its currency.

PRISONERS OF THEIR OWN DEVICE

In its annual report for 2008, the Central Bank of the Russian Federation revealed that it had reduced the share of dollars in its reserves from 47 to 41.5 percent between the end of 2007 and the end of 2008, while raising the share of the euro from 42.4 to 47.5 percent. Then in mid-2009, in a poke at the United States, the central bank's first deputy chairman, Alexei Ulyukayev, announced that Russia intended to reduce the share of dollar-denominated assets in its portfolio still further.

But where Russia can do pretty much as it pleases without causing too much trouble, China is different by virtue of the sheer size of its holdings. Its official dollar assets are roughly eight times Russia's. China is estimated to control nearly half of all U.S. treasuries in the hands of official foreign owners.[27] Some 65 percent of China's $2.5 trillion of reserves are in dollar-denominated assets.[28] China selling U.S. treasury securities in quantities sufficient to significantly alter the composition of its reserve portfolio would cause their prices to tank. To the extent that dollars still comprised a significant portion of its reserves, the People's Bank would suffer additional accounting losses. If it moved significant amounts of money into other currencies, the dollar would depreciate, making for further losses on those residual holdings.[29]

Since dollar depreciation would make U.S. imports more expensive, Chinese exporters would suffer. This is not a minor matter for a China that depends on exports for employment growth. It is a major consideration for a country that experiences some 70,000 civil disturbances a year.

Moreover, disruptions to the U.S. treasury market that sharply raise U.S. interest rates would not endear China to its American interlocutors. Transactions that cause the dollar to depreciate abruptly, leaving investors wrong-footed

Millions of U.S. dollars

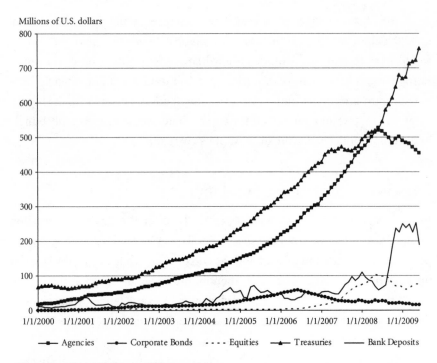

Figure 6.3. China's Holdings of U.S. Securities.
Source: Following Bertaut and Tryon (2007).

and roiling international markets, would not please other countries. One is reminded of Keynes's line, "When you owe your bank manager a thousand pounds, you are at his mercy. When you owe him a million pounds, he is at your mercy."

The sensible strategy under such circumstances is to adjust one's portfolio gradually and inconspicuously. This is, in fact, what China has been doing. It is yet another reason that the declining dominance of the dollar in reserve portfolios, to the extent that it occurs, will be gradual rather than sudden.

To be sure, Chinese officials feel pressure to do something. That the issue has become a flashpoint domestically is not surprising when one observes that China's foreign reserves amount to $2,000 per resident. They are the equivalent of a third of Chinese per capita income. In 2009 China's *Global Times* newspaper ran an online poll in which 87 percent of respondents called China's dollar investments unsafe. During his 2009 visit to China, U.S. treasury secretary Timothy Geithner felt compelled to address the issue before an audience of students at Beijing University, attempting to reassure them that

Chinese holdings of U.S. treasury bonds were secure. His answer drew hoots of laughter.[30]

China would like the United States to compensate it for any losses on its dollar-denominated securities, like the guarantee the British government extended to the members of the sterling area after the pound's 1967 devaluation. But it is hard to imagine any circumstances under which the U.S. Congress would agree.

Funny Money

Recognizing that selling dollars is risky and that, even if the transactions can be safely executed, it is not clear what to replace them with, the Chinese have begun exploring other options. In March 2009 Zhou Xiaochuan, the cerebral governor of the Chinese central bank, drew attention by arguing that the IMF's Special Drawing Rights should eventually replace the dollar as the world's reserve currency.[31] SDRs, recall, are the bookkeeping claims on the IMF first created in the late 1960s to supplement dollars in official international transactions. Zhao in his speech even made explicit reference to the Triffin Dilemma that provided the analytical underpinning for SDRs in the first place.[32]

SDRs quickly became something of an intellectual fad. China, Russia, and Brazil announced their willingness to buy $70 billion of SDR-denominated bonds as their contribution to topping up the IMF's resources.[33] A United Nations commission chaired by the Nobel laureate Joseph Stiglitz advocated an expanded role for an international unit resembling the SDR, although the members of the commission indicated a preference for it to be issued not by the IMF, of whose policies they disapprove, but by a new "Global Reserve Bank." How this would work, exactly, is unclear. As the commission dryly observed in its report, "in setting up such a system, a number of details need to be worked out."[34]

It is not hard to understand the appeal of this idea in the abstract. Empowering the IMF or some similar entity to provide bookkeeping claims in the quantities required by the expansion of global trade and finance would address the need for balance-of-payments insurance. Rather than having to accumulate dollars with which foreign loans could be paid off and foreign goods could be purchased in an emergency, governments could use their SDRs, since other governments would be obliged to accept them. Having SDRs satisfy this need would eliminate the exorbitant privilege enjoyed by the United States and make the world a safer financial place. By creating an alternative to existing national currencies, it would solve the dilemma of large reserve holders like China.

Minor Obstacles

At the moment, however, the SDR is only a bit player. Even after the April 2009 decision to proceed with the distribution of an additional $250 billion of SDRs to IMF members, SDRs still accounted for less than 5 percent of global reserves.

Even more fundamental than this question of scale is the question of utility. Reserve assets are attractive only if they can be used, and the usefulness of SDRs is limited. SDRs can be used to settle debts to governments and the IMF itself, but not for other purposes. They cannot be used to intervene in private markets because there are no private markets where SDRs are traded. They cannot be used to invoice and settle trade because no trade is invoiced and settled in SDRs.[35] Central banks will find it attractive to hold SDRs only when a significant fraction of trade is invoiced and settled in SDRs. They will find it attractive to do so if and when private lending and borrowing take place in that unit. Until then, central banks will have to convert their SDRs into dollars or euros when they want to use them, incurring additional cost and inconvenience. Under current arrangements this process takes a minimum of five days, which is an eternity in a crisis.

Making the SDR attractive would require building deep and liquid markets on which SDR claims can be bought and sold. It would be necessary to build markets on which governments and corporations could issue SDR bonds at competitive cost. Banks would have to accept SDR-denominated deposits and extend SDR-denominated loans. It would be necessary to restructure foreign exchange markets so that traders seeking to buy, say, Korean won for Thai baht first sold baht for SDRs rather than first selling baht for dollars.

Anyone serious about going down this road should familiarize himself with the earlier failed attempt to create a private market in SDRs. In 1981 the IMF sought to jump-start the market by reducing the number of currencies making up the SDR from sixteen to five. The sixteen had included the currencies of all countries accounting for at least one percent of world trade.

However, such a large number made the SDR hard to understand, and it included currencies like the Saudi riyal, the South African rand, and the Iranian rial that were not freely traded or for which forward markets did not exist. Banks refused to accept SDR-denominated deposits since they couldn't hedge the risk on forward markets; they couldn't protect themselves against losses due to exchange rate changes.

By simplifying the SDR basket to include only dollars, German marks, Japanese yen, French francs, and British pounds, the IMF thought it could solve these problems. Commercial banks seeking to test the market took out ads offering certificates of deposit in SDRs. Investment banks offered to underwrite SDR bonds on behalf of governments and corporations. There were a few modest indications of interest among investors in the first quarter of 1981. But with Paul Volcker at the Fed still at work wringing inflation out of the economy, this period was also one of high U.S. interest rates and a strengthening U.S. currency. The SDR depreciated by 7 percent against the dollar in the first quarter of 1981, and all interest on the part of savers and lenders dried up.

One might think that borrowers would have wanted to do business in a unit that became less valuable over time. Sweden in fact obtained a syndicated credit in SDRs in early 1981, but the only other governments that followed its example, the likes of Ireland and the Ivory Coast, were small potatoes. As the Federal Reserve Bank of New York put it in an understated assessment at the end of 1981, "nonbank investor and borrower interest has been modest to date."[36] It became even more modest subsequently.

It is easy to see why there was so little progress. The first private entity issuing an SDR bond or deposit incurred extra costs as a result of the instrument's illiquidity. The first private SDR, by definition, was not traded in a broad and deep market. Purchasers required additional compensation to hold it. And since liquid markets in claims denominated in national currencies already existed, private SDRs traded at a disadvantage.

Moreover, anyone who preferred borrowing or lending in a basket of currencies was apt to favor a tailor-made basket that would suit his or her financial needs more closely and whose components trade in more liquid markets. There was no particular reason that the weights attached to the five currencies making up the SDR basket would be the same as the proportions in which an investor would want to hold bonds denominated in those five currencies. If the diversification benefits of holding different countries' bonds appealed to an investor, he could roll his own portfolio. And since the costs of buying and selling private SDRs were high, SDRs had no cost advantage to offset the attractions of a bespoke portfolio.

Getting Serious

Building private markets in SDR-denominated securities will require sustained investments by the relevant stakeholders, in this case, governments. If China is serious about giving the SDR reserve-currency status, in other words, it should take steps to create a liquid market in SDR claims. It could issue its own SDR-denominated bonds in Hong Kong. This would be a more meaningful step than buying SDR bonds from the IMF. Those bonds will not be traded, so they will do nothing to enhance market liquidity. A Chinese government bond denominated in SDRs would be another matter. Like U.S. treasury bonds, that instrument would be actively traded by investors. And where China led, Brazil and Russia could follow.

The first governments issuing SDR bonds will pay a price, since investors will demand an interest-rate premium to hold them. Bondholders will demand additional compensation for the novelty of the instrument and its lack of liquidity. But nothing is free. That price will be an investment in a more stable international system. Time will tell whether countries like China are willing to pay it.

Then there is the question of exactly who will find it attractive to buy the securities that governments sell. Many government bonds are held by pension funds and insurance companies, since the maturity of those bonds matches the maturity of their obligations to their clients. Domestic government bonds have the advantage that they are in the same currency as the pension or insurance payments that the company makes to its customers. This relieves it of having to worry about changes in exchange rates.

SDR bonds, on the other hand, would not be in the same currency as those pension fund and insurance company obligations. If the dollar depreciates against the euro, a European insurance company with SDR-denominated investments but euro-denominated liabilities would quickly find itself in the soup.[37] One day, far in the future, policy holders and pensioners may be prepared to accept payouts in baskets of currencies. But putting the point this way is a reminder that the day when there is a deep and liquid market in SDRs, with adequate demand and supply sides, remains very far away.

A decision to create large numbers of SDRs on a regular basis to meet the global demand for reserves would also have to confront the delicate question of who gets them. When IMF members agree to increase the number of SDRs, they are allocated according to an agreed formula. But what formula should be used in the future? Would SDRs be allocated in proportion to currently existing reserves? Or mainly to the poorest countries with the most need? In the absence of a consensus about who gets the goodies, there is unlikely to be a commitment to ongoing SDR issuance on the scale needed to replace existing reserve currencies.

Finally, in a world where the SDR was the dominant international currency, the IMF would have to be able to move quickly to issue additional SDRs at times of crisis, much as the Fed and ECB provided dollar and euro swaps to ensure adequate dollar liquidity in 2008. Under current rules, countries holding 85 percent of IMF voting power must agree before SDRs can be issued.[38] This is not a recipe for quick action. IMF management would have to be empowered to decide on SDR issuance, just as the Federal Reserve can decide to offer additional dollar swaps. For the SDR to become more like a global currency, in other words, the IMF would have to become more like a global central bank and provider of emergency liquidity. Again, this is not something that is going to happen overnight.

The case for a global currency issued and managed by a global central bank is compelling in the abstract. A series of ambitious IMF managing directors, seeking to expand the ambit of the institution, have suggested moving in this direction. But as a practical matter, so long as there is no global government to hold it accountable for its actions, there will be no global central bank. No global government, which means no global central bank, means no global currency. Full stop.

At most, one can imagine a limited role for the SDR in supplementing existing reserve holdings. Because the SDR is defined as a basket of currencies, accumulating SDR claims will be another way for central banks to modestly adjust their reserve portfolios in the direction of fewer dollars. Issuing SDRs has the attraction that doing so is cheap. Since the SDR is simply a bookkeeping claim, it costs no real resources to produce. Countries seeking additional reserves do not have to forgo consumption and run export surpluses in order to acquire them. This is also a way of limiting the exorbitant privilege of future reserve currency countries.

But limiting is not the same as eliminating. Central banks will hold only a fraction of their reserves in this form, since SDRs are not liquid or readily used in market transactions. The SDR will not replace national currencies in central bank reserves because it will not replace national currencies in other functions.

Symbolic Gestures

Governor Zhou is aware of these difficulties. He has been around for a long time, having worked his way up through a series of Chinese banks and helped to run the country's State Administration of Foreign Exchange (SAFE). He attends the Jackson Hole retreat of the Federal Reserve Bank of Kansas City, where issues like the viability of the SDR as an international currency are discussed around the campfire.

One might ask, in light of this, what motivated Zhou to make his case for the SDR. One answer is that his SDR proposal was intended as a stalking horse for a Substitution Account through which the international community would take China's dollars off its hands. The idea of an account at the IMF through which SDRs would be substituted for dollars on the books of central banks was first raised in the late 1970s, an earlier period of angst over the prospects for the greenback.[39] It foundered then over the question of who would bear the losses on the dollars absorbed by the account. Since the U.S. government was not prepared to do so, the risk would have remained in the hands of IMF members as a group. But because it was those same IMF members who were anxious to get dollars off their books, this rendered the operation purposeless. It amounted to little more than shifting those dollars from one pants pocket to the other.

Recently there has been another flurry of interest in a 1970s-style Substitution Account to exchange SDRs for the dollars that central banks are anxious to sell.[40] But again the proposal is certain to founder over the question of who will absorb the losses to the account if the dollar depreciates against other currencies. If the members of the IMF, which operates the account, take the losses, then it achieves nothing. Almost 85 percent of shares in the IMF are owned by countries other than the United States—the same countries that are anxious for a Substitution Account to take some of their dollars. In contrast, if the United States agrees to compensate the IMF for losses to the account, it would open itself up to a very large financial liability, which it is not willing to do. Governor Zhou is savvy enough to understand this.

A more compelling explanation for Zhou's initiative is that he was engaged in symbolic politics. He wanted to signal China's unhappiness with prevailing arrangements. By delivering his speech on the eve of a G20 economic summit, he reminded other countries that China's views are to be reckoned with. By suggesting an enhanced role for the SDR, he was positioning China as an advocate of a rules-based multilateral system.

In addition Zhou was playing to his domestic audience. He was seeking to deflect criticism that the Chinese authorities, by failing to more actively seek out alternatives to the dollar, had not been careful stewards of their country's international reserves.

What China Is After

But perhaps the most fundamental reason that the SDR proposal will go nowhere is that China has a preferred alternative, namely establishing the renminbi as an international currency. Were the renminbi used widely in international transactions, China would be freed of having to hold foreign currencies to smooth its balance of payments or aid domestic firms with cross-border obligations. It could just print more or less of its own currency as called for, like the United States. It would enjoy all the advantages of a reserve-currency country.

It is clear that Chinese officials are thinking along these lines. To cite one example, Zhang Guangping, vice-head of the Shanghai branch of the China Banking Regulatory Commission, suggested to reporters in 2008 that the renminbi could become an international currency by 2020.[41]

But 2020 is a long way off. It is a long way off in that the renminbi will remain inconvertible for the foreseeable future. Inconvertibility means that foreigners can only use it to purchase goods from China itself, with a few exceptions. China permits the currency to be used in cross-border trade only with its immediate neighbors, countries like Mongolia, Vietnam, Cambodia, Nepal, and North Korea and the special administrative zones of Hong Kong and Macau. Even there only "select" trustworthy companies are permitted to settle their transactions in renminbi.[42]

These limitations are designed to prevent the value of merchandise imports and exports from being misstated as a way of circumventing China's capital controls. If a Hong Kong resident wanted to smuggle money into China in order to invest in apartments, he could overstate the value of the goods he was importing from Guangzhou, inflate his payment, and on his next trip to Guangzhou recover the funds from the company he was in cahoots with. Or if a businessman in Guangzhou wanted to ferry money out of the country, he could overstate his payments to an exporter in Hong Kong.[43] This is why only trustworthy importers and exporters are allowed to use the renminbi in cross-border trade. These restrictions insulate the Chinese economy from capital flow volatility. They allow Chinese officialdom to manipulate financial markets as they choose. But they also limit the renminbi's international use.

Brazil and China made a splash in 2009 by announcing that they were exploring ways of using their own currencies in bilateral trade.[44] But such explorations are mainly useful for advertizing the fact of that trade. What use would the typical Brazilian firm have for renminbi given that the Chinese currency cannot be converted into *reais*? A Brazilian firm will take renminbi for its exports only insofar as it imports from or seeks to invest in China—not your typical case. Brazil and Argentina reached a similar agreement to settle their bilateral trade in their own currencies in September 2008 but, revealingly, still use dollars in practice.

China is not Argentina. Its trade will continue to grow, and Chinese firms will encourage their customers to invoice and settle their transactions in renminbi, since doing so will protect them from currency fluctuations. Something analogous happened with Japanese trade in the 1980s. As Japanese firms acquired more bargaining power, they insisted that more of their exports be invoiced and settled in yen. Still, the share of Japanese exports invoiced and settled in yen never rose above 40 percent, the yen lacking the other attributes of an international currency. Given that the renminbi will likewise lack these attributes for the foreseeable future, it is not clear that it will do better.

Similarly, China's currency swap agreements with Argentina, Belarus, Hong Kong, Indonesia, South Korea, and Malaysia are not so much practical measures as a way for it to signal its ambitions. Other central banks can't use the renminbi to intervene in foreign exchange markets. They can't use it to import merchandise from third countries or to pay foreign banks and bond-holders. Contrast the $30 billion swap that the Bank of Korea received from the Federal Reserve in November 2008, which the Bank used to intervene in the foreign exchange market. China could become more consequential as a supplier of emergency credits if it offered other countries swap lines in dollars. But so much, then, for swaps as a device for enhancing the renminbi's international role.

With time China can strengthen the international role of the renminbi by developing liquid securities markets and liberalizing access to them. With time it can make its currency freely usable for financial as well as merchandise transactions. The question is: *how much time?* China has been feeling its way in this direction for more than a decade yet even now has moved only part of the way down the path. With good reason: reconciling financial stability with full freedom to buy and sell domestic and foreign assets has formidable prerequisites. Markets must first become more transparent. Banks must be commercialized. Supervision and regulation must be strengthened. Monetary and fiscal policies must be sound and stable, and the exchange rate must be made more flexible to accommodate a larger volume of capital flows.

China, in other words, must first move away from a growth model of which bank lending and a pegged exchange rate have been central pillars. This is easier said than done. Witness that the Chinese authorities' reaction to the 2008 crisis was to move in the opposite direction, ordering the banks to boost their lending and hardening the renminbi's peg to the dollar to sustain exports. All the evidence suggests, then, that China's move to more open financial markets will remain gradual.

SLOW BUT STEADY

Policy toward bond markets is a case in point. Until recently, renminbi-denominated bonds were sold only by Chinese banks and by multilateral banks like the World Bank and the Asian Development Bank, and only in China. The authorities were reluctant to allow foreign corporations to issue bonds, since doing so would have interfered with the government's ability to channel savings to Chinese industry (shades of Japan in the 1970s). If foreign companies offered Chinese investors more attractive terms, their savings would not automatically flow to Chinese banks, to be lent out to enterprises that the government deemed worthy.

In the summer of 2009 HSBC Holdings became the first foreign bank to sell renminbi-denominated bonds in Hong Kong. The following September the Chinese government then issued 6.3 billion of renminbi-denominated sovereign bonds there. The equivalent being less than $1 billion, this was a drop in the bucket, but it was an indication of what is to come. Then in July 2010 Hopewell Highway Infrastructure, a Hong Kong-based highway construction firm, became the first company other than a bank to receive authorization to issue renminbi-denominated bonds offshore.

A market in renminbi-denominated financial instruments in Hong Kong is one thing. So long as financial markets in Hong Kong and the mainland are separated by administrative controls, the actions of foreign investors would not compromise the ability of the government to channel funds to Chinese industries of their choosing. But a market in renminbi-denominated bonds in Shanghai fully open to foreign issuers would be another matter. It would destroy the ability of the Chinese authorities to channel savings to domestic industry. Chinese savers would regard these bonds, with their returns guaranteed in domestic currency, as an attractive alternative to the captive bank deposits that are funneled into industrial development. The very foundations of the Chinese development model would be threatened.

That said, Chinese policymakers are serious about transforming Shanghai into an international financial center by 2020. Doing so will require deeper and more liquid markets. It will require liberalizing the access of foreign investors to those markets, which will in turn imply other changes in the country's tried-and-true growth model. Liberalizing the access of foreign investors to China's financial markets will in turn require a more flexible exchange rate to accommodate a larger volume of capital inflows and outflows.[45] While these are not changes that can occur overnight, it is worth recalling how the United States moved in less than 10 years from a position where the dollar played no international role to one where it was the leading international currency. There is precedent, in other words, for the schedule that the Chinese authorities aspire to meet.

The creation of the Federal Reserve System and a market in dollar acceptances in New York were major institutional changes, but the changes to the Chinese economy required to make the renminbi convertible would be even more far-reaching. Whether China can complete them in as few as 10 years is an open question.

The other reason that 2020 seems a bit ambitious for elevating the renminbi to reserve-currency status is that even if China grows at a 7 percent annual rate for the next decade (slower than in the past, reflecting less favorable demographics, but still exceptional by historical standards), its GDP in 2020 will still be only half that of the United States at market exchange rates—market rates being what matter for international transactions. The renminbi will still have a smaller platform than the dollar from which to launch its international career. The liquidity of markets in renminbi will still not be comparable to markets in dollars.

This means that the share of reserves in renminbi will be limited. Renminbi reserves will be most attractive to countries trading heavily with China and doing their financial business there. They will be most attractive to countries for which fluctuations of the renminbi on the foreign exchange market matter most. This suggests that the practice of holding renminbi reserves will be disproportionately concentrated in Asia, much as the practice of holding euro reserves will be disproportionately concentrated around Europe.

Someday, perhaps, the renminbi will rival the dollar. For the foreseeable future, however, it is hard to see how it could match the currency of what will remain a larger economy, the United States. Regional reserve currency? Yes. Subsidiary reserve currency? Yes. But dominant reserve currency? This is harder to imagine.[46]

Going Buggy

Finally, there are some minor alternatives to be dismissed. Gold has its bugs. They argue that if there is a loss of confidence in the dollar—or even if there isn't—gold is an obvious asset for international investors, including central banks, to scramble into. In practice, of course, central banks have been scrambling in precisely the opposite direction for the better part of a century. Where gold accounted for nearly 70 percent of central banks' international reserves in

1913, its share today is barely 10 percent. In every year since 1988, central banks have been selling, not buying, gold.

Why they have done so is clear. Financial instruments are more convenient for emergency financial transactions. When a currency is under pressure and the central bank is forced to support it, it is simpler just to buy that currency for dollars than to first sell gold in order to obtain the requisite dollars. Gold is not a convenient instrument with which to purchase imports—how many foreign companies will be as inclined to accept it as they are a dollar-denominated check? It is not a convenient instrument with which to pay interest on foreign debts or to engage in other financial transactions.

The exceptions prove the rule. Late in 2009 the Reserve Bank of India bought 200 tons of gold from the International Monetary Fund.[47] This raised the share of gold in the Reserve Bank's reserve portfolio from 4 to 6 percent. Notice, however, how this was a sale of gold by an institution, the IMF, with reason to expect that it might actually have to use its financial resources. Starting in 2008 the IMF had to leap in with emergency financial packages for Hungary, Iceland, Latvia, and Ukraine. In response to the financial crisis, it needed to provide them with cash—actual dollars and euros. Shipping them gold bars wouldn't have been convenient.[48]

India, on the other hand, has a flexible exchange rate, restrictions on capital inflows and outflows, and a relatively sound banking system. At the moment its central bank has little need to use its foreign reserves in market transactions. Given worries about whether the dollar will hold its value, it therefore made sense for the Reserve Bank to modestly increase the share of its portfolio in gold.[49]

Will other central banks follow? In the wake of India's high-profile transaction, there were small purchases of gold on local markets by Venezuela, Mexico, and the Philippines and from the IMF by the central banks of Sri Lanka and Mauritius. Russia's central bank has reportedly purchased limited amounts of gold. But in early 2010 the IMF was forced to acknowledge that it had been unable to find buyers for the remaining 200 tons of gold it wished to sell. So much, then, for the mass migration of central banks into gold.

Again the big player, potentially, is China. Since 2008 China has added modest amounts of gold to its portfolio. Were it to move further in this direction, it could have important implications for the role of gold in central bank portfolios. But once more China faces the dilemma that its reserves, the majority of which are in dollars, are so large. Selling significant quantities of dollars for gold would push down the value of the greenback, creating losses on the dollars that the central bank has not yet sold and pushing up the cost of Chinese exports. Doing so would also push up the price of gold and hence the cost of obtaining more.

Gold bugs are forever. But it is not obvious that one can say the same for the monetary role of gold.

Timber

The other oft-mooted possibility is real assets. Several countries, China among them, have transferred a portion of their reserves to sovereign funds that invest in timber acreage, oil reserves and refineries, and other real assets. It might be possible for the United States to inflate away the value of its treasury securities, the argument goes, but not the value of timberland in New Zealand or petroleum in West Africa.

Again, this is a fine strategy for countries with more foreign reserves than they will ever use. It is unlikely that China will ever have to use more than a fraction of its $2.5 trillion of reserves to intervene in foreign exchange markets or to recapitalize banks with dollar liabilities. It makes perfect sense to lock up a share of those reserves in real assets. That those investments are illiquid is no big deal since there is little prospect that their Chinese owners will find themselves having to sell them in an emergency. It is no coincidence that Norway, which has accumulated more foreign assets through sales of natural gas than it will ever need to intervene in financial markets, was among the first to pursue this strategy, creating a sovereign wealth fund to invest in real assets.

But the situation is different for countries that foresee circumstances in which they might actually have to use their reserves. Selling timberland for dollars in a financial emergency is even more difficult than selling gold. Just ask Harvard University, whose endowment fund bought up large tracts of timber in New Zealand in the years leading up to the crisis. At 2006 valuations, timber accounted for 12 percent of the Harvard endowment's real estate portfolio. This created huge difficulties in 2008 and 2009 when the fund needed cash and couldn't easily sell its timber acreage. This is not a strategy for investors who value liquidity. It is not an investment strategy for central banks.

WEALTH OF ALTERNATIVES

So where does this leave us? It leaves us with the prospect of multiple international currencies. A world of multiple international currencies is coming because the world economy is growing more multipolar, eroding the traditional basis for the dollar's monopoly. Once upon a time, after World War II, when the United States dominated the international economy, it made sense that the dollar should dominate international monetary and financial affairs. The United States dominated world trade. Only it had deep and liquid financial markets. As an international currency, the dollar had no rivals.

Today more countries are consequential traders. More countries have liquid financial markets. The shift away from a dollar-dominated international system toward this more multipolar successor was accelerated, no doubt, by the 2008 crisis, which highlighted the financial fragility of the United States while underscoring the strength of emerging markets. But even before the crisis, it was clear that the tension between a multipolar economic world and a dollar-dominated international monetary system would have to be resolved. And even then, there was little question about the form this resolution would take.

The speed with which this world of multiple international currencies arrives will depend on the advantages of incumbency. Recall the argument that the competition for international currency status is subject to status quo bias. It pays individual exporters and bond issuers to use the same currency as other exporters and bond issuers. This works to maintain the status quo. And the status quo choice is the dollar.

But this mechanism is unlikely to carry the same weight in the future as the past. Once upon a time it made sense for importers, exporters, and bond underwriters to use the same currency as other importers, exporters, and bond underwriters, since doing otherwise could create confusion for their customers. The difficulty of obtaining up-to-date information on the value of different currencies and the high costs of switching between them meant that it paid to use the same unit as everyone else. The currency in which everyone transacted had the most liquid markets as a result of the fact that everyone transacted in it. The dominance of the leading currency was self-reinforcing.[50] International currency status was a natural monopoly, like municipal water supply or electricity.[51]

The twenty-first century is different. Everyone now carries in his pocket a device capable of providing the real-time information needed to compare prices in different currencies. Comparing the prices of bonds or the cost of trade credit in dollars and euros is no longer a problem. Changes in technology have allowed for freer competition in other industries long assumed to be natural monopolies, like electricity and telephony. Why should international finance be any different?

In addition, the sheer size of the twenty-first-century world economy means that there now is room for more than one market with the liquidity that makes for low transactions costs. Again, the natural-monopoly argument for why there should be only one consequential international currency has become less compelling as a result of economic and financial development.

Forecasts are risky, especially when they involve the future. But there is little uncertainty about the identities of the leading players in this new, more multipolar system. The dollar, the currency of the single largest economy with the most liquid markets, will remain first among equals. The euro, the currency of a monetary zone whose economic size approaches that of the United States, will become more attractive, particularly on the periphery of Europe, if not now, then once Europe has sorted out its problems. China, for its part, is already encouraging select nonresidents to use its currency to invoice and settle merchandise transactions. In the not-too-distant future, perhaps in as few as 10 years, the renminbi will be an attractive unit, especially in Asia, for use by international investors and central banks.

While the dollar, the euro, and the renminbi will be the leading international currencies, they may not have the field to themselves. The same arguments suggesting that there is room for three international currencies suggest that there is room for more than three. The additional candidates are not likely to be the currencies of demographically challenged countries like Japan and Russia. Size matters for the depth and liquidity of financial markets. And assuming the continued convergence of living standards, population will be a key determinant of economic size.

This points to India's rupee and Brazil's real as additional runners. Like China, both India and Brazil have work to do before their currencies are used internationally. Like China, they continue to restrict foreign participation in their financial markets, thereby limiting the attractions of their currencies for international use. Like China, their financial systems are bank based: they have a way to go in building liquid markets in the bonds and bills that central banks and other international investors find attractive. Still, their favorable demographics suggest that their currencies, like China's, may acquire growing roles. That their economies are smaller than China's and that they engage in less foreign trade and investment suggest more limited international use of their currencies. But they are coming.

None of this means that the dollar will lose its international currency status, only that it will have rivals. It will have to compete for business because exporters and investors will have a growing range of alternatives. That said, there is no reason that it shouldn't succeed at that competition—barring a homegrown economic disaster of the first order.

CHAPTER 7

DOLLAR CRASH

But what if the dollar does crash? What if foreigners dump their holdings and abandon the currency? What, if anything, could U.S. policymakers do about it?

It would be nice were this kind of scenario planning undertaken by the Federal Reserve and Central Intelligence Agency, although recent events are not reassuring about the capacity of U.S. officialdom to anticipate the worst. Were it undertaken, it would have to start with what precipitated the crash and caused foreigners to abandon the dollar.

One trigger could be political conflict between the United States and China. The simmering dispute over trade and exchange rates could break into the open. American politicians who see China's failure to revalue its currency more quickly as giving it an unfair competitive advantage, resulting in a chronic trade imbalance and U.S. unemployment, could impose an across-the-board tariff on imports from the country. Beijing would not take this lying down. Or the United States and China could come into conflict over policy toward rogue states like North Korea and Iran. Imagine that the United States took military action against one of those regimes, contrary to the wishes of Beijing. Again, China might be tempted to do something significant to register its protest.

One way for China to vent its anger and exert leverage over the United States would by using its financial weapon. Official Chinese agencies hold 13 percent of all U.S. government securities. Dumping them would send the bond market into a tizzy. As soon as they realized that the Chinese government was selling, other investors would pile on. Interest rates in the United States would spike. The dollar would crater. This demonstration of its vulnerability could cause exporters, importers, and investors to abandon the dollar permanently.

How plausible is this scenario? Some history may help to frame the answer.

EAST OF EDEN

One instance where the financial weapon was used to advance geopolitical ends, by none other than the United States, was the 1956 Suez Crisis. In the era before supertankers, 70 percent of Western Europe's oil passed through the Suez Canal (modern supertankers are too large to navigate the channel). Transiting the canal reduced the cost of transporting tin and rubber from the British colony of Malaya and more generally of shipping goods between Asia and Europe. Hence Britain maintained a garrison of 80,000 troops at Suez and, together with France, exerted financial control of the Suez Canal Company.

Egypt, experiencing the same upsurge of nationalism as other Third World countries, sought to revoke the lease of the Franco-British consortium starting in 1952. Following the military coup that overthrew the monarchy on July 22 and brought General Gamal Abdel Nasser to power, Egypt's relations with Britain and more generally with the West grew increasingly strained. In 1954 Nasser obtained agreement by Britain to withdraw its troops from the canal garrison. He upped the ante by recognizing the People's Republic of China in 1956.

The United States, allied with Taiwan and hostile to mainland China, responded by halting financial support for Egypt's Aswan Dam project. Britain had engineered the dam, British hydrologists having been involved in earlier projects at Aswan. But the United States financed it, reflecting Britain's straitened circumstances. The Eisenhower administration's abrupt decision betrayed the influence of the brusk cold warrior John Foster Dulles. The president was recuperating from intestinal surgery at the time, putting the hard-edged Dulles effectively in charge of foreign affairs.

Dulles was confident that Nasser would back down, but the Egyptian president was unwilling to compromise. The High Dam was his pyramid, the symbol of the proud modern Egypt he was seeking to create. Nasser therefore retaliated by revoking the Anglo-French concession at Suez and nationalizing the canal. The 70,000 French shareholders in the Canal Company were predictably outraged. A further grievance of the French government was Nasser's support for the Algerian rebellion, which aggravated France's political and military problems in North Africa.[1]

In response the French negotiated a secret pact with Israel. The Israelis had long objected to Nasser's interference with their shipment of goods through the canal. More immediately they were alarmed to learn that Egypt had just purchased a shipment of MiG fighters from the Soviet Union. (The planes came via the Soviets' client state Czechoslovakia, but no matter.) The information acquired new urgency with the arrival in Egypt of Russian and Czech pilots to fly the planes.[2]

After a series of cloak-and-dagger meetings with the French, Britain joined the alliance. When on October 29 Israel preemptively launched an incursion into Sinai, Britain and France moved to seize the canal, ostensibly to protect it from both Israeli and Egyptian forces. British and French planes bombed Egypt's airfields. (So much for the MiGs.) Nasser responded by sinking all forty-seven ships transiting the canal, closing it to shipping. Although goods and petroleum from Asia and the Middle East could still reach Europe via the Horn of Africa, the extra cost and time were enormous. Nasser's action produced among other things a horrific naval traffic jam in Cape Town, as three times the normal number of ships began arriving there for refueling.[3]

Although French paratroopers and British commandos were able to seize control of the canal at low cost to themselves, the damage had been done. In particular it had been done to the special relationship between the United States and Britain. Rather out of character for such a skilled diplomat, Conservative prime minister Anthony Eden had not obtained Eisenhower's agreement prior to launching the operation. He simply assumed that the U.S. president would support action against an Egyptian government that had recognized a Chinese regime actively hostile to America's Taiwanese ally.

Part of the explanation may have been Eden's blind fury with Nasser. Eden was notoriously vain, emotional, and given to fits of anger. He had tendered an emotional resignation as foreign secretary in 1938 when the prime minister, Neville Chamberlain, approached the Italian dictator Benito

Mussolini behind his back. It didn't help that Nasser's nationalization of the canal discredited the British policy of conciliation of which Eden had been the principal architect. During his third stint as foreign secretary in 1951–1955 (the second having been during World War II), Eden had personally negotiated the withdrawal of British troops from their Suez base.

Nasser having poked a stick in his eye, Eden now set his mind on toppling the Egyptian leader. Half measures would not do. As he put it in response to a memo from Anthony Nutting, his minister of state for foreign affairs, advocating a more diplomatic approach, "What's all this poppycock you've sent me? . . . What's all this nonsense about isolating Nasser, or 'neutralizing' him, as you call it? I want him destroyed, can't you understand? I want him removed. . . . And I don't give a damn if there's anarchy and chaos in Egypt."[4]

Misunderstanding also flowed from the fact that Eden never developed much of a relationship with the U.S. ambassador to London, Winthrop Aldrich—who happened to be the son of the Nelson Aldrich who played a leading role in the founding of the Fed and the dollar's rise to international prominence. Normally the American ambassador would have been a conduit for information on the views of the president and the State Department. But Eden was on cool terms with Aldrich, who seemed more interested in London society than foreign policy.

A final factor was Eden's reliance on Harold Macmillan, his chancellor of the exchequer.[5] Macmillan was blindly confident that Britain could depend on its special relationship with the United States. Macmillan had his own personal relationship with the United States, his mother having been born in Indiana. He also had a special relationship with the American president, having served as wartime liaison between Prime Minister Churchill and Eisenhower when the latter was supreme allied commander of the North African theater. Macmillan was smuggled into the White House to meet with Eisenhower on a trip to Washington to attend the annual meetings of the International Monetary Fund and World Bank shortly before the Suez invasion. Whether Suez was discussed is disputed, but Macmillan, when cabling his prime minister, left no doubt about the views of the American president. "Ike," he wrote, "is really determined, somehow or other, to bring Nasser down."[6]

Wishful thinking this. The last thing Eisenhower and his State Department wanted in the wake of the Soviets' suppression of the Hungarian Revolution was to side with an occupying power. Dulles was critical of anything that smacked of colonialism, which he saw as weakening the United States in the Cold War. Meanwhile the U.S. Treasury, under George Humphrey, Eisenhower's closest friend in the Cabinet, opposed extending American support because of its budgetary implications.

The British also misunderstood U.S. electoral politics. The fact that Eisenhower was running for reelection in November 1956 gave them confidence that he would stand with Britain and Israel against the Egyptians. In fact, the American electorate had little appetite for another military adventure. For Eisenhower, who was campaigning on his record as a peacemaker, opposing the Suez incursion was a political winner. To British surprise, the United States demanded an immediate halt to military operations.

Less Than Sterling

Such was the geopolitical context. The financial background was the vulnerability of sterling. Britain's foreign creditors still sought to shed the financial claims they had acquired during World War II, and the country's increasingly porous capital controls gave them the opportunity to do so.[7] Meanwhile high wages, low productivity, and adversarial labor relations prevented Britain from developing a strong export economy to offset its weak finances. Even before the Suez incursion, British reserves had fallen perilously close to the $2 billion viewed as the minimum safety level.[8] Against this backdrop, an expensive and uncertain military campaign was risky.[9] Closure of the canal would increase the cost of shipping and raise the price of imported oil. The Suez adventure thus catalyzed market doubts about the sustainability of the $2.80 pound-dollar exchange rate.

A fall in that exchange rate might have far-reaching consequences. Commonwealth countries, as well as Northern European countries accustomed to tying their currencies to the pound, would have to decide whether to follow. They might choose instead to maintain their link to the dollar, the currency of a stronger economy and larger trader. If so, the cohesion of the sterling area, and the practice on the part of its members of banking in London, would be casualties.[10]

Even before the Suez operation, then, the Eden Government knew that in order for the $2.80 sterling-dollar exchange rate to hold, it would need help from the IMF. This was where Eden and Macmillan were confident they would receive unconditional American support. And it was where their judgment proved fatally wrong. The State Department warned that the United States would support a request for assistance only in return for a commitment by the British Government to withdraw its troops. On November 2 the United States then introduced a cease-fire resolution in the UN General Assembly. By making public the spat between the United States and the UK, this action precipitated a run on the pound.[11] The attack intensified when the United States made clear that it was insisting on not just a cease-fire but the physical withdrawal of troops.[12]

At this point Macmillan, who had been the staunchest supporter in the Cabinet of military action against Nasser, abruptly switched sides. He was accused of inconsistency, even duplicity, by the opposition. "First in, first out Macmillan" was the way they put it. But as financial water carrier for the government, he could hardly have done otherwise. His real failing was his earlier overconfidence about the prospects for American help.

For two weeks the British Government prevaricated, accepting the cease-fire but agreeing to withdraw only one battalion. Capital controls slowed the loss of reserves, but speculators, seeing devaluation as increasingly likely, found ways around them. Foreign purchasers of British goods delayed paying, given the likelihood that that the pound was about to be reduced in value.[13] Sellers of goods to Britain insisted on being prepaid.

Climbing down was painful. A group of Conservative backbenchers known as the "Suez group," reluctant to acknowledge that Britain was no longer a geopolitical power of the first rank, opposed all troop withdrawals. The Eden Government sought a commitment on financial assistance that could be used to secure Cabinet consensus on withdrawal. But the Eisenhower administration continued to demand a British commitment to withdraw by a date fixed. The British worried that setting a date might mean disorderly withdrawal, jeopardizing the safety of the troops. Eden, in poor health and now suffering from exhaustion, flew off for an extended period of recuperation at Goldeneye, the holiday home of the novelist Ian Fleming in Jamaica. This did not inspire confidence in his government.

Everyone knew that the crisis would come to a head on December 4, when Macmillan would make his regular monthly announcement of Britain's reserves. It would show gold and dollar holdings below $2 billion, almost certainly triggering the final run on the pound. Under pressure of time, the Eden

Government offered increasingly firm commitments to withdraw while still trying to avoid being pinned down to a date. It temporized with convoluted language, promising Washington, "[We] have decided to go without delay and we intend to go without delay."[14]

But the Americans held all the cards. They could force concessions simply by doing nothing. On December 2, with the chancellor's speech two days away, the Cabinet agreed to a December 22 deadline for the withdrawal of troops. On December 3, Secretary Humphrey, back in the office after a short vacation, agreed to support a British drawing from the IMF.

When Macmillan reported on December 4 that the Bank of England's reserves had fallen below $2 billion, he was therefore able to announce American support for Britain drawing its entire $1.3 billion credit line at the IMF.[15] On December 10, with U.S. support, Britain's application to borrow was approved; of the sixteen members of the IMF Executive Board, only the director representing Egypt abstained.[16] This action marked the end of the financial crisis. It also marked the end of the era when a country that had once been economically strong, Britain, could pursue a foreign policy independent of a now stronger partner, the United States.

A Parallel Too Far

This history is suggestive for those contemplating the financial implications of a foreign-policy conflict between the United States and China. But the only thing it has in common with a potential Sino-American conflict is the vulnerability of the currency of one of the principals. One important difference is that a China that caused the U.S. bond market and dollar to crater would be inflicting significant financial damage on itself, since it would be pushing down the value of its dollar assets. The American government's holdings of British securities were barely $1 per American resident in 1956. Financial losses to American investors as a result of a decision not to support sterling would have been negligible. The United States could credibly threaten steps that might lead to a sterling crisis without worrying about self-inflicted financial losses.

Today, in contrast, Chinese holdings of U.S. government and agency securities exceed $1,000 per resident. Losses to China from a decision to use those holdings to advance geopolitical ends would be harder to ignore. Given the magnitude of its holdings, it is not clear who would be hurt more. There is no ruling out that China might take precipitous action in a fit of pique. But it is more likely to think twice.

Similarly, the United States when tightening the screws did not have to worry about damaging its access to foreign markets. Its merchandise exports were barely 5 percent of U.S. GNP. Less than a twentieth of those exports—5 percent of the 5 percent—went to Britain. Even if sterling depreciated sharply and the British economy went into a tailspin as a result of America's failure to help, the impact on the U.S. economy would have been modest. Even had Britain retaliated by slapping tariffs on U.S. exports, there would have been only a minor impact on the United States. Knowing this, the United States was undeterred in using its financial weapon.

Contrast China today, 40 percent of whose GNP is in the form of exports, a quarter of which go to the United States. A sharp fall in the dollar that created financial problems for the United States would hit Chinese exporters in the pocketbook. The fallout from the 2007–2008 crisis just hints at the consequences. Chinese exports fell by 17 percent in 2009 as a result of the crisis in the United States. The Chinese authorities were able to prevent a significant economic slowdown by applying the single largest fiscal stimulus, as a share of GNP, of any country. They were aided by the fact that their trading partners, including the United States, did not resort to overt protectionist measures, and that governments around the world cooperated in applying monetary and fiscal stimulus to stabilize the global economy.

The situation would be different in the event of a Sino-American conflict. The U.S. would respond with trade sanctions if China was seen as using its financial weapon to roil U.S. markets. The damage to China's exports would be more serious than in 2008–2009. Stabilizing the world economy would be harder, given the inability of the two countries to cooperate. The potential for wider damage would cause China to hesitate.

MARKETS OUT OF CONTROL

Instead of geopolitics, the trigger for a dollar crash could be a sudden shift in market sentiment. Investors might wake up one morning and decide that holding dollars was a losing proposition. With the smart money leading the way, other investors would follow. If we know one thing about investors, it is that they are erratic. Markets can crash. Investors can run with the herd. Currencies can fall prey to investor panics.

A sharp fall in the dollar in a short period—say, a 50 percent fall like that experienced by the Korean won following the failure of Lehman Bros.—would catch some investors off-guard. Anyone still holding dollars would suffer catastrophic losses. There could be a cascading wave of defaults. The solvency of institutional investors and the stability of the global financial system could be placed at risk.

And even if this risk was contained, there would be other fallout. The other currencies into which investors piled would appreciate sharply. Europe's competitiveness problems would be aggravated. Rising unemployment, laid at the doorstep of a depreciating dollar, could trigger a protectionist backlash.

In the wake of these events, foreigners would come to think twice about using an unstable dollar. Exporters would shift to other currencies for invoicing and settling their trade.[17] Bondholders would shun dollar-denominated claims. This would be the tipping point where the dollar lost its international currency status. America's exorbitant privilege would be no more.

Only one thing is wrong with this scenario. It assumes that the Fed wouldn't intervene to support the dollar. Under normal circumstances the Fed doesn't intervene in foreign exchange markets. Instead it targets price stability and employment growth. But this panic would not be normal circumstances. In the face of a plunge that it saw as resulting from panic, the Fed would surely step in to support the dollar, buying it up on foreign exchange markets. It would make it more expensive for investors to bet against the currency by raising interest rates. And if it was right that the cause of the dollar crisis was panic pure and simple, the currency would recover. Panics do not last forever. Investors eventually realize they have overreacted. The Fed's intervention would be a plausible occasion for their coming to their senses. With the Fed buying low and selling high, its intervention might even be profitable.

To carry out this operation, the Fed would need help from its friends. Its capacity to buy dollars is limited by its reserves of foreign currencies, which are small relative to the scale of the problem. The situation would not be unlike the 1960s when the United States required assistance from Germany and other European countries to maintain the dollar's peg to gold.[18]

Back then, of course, it was mainly our friends holding our financial liabilities. The fact that the geopolitical interests of China, Russia, and the oil-exporting countries of the Middle East, U.S. creditors all, are not fully aligned with ours leaves one less confident now that their help can be counted on.

Geopolitics notwithstanding, foreign governments have the same interest as the U.S. Treasury and the Fed in preventing a self-fulfilling run on the dollar. They will not want to see their firms experience a serious loss of competitiveness. They will not want to see investors suffer gratuitous balance-sheet damage. Given their shared interest in the stability of a global system in which the dollar plays a leading role, they too will have an incentive to intervene. And in the scenario where intervention is profitable for the Fed, it is profitable for other central banks. Again, the self-interest of all those concerned would work to prevent problems from getting out of hand.

Deficits Out of Control

Thus, the plausible scenario for a dollar crash is not one in which confidence collapses on the whims of investors or as the result of a geopolitical dispute but rather because of problems with America's own economic policies. The danger here is budget deficits out of control.

Chronic budget deficits have frequently been the precipitant for crises. Recent experience in Greece, Portugal, Spain, and elsewhere in Europe illustrates how the process works. The longer a government runs deficits, the higher its debt and interest payments mount. Those payments lay claim to a growing and ultimately excessive share of available tax revenues. Investors may be lulled into complacency for a time by the government's promise to put its fiscal house in order, if not today, then tomorrow. But one morning they will wake up with a start and conclude that the debt is unsustainable. They will sell its bonds en masse, and its currency will collapse on the foreign exchange market.

The implications for the United States would not be pretty. Bond prices would plunge as investors scrambled to get out. Interest rates would spike. With foreign investors among those liquidating their positions, the dollar would collapse to lower levels. If this happened all at once, the results could be devastating.

The Fed may again step into the breach, buying up bonds to support the market and prevent treasury yields from spiking.[19] But in contrast to the previous scenario, in this case the Treasury will at the same time be flooding the market with additional debt. The Fed will be compelled to buy this debt, too, if private demand has evaporated. Investors will see this as a process without end. They will see the Fed's bond purchases and the cash that it is pumping into the economy as auguring inflation, which will mean further dollar weakness, and worse. The decline in the currency will feed on itself. In the face of these problems, there really could be mass migration away from the dollar.[20]

The fate of the dollar ultimately hinges, in this case, on U.S. budgetary policy. And here are there are grounds for concern. Three, actually. First is the deterioration in the fiscal position prior to the financial crisis. The 2001 and 2003 tax cuts pushed revenues to their lowest level as a share of GDP since 1950, while the decision to add a prescription drug benefit to Medicare and fight two expensive wars eliminated any pretence of cutting spending. Together these tax cuts and unfunded spending increases pushed the budget from surplus in 2000 to a structural deficit of 4 percent of GDP in 2007–2008. Given the interest that now has to be paid on the resulting debt, the impact on the deficit only rises with time.

Second, there are the eye-popping deficits resulting from the financial crisis. Budget deficits were unavoidable under the circumstances; tax receipts

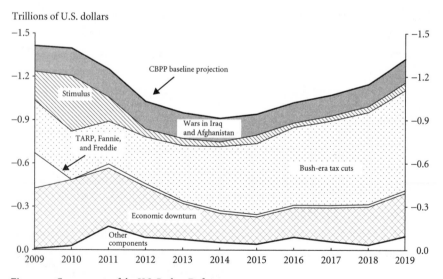

Figure 7.1. Components of the U.S. Budget Deficit.
Source: Center on Budget and Policy Priorities analysis based on CBO estimates as of February 17, 2010.

collapsed, and the government had no choice but to step up and replace some of the private spending that evaporated in the crisis. But the resulting deficits were enormous: the 11 percent of GDP deficit in 2009 was not just unprecedented in peacetime; it was larger than the national income of all but six other countries in the world. The 2010 deficit was larger. The official line is that these deficits will now be reversed out in short order, but whether this maneuver can be accomplished is dubious at best.

Third, there is the prospect of even larger deficits once the baby boomers start retiring in large numbers around 2015, raising health and pension costs. This is what the country's efforts at health-care reform are all about.

But it is not necessary to look that far ahead to see trouble. The current trajectories of revenues and spending imply that federal government debt will have risen from 40 percent of GDP before the crisis to 75 percent by 2015, net of obligations to social security and other government trust funds.[21] Debt ratios will rise even faster if the economy's growth potential has been permanently damaged by the crisis, as many observers believe. Growth 1 percentage point slower would raise the debt/GDP ratio by 5 additional percentage points by 2011 and by 10 additional percentage points by 2015.

It will not be easy for the United States to cope with a debt/GDP ratio of 75 percent. This sort of burden is manageable for a government that takes 30 to 40 percent of national income in taxes, as is typical in Europe. But it is more difficult for a U.S. government whose tax revenues are only 19 percent of GDP in a normal year.

With one out of every five tax dollars committed to interest payments, it will be tempting to maintain other services by running deficits and issuing additional debt.[22] At some point, however, investors will recognize this behavior for the Ponzi scheme it is. They will understand that U.S. alternatives ultimately reduce to measures to drive down the real value of the debt, presumably by inflating it away. Since investors look forward, they will want to close out their positions before this inflation happens.

If foreign investors refuse to accumulate additional dollar securities as they flow onto the market, U.S. interest rates could rise by a full percentage point.[23] More alarmingly, foreign investors could become unwilling to hold dollar securities, period. Selling their holdings will have even larger interest-rate and exchange-rate effects than simply refusing to absorb additional issues. Anticipating continued dollar depreciation, residents of other countries will see no reason to risk pricing their exports in dollars. They will not accept payment in that form, just as Britain's creditors refused to accept sterling in 1956.

If history is any guide, this scenario will develop not gradually but abruptly. Previously sanguine investors will wake up one morning and conclude that the situation is beyond salvation. They will scramble to get out. Interest rates in the United States will shoot up. The dollar will fall. The United States will suffer the kind of crisis that Europe experienced in 2010, but magnified. These events will not happen tomorrow. But Europe's experience reminds us that we probably have less time than commonly supposed to take the steps needed to avert them.

Doing so will require a combination of tax increases and expenditure cuts. At 19 percent of GDP, federal revenues are far below those raised by central governments in other advanced economies.[24] With spending on items other than health care, Social Security, defense, and interest on the debt having shrunk from 14 percent of GDP in the 1970s to 10 percent today, there is essentially no nondefense discretionary spending left to cut. One can imagine finding small savings within that 10 percent, but not cutting it by half or more in order to close the fiscal gap. It is wishful thinking to believe that there exists that much waste and fat. And after 2015, as the baby boomers retire, current budget plans imply federal government spending on the order of 25 percent of GDP. Under current law, federal spending will rise to 40 percent of GDP over the subsequent quarter century, which is just a way of saying that current law cannot remain unchanged.[25]

A new era of peace and reconciliation may descend on the world, allowing for additional reductions in defense spending. Or there may be agreement on further health-care reform that significantly bends the cost curve for service delivery. It is not clear which scenario is more fanciful. It hard to avoid the conclusion that restoring fiscal balance will require dealing with entitlements. It will require agreement to limit pension costs by raising the retirement age. The problem of funding Social Security can be alleviated by liberalizing immigration policy. There will also have to be agreement on what American politicians euphemistically refer to as "revenue enhancement." One can imagine imposing higher gasoline taxes at the pump or auctioning off greenhouse gas permits. One can imagine the imposition of a value-added tax. But with a Republican Party unconditionally opposed to all new taxes, a Democratic president who campaigned on a promise not to raise the taxes of the middle class, and a well-organized American Association of Retired Persons to lobby against Social Security and Medicare cuts, it is uncertain whether any of these sensible outcomes can be produced by normal congressional politics.

Hence the allure of taking the decision out of the hands of the Congress and placing it in those of a benevolent bipartisan commission. Congress would provide the mandate—it would specify the pace at which the commission was instructed to close the deficit. All taxes and spending programs would be on the table, including Social Security, Medicare, and Medicaid. Unlike the Congress, where every member represents his or her own narrow constituency, this commission could proceed with the national interest in mind. The Congress would be presented with a package in which everyone's ox was gored, but only slightly. The commission's recommendations would then be voted up or down by the House and Senate without amendment.

This is not an unreasonable idea, but neither is it guaranteed to work. If the Congress is reluctant to see taxes raised or spending cut, it will hesitate to give a commission true independence. It will be reluctant to bind itself to accept or reject its recommendations in a single up-or-down vote. A bipartisan commission created by executive fiat that lacks buy-in from the opposition and whose recommendations the Congress is not bound to accept or reject without amendment is unlikely to have much effect. Even if the Congress does commit to either accepting the commission's recommendations or else leaving the government without a budget and incapable of providing essential services, one should not underestimate the capacity of legislators to do the wrong thing. For anyone dubious of the proposition, I have just one word for you: California.

In the end there is no substitute for achieving political consensus in the Congress and nationally on how to solve the fiscal problem. Procedural changes can help. But meaningful reform will require political consensus on the ends to which procedural changes are the means. A dollar crisis could be the event that precipitates the necessary reforms. Better, of course, would be the mere possibility of a dollar crisis.

This said, the United States is not the only economy with fiscal challenges. Europe and Japan have even heavier debts. The euro area, having received an early wake-up call, is now making strenuous efforts to put its fiscal house in order, but it will be years before we learn whether it succeeds. Japan, confident that it is safe because its debt is held almost entirely by its own residents, has barely begun doing likewise. The task for both is complicated by slowly growing labor forces and rapidly aging populations. The dollar's prospects may be bleak, but, as always when thinking about exchange rates, it is necessary to ask: bleaker than what? People have been wrong before when betting against the U.S. economy. They have been wrong before when betting against the dollar. They could be wrong again.

Or they could be right, in which case the dollar's exorbitant privilege will be no more.

LIFE UNDER PRESSURE

If the dollar loses its international status, foreign investors will have little appetite for dollar claims. When lending to an American company, they will lend in other reputable international currencies. They will demand that American corporations issue bonds and commercial paper in those other currencies. Skeptical that the dollar will retain its value, they will lend to the U.S. government only if the Treasury issues bonds denominated in foreign currencies.

American economic policy will have to be adapted accordingly. Most obviously the Fed's benign neglect of the exchange rate will have to be abandoned. Customarily the Fed focuses on inflation and employment growth.[26] It attempts to strike a balance between these dual objectives. It concerns itself with the exchange rate only insofar as there are implications for these other variables.[27] When a Fed chairman actually says something about the currency, as Ben Bernanke did in November 2009 in response to a bout of dollar weakness, the markets take notice precisely because the subject is addressed so rarely.[28]

This is in contrast to countries lacking America's exorbitant privilege. When they borrow abroad, they borrow in someone else's currency, since the lenders have no particular use for their national money. If the local currency then depreciates, borrowers get smashed, since their foreign-currency obligations become more expensive to service and repay. And, knowing this, the central bank is forced to jack up interest rates to limit the depreciation. This is the "fear of floating" syndrome in emerging markets whose liabilities are in someone else's money.[29] It forces central banks to compromise their pursuit of other goals in order to keep the exchange rate from moving excessively. Insofar as they are forced to more closely align their interest rates with those in the rest of the world in order to keep the exchange rate stable, it gives central banks less room for maneuver.

A Fed constrained in this way would not be able to cut rates to low levels as it did to counter the recession that followed the collapse of the high-tech bubble and 9/11. With interest rates significantly lower in the United States than other countries, the dollar declined by 30 percent between 2001 and 2004. Given America's exorbitant privilege, the Fed could treat this depreciation with benign neglect. Since U.S. international competitiveness was enhanced, it could see depreciation as part of the solution rather than part of the problem.

If we find ourselves in a new world where significant amounts of U.S. debt are in other currencies, the Fed will no longer be able to disregard the financial consequences. Well before the dollar's fall reached 30 percent, the Fed would be forced to raise rates. American monetary policy would have to hew to the line set by foreign central banks. Welcome to the club, the Fed's friends in less developed countries would no doubt say. In this way the United States would resemble an emerging market.

Moreover, the United States would be dependent on the generosity of others in the event of a crisis. When in 2008 banks stopped lending and financial markets seized up, the Fed could provide emergency liquidity to cash-starved banks and firms because their bills were denominated in dollars that the Fed could print. Contrast this situation with South Korea, where banks and firms had borrowed abroad in dollars. The capacity of the Bank of Korea, the country's central bank, to provide banks and firms with the resources needed to avoid defaulting on their dollar obligations was limited to the Bank's dollar reserves—since the Bank of Korea can only print won. When in November 2008 the Bank's reserves fell to the psychologically important $200 billion regarded as the prudent minimum, indicating that it might be forced to halt such lending, panic set in.[30] (Recall that $2 billion was seen as the prudent minimum for the Bank of England's reserves in 1956; add two zeros and you have Korea.) Foreign banks refused to roll over their loans. The won collapsed on the foreign exchange market. The situation stabilized only when the Fed announced that it was loaning its Korean counterpart $30 billion, enabling the Bank of Korea to lend dollars to banks and firms with bills in dollars to pay.[31]

In a world where American banks and firms are forced to borrow abroad in foreign currencies, the Fed will find itself in the position of the Bank of Korea. In a crisis where foreign banks stop lending and financial markets seize up, not only will U.S. banks and firms be unable to get their hands on the foreign currencies needed to keep current on their debts, but the Fed will not be able to help them, since it can't print those foreign currencies. It will have to rely on foreign central banks to provide it emergency loans like those the Fed provided them in 2008. Financial stability will hinge not just on the Fed doing the right thing, but on foreign central banks doing the right thing. America's fate will be in foreign hands. Foreigners may seek to exact a price from the United States in return for their assistance. In a crisis the United States will have little ability to resist.

The U.S. government could also, in principle, appeal to the International Monetary Fund, the other important source of emergency liquidity in the 2008 crisis. For foreign critics of the IMF who have long accused it of imposing on them U.S. wishes, this is a delicious possibility. But American financial markets are large relative to the resources of the IMF. Unless the Fund was very considerably expanded, which is unlikely, it would lack the capacity to provide emergency liquidity on the scale that would be required by U.S. banks and markets.

Tighter Belts

How much difference will it make for American living standards if foreign central banks and governments no longer turn to the United States and the dollar for reserves and no longer finance U.S. external deficits so readily? No question, Americans will have to tighten their belts. We will no longer be able to consume and invest a trillion dollars more than we produce each year simply because central banks and other foreign investors have a voracious appetite for dollars that require no real resources to supply. It will no longer be possible for us to import goods and services amounting to $1 trillion in excess of what we export. The days will be over when the United States can run a current account deficit of 6 percent of national income without tears. The United States will have to cut its trade deficit. It will have to export more.[32]

Doing so will mean making our exports more attractive. Their cost will have to be lower, their quality higher. This can be accomplished by raising the efficiency of American industry or limiting payments to the factors used in their production. Raising efficiency—increasing the quality and quantity of the output produced by our firms and workers—is of course the happier alternative. Unfortunately, increases in efficiency can't be willed into existence; they have to be achieved. And in order to deliver an improvement in the U.S. trade balance, they have to be achieved faster than in countries with which we compete.

Here the United States has some obvious strengths. It has large numbers of university-and industry-based scientists, many attracted from other countries. With high-powered incentives for entrepreneurs and an agile venture capital industry, it has a demonstrated ability to develop innovative technologies. With low hiring and firing costs and flexible labor markets, it is quick to commercialize those innovations. The United States also has an abundance of fertile land that supports a profitable agribusiness sector, something that is increasingly valuable in a food-scarce world.

But much of the country's physical infrastructure is antiquated and difficult to modernize, partly by virtue of the fact that it is under the jurisdiction of a multitude of state and local governments or in private hands. Freight railways own much of the track used by Amtrak, for example. Contrast the difficulty of building a high-speed train line from New York to Chicago with China's rapid completion of a high-speed link between Beijing and Shanghai—or for that matter with France's, Germany's, and Spain's high-speed trains. China plans to build as much as 8,000 miles of high-speed rail by 2020. In the United States, meanwhile, intercity rail service is now actually slower than in the 1940s. Market economies have their strengths, but when it comes to some tasks it helps to be a planned or, like Europe, mixed economy. Were Dwight Eisenhower to come along today and propose building the interstate highway system, no doubt he would be accused of socialism.

Similarly, the United States is no longer the beneficiary of an increasingly well-educated labor force. The current generation is the first in more than a century whose educational attainment does not significantly exceed that of its parents. Claudia Goldin and Lawrence Katz estimate that the educational attainment of an American born in 1975 is just six months more than that of his or her parents born in 1951. By comparison, the educational attainment of an individual born in 1951 was more than 2 years greater than that of a person born in 1921.[33] Meanwhile a variety of middle-income countries with which the United States competes continue to boost their levels of education. The gap is closing. And for those who go straight from secondary school to work, the United States lacks effective vocational training like that which exists in Europe.

Nor can the United States count on high levels of private investment. The additional public debt inherited from the financial crisis will have to be serviced. Servicing it will mean higher taxes. Ensuring that new bonds are willingly taken up when existing bonds mature will require higher interest rates. Higher taxes and interest rates are burdens for investors. They do not bode well for capital formation. They do not bode well for the dollar.

These problems can be fixed. Together with economic growth, budget surpluses can reduce public debt relative to taxes and national income. But even if the will exists, completing the task will take time. Decaying roads and bridges can be repaired. New ones can be built. But this revitalization, too, can occur only over a period of years. The country can invest more in education, but again time will have to pass before the graduates receive their degrees and enter the labor force.

It is not clear that the markets will wait. If they don't, the country will have to adjust in other ways. Absent a miraculous acceleration in productivity growth, the only way of exporting more will be by limiting costs. Employers can cut back on wages and nonwage costs like health insurance. But after a decade in which average labor compensation has stagnated and fringe benefits have been cut to the bone, there will be resistance to going down this road.

Alternatively, the adjustment can be left to financial markets. That is to say, the competitiveness of American exports can be enhanced by allowing the dollar to decline. Again, the result will not be pleasant. Walmart shoppers will pay more for their Chinese-made clothes. Your high-definition TV will become more expensive. But if the United States now has to export more as a result of no longer being the exclusive provider of international reserves to the world, this change is unavoidable.

Germany illustrates the point. Following strong spending growth in the 1990s when pent-up demand was released by German reunification, domestic demand stagnated. In Germany then, as in the United States now, the party could not last forever. As demand growth slowed, Germany had to export more for employment to rise. Fortunately, the country's big trade unions, starting with IG Metall, the metalworkers' union, understood the challenge. They agreed with management and government on a policy of wage restraint. They agreed to allow wages to grow more slowly, especially in the country's eastern states, where output per worker was less.

Between 2003 and 2010, average hourly earnings Germany-wide rose by less than 1 percent per annum. Combined with respectable productivity growth, this policy of restraint reduced the cost of labor. Germany was able to boost its foreign sales at a double-digit pace. With exports increasing half again as fast as imports, it was able to strengthen its international accounts. Germany's example illustrates the kind of adjustment now required of the United States.

But the other side of this coin is the continuing stagnation of living standards. From the trough of the business cycle in 2003 to the eve of the financial crisis in 2007, the consumption of German households rose by just 1 percent. While Germany's example shows that adjustment is possible, it also shows that it comes at a cost.

Still, a decline in the dollar need not have a catastrophic impact on American living standards. The historical rule of thumb is that reducing the current account deficit by 1 percent of GDP requires the dollar to depreciate by 10 percent.[34] Cutting the external deficit from 6 to 3 percent of GDP, which is what is required, would thus mean a 30 percent fall in the dollar against other currencies.[35] The first third of this adjustment was accomplished, as it were, in the course of 2009, with the dollar falling 10 percent in the 11 months following President Barack Obama's inauguration.

The dollar's 2009 fall was disquieting, but there was no collapse of American living standards. The dollar exchange rate has regularly risen or fallen by 10 percent in a year. It has periodically fallen by as much as 30 percent in 2 or 3 years. It fell that much, adjusted for inflation, between 2001 and 2004, and there was no existential threat to the American way of life. It fell even faster between 1985 and 1988. While this 1980s episode was not a happy one, it did not produce an apocalyptic fall in U.S. living standards. To the contrary, the dollar's fall only modestly affected the prices American consumers faced at the mall.[36]

DOLLAR DECLINE AS ELIXIR?

Some will argue that dollar depreciation and rebalancing the U.S. economy toward exports are to be welcomed, not resisted. Their argument is that the strong dollar that resulted from America's exorbitant privilege has contributed to the hollowing out of American manufacturing industry. It has slowed learning on the job, there being fewer manufacturing jobs from which to learn, and delayed improvements in efficiency. All the while, other manufacturing-heavy economies, from Germany to China, were sprinting ahead.

Now, with a weaker dollar, the argument goes, the United States will produce more manufactured goods for foreign consumption and fewer fast-food meals for American households eating out less. With households tightening their belts (in both senses), there will be more good jobs and fewer McJobs. The distribution of income will be more equitable. Another way of thinking about this change is as a shift in the composition of what America exports from the treasury, agency, and derivative securities purchased by foreign central banks and private investors, toward John Deere earthmoving equipment, Boeing Dreamliners, and—who knows—maybe even motor vehicles and parts.

This shift will also help to redress the problem of income inequality, the advocates of a weaker dollar contend, since manufacturing uses more blue-collar labor than does financial services. The growth of income inequality in the United States in the last decade was largely accounted for by the exceptional increase in the compensation of the top 0.01 percent of earners. Suffice it to say that these folks were not assembly-line workers. A substantial share of that top-earning group was made up of the managing directors and executives of investment banks, hedge fund managers, and private equity and venture capital professionals.[37] With the United States now producing and exporting fewer financial services, and with more blue-collar workers in good manufacturing jobs, it is argued, this trend will be reversed.

Other countries have boosted their manufacturing sectors by keeping their exchange rates low and exporting more of what they produce. The proposition is that the United States should meet fire with fire, not simply restraining the growth of labor costs à la Germany but also actively lowering its exchange rate in the manner of China.

Why That Won't Work

Were it only true. It would be nice if a lower dollar could miraculously rejuvenate American industry and create large numbers of manufacturing jobs while narrowing income inequality. But the circumstances of the United States are not the same as Germany's. Having long been the producer of capital goods for much of Europe, Germany is a dominant supplier of production equipment, now also to emerging markets. While it has other economic and financial problems, with a well-developed system of apprenticeship training providing legions of skilled mechanics, it never allowed its manufacturing sector to wither. Attempts to grow U.S. manufacturing employment would have a less favorable starting point.

The circumstances of emerging markets like China differ even more radically. China has been able to grow its manufacturing employment and raise the incomes of its unskilled masses by shifting rural peasants into assembly operations where they can learn the requisite skills in a matter of days. This is not unlike the situation in Highland Park, Michigan, a century ago when Henry Ford built the first assembly line. The simplicity of the technology used to produce the Model T, by our contemporary standards, made it possible to train up workers, many of whom were immigrants or straight off the farm, in less than a week.

The situation in the United States today is different. Manufacturing has migrated to developing countries—thankfully so, for this is what we mean by economic development. The spread of industrialization is lifting two-thirds of the world's population out of poverty. Developing countries increasingly dominate industries that rely on unskilled and semiskilled labor that can be trained up in a week, since this is what they possess in abundance. This also means that the U.S. equivalent of China shifting a rural peasant into assembly operations is shifting a worker from the counter of a fast-food restaurant to the foundry of a semiconductor fabrication plant. But this is not how the world works. Manufacturing activities in which the United States is internationally competitive require skilled workers, not hamburger flippers. Given time, more Americans can acquire the skills and training to work in a semiconductor fab. But the fundamental constraint is imparting the skills, not simply lowering the cost of their labor.

Another way of seeing this point is to observe that manufacturing only accounts for a slim majority of U.S. exports of goods and services. Services, excluding interest payments on debt to foreigners but including things like the underwriting services of investment banks and insurance companies, the design services of engineering firms, and the business services of software companies and management consultancies, account for fully 30 percent. Most of the services the U.S. exports are provided by well-educated, high-skilled workers. Agriculture and products based on raw materials account for another 15 percent of exports.[38] The United States, with its abundant, fertile land, has long been an exporter of agricultural products. But these are the exports of capital-intensive agribusiness, which employs relatively few workers, not of the late lamented family farm.

None of this should come as a surprise. The United States has abundant capital and skilled labor by the standards of emerging markets. Capital and skilled workers are the inputs used most intensively by its export industries and sectors.[39] If you ask which U.S. plants have shut down as a result of Chinese competition, the answer is low-productivity plants with lots of production workers.[40] An exchange rate 30 percent lower is not going to be of much help to an unskilled or semiskilled worker in the United States competing head to head with Chinese labor, especially when labor productivity in China is growing by 6 percent per annum.

Ramping up U.S. exports is desirable on any number of grounds. But it will benefit mainly capital and skilled labor, since they and not the unskilled workers whose jobs have migrated to developing countries are the factors used intensively in the production of those exports. Changes in exchange rates cannot solve all problems. If Americans are concerned, as they should be, with income inequality, they will need to address it through other means, be they changes in the tax code and caps on bankers' bonuses or more investment in education and training.

LEVERAGING UP

Concern with the consequences of the dollar losing its exorbitant privilege is not limited to the pocketbook. A weaker dollar, security specialists warn, will make it more difficult for the United States to project strategic influence and pursue foreign policy goals. Maintaining a foreign military presence will become more expensive. We will have less foreign aid money with which to win friends and influence people. American companies will be less able to make the strategic investments in, inter alia, West African oil refineries that cause countries anxious to attract our capital to take note of our preferences. Devalued dollars will be less capable of buying the cooperation of foreign governments.

Other countries with stronger currencies meanwhile will be doing all the things that we can no longer afford. China is investing in the Greater Nile Petroleum Operating Company that controls Sudan's oil fields, making it harder for the United States to pressure Khartoum to abandon its human rights violations in Darfur. Whereas the United States is cutting the budget for Radio Free Europe/Radio Liberty, China Radio International provides 19 hours of daily programming from its transmitter in Kenya.

And as a net foreign debtor, America will depend on the generosity of others, creating a pressure point for them to exploit. Not only will other countries grow more assertive, but the United States will be more reluctant to cross them. Foreign debtors have weak currencies. And no foreign debtor, it is said, remains a great power for long.

Such warnings make sensational newspaper copy, but they misdiagnose the problem. The shift from a world where the dollar was the dominant international currency to one in which is now obliged to share that role will in fact have only minor implications for the ability of the United States to pursue its geopolitical goals. It is hard to see how having to narrow our current account deficit by 3 percent of GDP, which would be the implication of other countries no longer relying primarily on dollars for their reserve needs, would fundamentally transform America's position in the world. It is hard to see how a dollar exchange rate 30 percent lower—a 30 percent fall, recall, being what is required to narrow the U.S. current account deficit by that amount—could make such a difference, given that the dollar has risen or fallen that much before without cataclysmic effects.

The fundamental determinant of U.S. strategic leverage is the basic economic and fiscal health of the nation. A nation whose economy does not grow loses political and strategic power. A government unable to raise sufficient revenues or rein in other expenditures will be unable to finance an adequate defense budget. It is this fact and not whether the dollar remains the world's dominant reserve currency that is confronting the Pentagon with a further decline in U.S. defense spending from an already historically low 4 percent of GDP. And what is true of military power is true of soft power, what with China now sending more government-funded doctors than the United States to many parts of Africa. It is the cash-strapped fisc and not whether or not the dollar is the dominant reserve currency that prevents the

United States from spending more on foreign aid or hosting more Fulbright scholars.

With the emerging markets in which two-thirds of the world's population live growing faster than the United States, U.S. defense spending as a share of global output is shrinking even faster than U.S. defense spending as a share of U.S. output. This is simply a matter of arithmetic. It is also a reminder that the fundamental factor that has rendered the U.S. less dominant geopolitically is the same thing that has rendered the dollar less dominant financially, namely that the world is growing more multipolar. It is a reminder of the other thing the United States must do to maintain and strengthen its capacity to project geopolitical leverage besides putting its fiscal house in order, namely enhance its economic health generally. Britain's loss of great-power status after World War II occurred not so much because she emerged from the war as a net foreign debtor as because her subsequent economic performance was dismal, leaving H.M. Government strapped for cash. It was this economic malaise, and not simply that Britain was a net foreign debtor, that forced the UK to withdraw from Greece in 1947. It was this, and not just that Britain owed the U.S. money, that led to its climbdown from Suez in 1956.

The point is that it is not the exchange rate or the net foreign investment position as much as the fundamental underlying health of the economy that matters for geopolitical leverage. If one wants a single unified explanation for the behavior of the exchange rate and the net foreign investment position, it would again be the fundamental underlying health of the economy. Whether the dollar rises or falls by 30 percent will matter much less for U.S. strategic influence than whether U.S. economic growth averages 2 or 4 percent per annum over the next decade.

Again, there is a more alarming scenario: instead of the dollar declining gradually to somewhat lower levels, there is a dollar crash. In this case all bets are off. Here it is important to remember that the only plausible scenario for a dollar crash is one in which we bring it upon ourselves. This also means that it is within our grasp to avoid the worst. The good news, such as it is, is that the fate of the dollar is in our hands, not those of the Chinese.

NOTES

CHAPTER I

1. Bellman, Chan, and Watcharasakwet (2009).

2. Defined as foreign currency debt sold outside the issuer's home country.

3. This refers to the combined GDP of the United States, UK, France, Germany, Italy, Austria, the Soviet Union, and Japan as calculated by Harrison (1998), p. 10.

4. Figures for 2008 from UNCTAD's *World Investment Report* (2008), while the 1945–1980 estimate is from Jones (2005).

5. In this case, that risk arises if the dollar depreciates against the franc, reducing the value of the bank's assets (its loans) relative to its liabilities (its deposits).

6. Of course this $500 billion is a stock rather than a flow; foreigners need to obtain it only once.

7. See Gourinchas and Rey (2007) and Habib (2010).

8. The dollar did, in fact, strengthen sharply when problems in the subprime market spiked in August 2007, but the trend over the course of 2007 was downward. For more on this episode see chapter 6.

9. When their value is expressed in dollar terms.

10. In other words, the dollar value of our foreign investments rose by that amount with no corresponding change in the value of our foreign debts.

11. http://www.facebook.com/notes.php?id=24718773587.

CHAPTER 2

1. The utility of trading wampum with the Indians had been discovered by Dutch settlers on Long Island and was introduced to the Massachusetts colonists by an itinerant Dutch trader.

2. While similarly expressing those obligations in pounds, shillings, and pence.

3. There was also "country pay," which permitted debtors to choose from a basket of commodities at rates set by the colonial legislature.

4. An isolated exception was the mint opportunistically established by Massachusetts in 1652. King Charles ordered it closed in 1682.

5. In addition to piracy, the colonists engaged in privateering, the officially sanctioned commandeering and looting of the ships of enemy powers. Conveniently Spain, whose ships carried the richest cargoes, was the principal enemy power.

6. The expression "two bits" to refer to a quarter of a dollar derives from the fact that the smaller 1-real piece was worth almost exactly the same as the English sixpence, popularly known as a "bit."

7. Michener (1987) concludes that the vast majority of the money circulating in the colonies was in the form of coin.

8. When states issued bills subsequently, they bore a rate of interest. While close substitutes, they therefore were not exactly money. Such was the case in 2009, for example, when the State of California, its legislature in a budget deadlock, issued IOUs.

9. Any holder of gold or silver was entitled to have it coined free of charge by the Mint. If the holder insisted on the equivalent in coin immediately, then a 0.5 percent charge was levied.

10. Cited in McIvor (1958), p. 39.

11. Powell (1995), p. 30.

12. See Williams (1968).

13. The example on which I draw is from Nussbaum (1957).

14. See Laughlin (1912), p. 99; Phelps (1927), pp. 57–58.

15. Certain state-chartered banks were permitted to open foreign branches, but they rarely did.

16. Cleveland and Huertas (1985), p. 81.

17. In addition it maintained a branch in London. In 1913 IBC was joined by a second specialized banking company, the Continental Banking and Trust Company of Panama, established under the laws of West Virginia, with four branches abroad.

18. One more trust company, Bankers Trust, figures importantly in our story. The idea of creating a trust company owned by commercial banks (a "Bankers Trust") was conceived in 1903 by Henry Davison, who offered the position of secretary to Benjamin Strong in 1904. Both men play prominent roles in what follows. Many years later, in the 1990s, Bankers Trust became the subject of notoriety because of its pioneering and questionable use of derivatives (Partnoy 2003).

19. Specifically, they were not permitted to discount trade acceptances in the manner of British banks. Nor were most banks authorized to accept drafts or bills of exchange.

20. Most state banking legislation similarly prohibited state-chartered banks from dealing in trade acceptances or failed to provide explicit authorization, leading the

courts to rule against those attempting to do so. While state trust companies could in principle engage in acceptance business, they did so only to a limited extent.

21. King (1936), p. 311. "Purchases" should be understood to include both rediscounts and purchases for the Bank's own account on the open market. This was also a way for the Bank of England to influence gold inflows and outflows, since by making trade credit more or less expensive it could affect the volume of merchandise imports and exports. This particularly impressed Benjamin Strong, who as founding governor of the Federal Reserve Bank of New York used the resources of that institution to actively develop the dollar acceptance market. See Chandler (1958), pp. 88–89 and pp. 28–30 below.

22. See Govan (1959). The bank was forced to suspend payments in 1839 and eventually declared bankruptcy as a result of loss-making investments in cotton and large loans to its own officers. Biddle was arrested and charged with fraud.

23. Flandreau and Jobst (2006) count the number of national markets in which exchange rate quotations for the various foreign currencies were available in 1900. The dollar ranks behind all these other currencies.

24. Stephenson (1930), pp. 333–34.

25. According to some accounts, Charles Norton, president of the Morgan-affiliated First National Bank of New York, rather than Strong was the sixth participant, although Vanderlip in his memoirs lists Strong rather than Norton. Wicker (2005) speculates that neither was present.

26. Cited in Broz (1997), p. 191.

27. Published as Lindbergh (1913).

28. A 1919 amendment known as the Edge Act allowed any national bank to form or invest in a foreign banking corporation, an arm that engaged in foreign banking operations while not also undertaking domestic banking business. This was an opportunity for smaller banks to enter the foreign field with the help of larger, more sophisticated partners.

29. See Cleveland and Huertas (1985). Even more important for providing trade finance was the Guaranty Trust Company, which, as we have seen, was one of the few U.S. financial institutions with foreign branches even before the passage of the Federal Reserve Act. So too was J.P. Morgan and Company, which had the not inconsequential advantage of serving as purchasing agent for the French and British governments in the United States.

30. It did so using American credits and the securities of British residents that, like the residents themselves, were drafted into the war effort. The government sold these mobilized securities in New York and used the proceeds to purchase U.S. treasury bills as needed to limit depreciation of the sterling exchange rate. The sale of Britain's dollar securities was probably the main factor supporting the sterling-dollar exchange rate in this period; it was also one of the main mechanisms through which the United States was transformed from international debtor to international creditor (Brown 1940).

31. This does not count the thirty-eight foreign branches of the ubiquitous American Express Company, which provided a number of bank-like services.

32. There was then some retrenchment as U.S. trade fell off and foreign competition intensified; by 1926 the number of foreign branches had fallen to 107 (Phelps 1927).

33. American Acceptance Council (1931), p. 17.

34. Technically, to offer repurchase agreements and carry bills on their own accounts. In 1921 it then allowed the reserve banks to rediscount acceptances running as long as 6 months to maturity. In 1922 it gave the reserve banks discretion over the eligibility of acceptances for rediscount.

35. Chernow (1993), p. 224.

36. So estimates Phelps (1927), p. 174.

37. See Mintz (1951).

38. The irony being that Britain by this time had gone off the gold standard, freeing up other policies and vitiating the argument for a tariff. Sometimes economic arguments take on a life of their own.

39. The 36 percent figure is from the fourth quarter of 1929 to the fourth quarter of 1932.

40. Face value, from Lewis (1938), p. 629.

41. Not just municipalities but also drainage districts. Starting in 1909 Tennessee counties were permitted, with county court authorization, to create special administrative districts to construct ditches for draining farmland. The districts could issue bonds to be paid off with future taxes on the landowners benefiting from their activities. Every single drainage-district bond with which Caldwell was involved eventually fell into default. That the company was still warehousing a number of these bonds on its own balance sheet and those of the banks with which it was connected led directly to the subsequent financial problems of both.

42. Quoted in *Time* magazine (October 5, 1931).

43. The remainder was French francs, which accounted for a nonnegligible share of reserves for the first time since World War I, France being the only significantly sized country that remained on the gold standard. The Depression came late to France, which had stabilized its currency later than Britain, and at this point remained relatively mild; France could therefore afford to indulge in its preference for maintaining gold convertibility. There had also been the experience of high inflation in the first half of the 1920s, which left French politicians and their constituents reluctant to contemplate alternatives (see chapter 3).

CHAPTER 3

1. Excluding the Soviet bloc, which became, with the intensification of the Cold War, increasingly self-contained and, from the point of view of international monetary relations, irrelevant.

2. This being the level at which FDR stabilized the price of gold in 1934. The U.S. reaffirmed its commitment to that price after World War II and maintained it when declaring the dollar's par value to the International Monetary Fund (see below).

3. With the eruption of World War II, most non-British members of the sterling area went off sterling. Membership then became a precise legal status as Britain put in place comprehensive exchange-control regulations around the whole group of sterling countries. Restrictions for foreigners were not applied to countries that, in addition to keeping their currencies pegged to sterling and maintaining their reserves in London, also promised to enforce a system of exchange controls similar to Britain's. This was done with the express goal of preserving sterling's international functions after the war.

4. To be precise, $6.3 billion in sterling versus $3.0 billion in dollars (Triffin 1968, table 2.2).

5. This as of December 1945. The two-thirds figure refers to net UK sterling liabilities held abroad.

6. The fear of the American negotiators was that their retention would allow the UK to offer commercial preferences to the Commonwealth and Empire as it had in the 1930s.

7. While convertibility was supposed to cover only newly earned sterling, it was not hard to relabel existing balances, which were an order of magnitude greater than those earned from mid-1946.

8. The value of sterling reserves had fallen only slightly, from $6.4 billion to $6.2 billion. The value of dollar reserves, meanwhile, had risen from $3.0 billion to $10.4 billion.

9. The methods will sound disturbingly familiar to modern ears. As Pierre-Henry Simon described in his book *Contre la Torture*, "on the afternoon of Dec. 3 some gendarmes invited some solders to watch tortures of two Arabs arrested the night before. The first torture consisted in suspending the two men, entirely nude, by their feet, hands tied behind their backs, and lunging their heads into a pail of water for long periods to make them talk."

10. These came all but automatically since wages were indexed to the price level by government decree. That devaluation, by raising the prices of traded goods, will do nothing to restore a country's international competitiveness when wages are indexed to those prices is intuitive. And, like many things intuitive, it is also the subject of a theoretical literature (e.g., Sachs 1980).

11. For more on this see p. 52 below.

12. The last time Germany experienced significant balance-of-payments problems was in 1951, when the Korean War drove up the prices of its imported raw materials. Temporary foreign assistance allowed it to bridge the gap, after which the trade accounts shifted into strong surplus.

13. It also prohibited the payment of interest on foreign bank deposits. These measures were put in place in June 1960, when Germany experienced strong inflows from the United States, and remained in place into 1969.

14. Craig (2004), p. 39.

15. Skidelsky (2001), p. 124.

16. White was also a fellow traveler who looked the other way when others at Treasury passed sensitive information to the Soviets, and may have even passed sensitive information himself. It was not that White was disloyal to the United States—to the contrary, he fought hard for American interests, including in his monetary negotiations with the British—but that he saw the Soviet Union as a critical wartime ally in the fight against Fascist Germany.

17. This was the so-called Scarce Currency Clause, which in any case was never invoked.

18. The $16 trillion figure is obtained by taking half of global imports and exports between 2006 and 2010.

19. Deposited, that is, in proportion to their quotas. White and his colleagues flirted with the idea of an international accounting unit, which they called "unitas" perhaps in order to make it marketable to the Congress. But this was a mere accounting unit in which to denominate the Stabilization Fund's assets and liabilities. It was never seen as a true international currency that the Fund would have the power to create.

20. Hence the name Bretton Woods System.

21. The Anglo-American loan was actually agreed to by the two governments in late 1945 but ratified by the U.S. Congress in mid-1946.

22. For example McKinnon (1996).

23. The commitment to convert dollars into gold was extended only to official foreign holders—that is, to central banks and governments. The United States' liabilities to those central banks and governments first exceeded U.S. monetary gold stocks only in 1963. But there was scope for arbitrage—for private holders to "put" their dollars to their central banks, heightening the pressure on those central banks to reduce their exposure in turn (Garber 1993).

24. See Triffin (1947).

25. The same will be true of the People's Bank of China once the renminbi becomes a consequential reserve currency.

26. This problem had been solved before 1913 by a fall in the overall price level as economies grew, which raised the real price of gold, given that the nominal price was fixed by gold standard statutes. This raised the relative price of gold and encouraged investment in the gold-mining industry, boosting supply (as described by Barro 1979). The same mechanism had worked in the 1930s, when the collapse of price levels had given impetus to gold production, but also precipitated a painful depression. Now, however, governments and central banks in general, and the U.S. central bank and government in particular, were preoccupied by the other effects of deflation, namely recession and unemployment. And they were firmly committed to preventing these things from happening. Hence the mechanism that had ensured a reasonably elastic supply of monetary gold under the gold standard was no longer operative.

27. The U.S. contributed 50 percent of the resources of the pool. France, Germany, Italy, and the UK each contributed 10 percent, Belgium, the Netherlands, and Switzerland about 3 percent. The pooled resources of the participants would then be used to sell gold whenever its price threatened to rise above $35 an ounce (equivalently, when there was a danger that the dollar would depreciate).

28. The Soviet Union's exceptional gold sales were prompted by a harvest failure, South Africa's by balance-of-payments weakness.

29. One is reminded of President Obama plucking Secretary of Defense Robert Gates from the Bush cabinet to reassure the security establishment.

30. As noted by Mayer (1980).

31. In 1974 it would be redefined as a basket of currencies. Then in 1981 it was redefined again (for more on this see chapter 6).

32. In this he echoed the words of C. H. Minor in 1931 (chapter 2 above, p. 35).

33. Cited in Rueff (1971), p. 155.

34. As described in James (1996).

35. Chairman of Bernstein-Maccaulay, Inc., quoted in the *New York Times* (August 25, 1971).

36. Cited in Meier (1974), p. 182.

37. Reeves (2001), p. 286.

38. On his resistance, see Greider (1987), p. 342.

39. Later, when Colson found religion, he made a pilgrimage to Burns's office to ask forgiveness (Safire 1975, pp. 495–96).

40. It was said that they "recycled" their earnings in New York, in a usage that made the reflux of funds into dollars seem inevitable. IMF data (as in Chinn and Frankel 2007) indicate a substantial increase in the dollar's share between 1973 and 1977. But this comes at the expense of "unspecified" currencies. One suspects that what might naively be interpreted as an upward trend in the dollar's share is simply more countries divulging the currency composition of their reserves to the Fund.

41. Some argue that the shift was no coincidence—that, in a telling sign of how a country's policies can be influenced by foreign powers that hold its debts, veiled threats from OPEC about dumping the dollar compelled Carter to attach a higher priority to fighting inflation and shift from Miller to Volcker (Harris 2009). But see also chapter 7.

42. The secret-agent phrase is from *Time* magazine.

43. More sharply even than Carter presumably expected; the Georgian criticized Volcker's austere policies as "ill advised" in the 1980 presidential campaign that he ultimately lost to Ronald Reagan.

44. Akinari Horii, then a young staff economist at the Bank for International Settlements (and eventually deputy governor of the Bank of Japan), provided the most detailed study of the question. Adjusting for changes in the distribution of reserves across country groups and statistical inconsistencies, he concluded that there was no net diversification out of dollar reserves between the end of 1972 and the end of 1979 (Horii 1986).

45. Saudi Arabia began accumulating deutschmarks and yen, but only on the margin as it continued adding to its reserve stockpile if only to avoid contributing to the dollar's weakness. The analogy with China's dilemma and behavior today will be clear. And Saudi purchases of deutschmarks and yen were in any case constrained by the limited availability of relevant instruments. Its reserve managers purchased mainly nonmarketable government bonds made available in limited amounts by the central banks of the two countries.

46. It stabilized at only slightly lower levels than in the late 1960s before the eruption of monetary turbulence.

47. As quoted in the *New York Times* (November 20, 1979).

48. For more on French problems and policies see chapter 4, pp. 83–84.

49. See Tavlas (1998).

50. Again circa 1990, with the yen, at 13 percent, accounting for the next largest share.

CHAPTER 4

1. See Marsh (2009), p. 14, for more.

2. Helmut Schmidt, the German chancellor who was one of architects of the European Monetary System, recognized the connection: "We had a currency union up to 1914 in Western Europe—the Gold Standard. From a historical point of view, I would draw a direct parallel." Marsh (2009), p. 69.

3. The Treaty of Rome, the Community's founding document, did not explicitly endorse the creation of a monetary union, but it identified exchange rates as a matter of "common interest" and provided for a Monetary Committee to advise governments on monetary matters. The Monetary Committee would be made up of two members from each member state together with two representatives of the Commission. There was then a proposal from the European Commission under Walter Hallstein in 1962 for a three-stage transition to a single currency to be completed over 10 years, but it was met by silence from governments and dropped. But the idea of a three-stage transition to be completed over 10 years would reappear in 1970 and, more consequentially, in 1989, as described below.

4. In the words of Strange (1980), p. 46.

5. Kloten (1980), p. 181.

6. Dyson (1994), p. 70. In the importance that he attached to a single European currency that could rival the dollar, it is perhaps germane that Giscard could trace his lineage back to Charlemagne, who had himself unified Europe monetarily, after a fashion.

7. Marsh (2009), p. 50.

8. The previous policy of pegging had meant buying the dollars that flooded into the country for DM increased the German money supply, the variable viewed by German authorities as a key indicator of prospective inflationary pressure.

9. See chapter 3, pp. 61–62.

10. Szulc (1972).

11. The Bretton Woods term, "parities," was jettisoned in favor of "central rates," implying that the additional room for maneuver would actually be used.

12. As described in chapter 3, pp. 61–62.

13. Sweden joined later.

14. Denmark came back in, temporarily, after a majority of Danes supported the referendum on EC accession voted on later in 1972.

15. Dyson and Featherstone (1999), p. 294.

16. On Triffin see also chapter 3, pp. 49–50. Jenkins was also influenced by the McDougall Report on fiscal federalism initiated by the Commission and completed earlier in the year. Michael Emerson, the secretary to the committee that produced the McDougall Report, was a member of Jenkins's cabinet.

17. The Callaghan Government had bigger problems, namely unemployment. It was aware that Germany would set the tone for monetary policy in the EMS and worried about the implications for British growth and unemployment, given that the domestic economic backdrop was highly unfavorable. It preferred to see Europe solve its monetary problems by negotiating with the United States to stabilize the dollar. In part this reflected the fact that the UK traded more heavily with the United States and other countries whose currencies tracked the dollar than did the continental Europeans, so a European currency bloc that delinked from the dollar and ultimately threatened it worked against British interests. Dyson and Featherstone (1999), p. 549.

18. Marsh (2009), p. 79.

19. This time, however, countries with special needs might be allowed to operate wider bands.

20. Emminger wrote Schmidt summarizing their understanding. "The autonomy of the Bundesbank in monetary policy would particularly be put in jeopardy if strong imbalances within the future EMS [European Monetary System] resulted in extreme intervention obligations which then threaten the value of the currency. This would make it impossible for the Bundesbank to carry out its legal obligations. Referring to repeated assurance from the chancellor and the finance minister, the Bundesbank is starting from the premise that, if need be, the German Government will safeguard the Bundesbank from such a situation of constraint, either by a correction of the exchange rate in the EMS or, if necessary, by discharging the Bundesbank from its intervention obligations." Emminger (1986), pp. 361–62 (translated here from the German).

21. Ibid.

22. Save the Danish krone, which was devalued by 5 percent.

23. Kohl had been drafted in the final weeks of the war, but he was never sent to the front.

24. This according to Painton, Bonfante, and Sancton (1983).

25. See chapter 6, pp. 132–133.

26. Among those opposed was a director of the French Treasury, Jean-Claude Trichet, who would subsequently become president of the independent ECB.

27. As recounted in Marsh (2009), p. 135.

28. She may have also believed that, with sterling in the ERM, London could better stake its claim as the financial center for Europe. And she may have also been of the view that Britain could more effectively shape Europe's monetary future from the inside than the outside.

29. With some exceptions for countries like Portugal, Spain, and Ireland with lingering financial problems (as explained below).

30. More so since much of this debt was short term. A 1 percentage point increase in the central bank's discount rate added a full 1 percent of GDP to the government's budget deficit.

31. Schlesinger's comments reflected the Bundesbank's decision in the second week of September to invoke the Emminger letter of 1978 (see note 20 above) and assert its right to limit its intervention on behalf of weak ERM currencies. Given this, to say that further devaluations could "not be excluded" was an understatement.

32. When one recalls this history, it becomes less surprising that Trichet, as president of the European Central Bank during the 2010 crisis, agreed that the bank should purchase Greek, Portuguese, Spanish, and Irish bonds in the interest of euro-area solidarity.

CHAPTER 5

1. Evans (2007) is an early account of how equity tranches were hawked to public pension funds by Bear Stearns at a meeting held, appropriately, in Las Vegas.

2. The AAA rating also rendered the tranche more attractive to commercial banks, which had to hold less capital against supposedly investment-grade assets.

3. Tett (2009) suggests that AIG's managers found it irresistible to engage in regulatory arbitrage (unlike commercial banks, they were not required to hold capital against their positions). Others (e.g., Lewis 2010) suggest that the problem was inadequate internal controls and simple lack of competence.

4. The prominent losses were those of the two Bear Stearns hedge funds noted above. Earlier in 2007 two other funds, HSBC Holdings PLC and New Century Financial, had disclosed that they had taken losses on subprime investments, but it was the failure of the two Bear Stearns funds that really got the markets' attention.

5. Rubin and Weisberg (2003), p. 288.

6. In testimony before the Senate (Summers 1998).

7. For a summary of the views of the academic Summers, see Shleifer and Summers (1990).

8. Rubin and Weisberg (2003), p. 98.

9. Rubin and Weisberg (2003), pp. 287–88.

10. The deals in question are known in the trade as "over the counter" transactions (see the Summers quote above), and the problem they created is technically known as "counterparty risk."

11. A central clearinghouse would have required dealers to post collateral (called "initial margin") for every contract cleared through them, cutting into their profits.

12. See Greenspan (1998).

13. Specifically, Greenspan recommended, reluctantly ("as much as I would prefer it otherwise"), that securitizers should be required to retain a meaningful part of the securities they issue. His statement and the hearing transcript are at http://oversight. house.gov.

14. 1994 was also the year when the same institution, J.P. Morgan, made the "breakthrough" that led to the growth of the market in credit default swaps (see Tett 2009).

15. These different securities were known in the trade as "on-the-run" (most recently issued) and "off-the-run" (previously issued) treasuries.

16. On the transition from Miller to Volcker, see chapter 3, pp. 65–66. An influential study of the causes of the Great Moderation is Ahmed, Levin, and Wilson (2002). The authors conclude that good luck (fewer oil shocks) was more important than good policy for explaining the decline in volatility, while the opposite is true for inflation volatility. A third factor they consider is changes in the structure of the economy, such as improved inventory management practices, which according to their estimates played a subsidiary role in the decline in volatility.

17. Kohn (2009), p. 39.

18. The speech in question was Greenspan (2002). The fear that the events of 9/11 would deter investment was of course a further factor in the decision to cut rates so dramatically.

19. Taylor then continued to use the relationship as he had originally estimated it on data for 1987–1892 to characterize appropriate policy immediately preceding and during the crisis. Others like Rudabusch (2009) instead re-estimate the relationship using more recent data. But which Taylor Rule one uses makes little difference for the characterization of monetary policy in 2002–2005.

20. A point that Chairman Bernanke has made in his defense (in Bernanke 2010).

21. In particular, the United States in the early years of the decade did not experience the same severe banking problems as Japan, problems that coming on the heels of a burst stock-market bubble consigned its economy to chronic deflation.

22. Then, when fears of deflation were vanquished, the risk-management approach dictated a gradual approach to normalizing the level of rates, now to avoid aborting the recovery.

23. Between 2001 and 2004, the gap between the rates on adjustable-rate mortgages (ARMs) keyed to the 1-year interest rate and conventional 30-year mortgages nearly doubled—as did the share of new mortgage borrowers opting for ARMs. Greenspan (2010) objects that ARM originations in fact peaked two years before the housing market, so they could not have been responsible for the bubble. Bernanke (2010) objects that the absolute gap between rates on ARMs and conventional mortgages, while growing, was still not that large.

24. See Taylor (2007). And with more homeowners refinancing mortgages at low rates, employment in the mortgage-underwriting business doubled. When eventually interest rates were allowed to rise and this refinancing business dried up, other more creative uses had to be found for all this personnel. They were found in the subprime market.

25. In some countries, Switzerland for example, the fixed payouts are a result of statute rather than contract.

26. It will also be evident among conduits and special-purpose vehicles that issue commercial paper to fund their investments in speculative assets. The effect will be less, though by no means absent, among commercial banks relying on retail deposits for most of their funding. That the expansion of balance sheets should be proportionately greater among broker-dealers than commercial banks is emphasized by Adrian and Shin (2010).

27. Rudabusch, Swanson, and Wu (2006) find that the decline in bond market volatility, arguably an indicator of the improved performance of the Fed in stabilizing inflation expectations, was an important factor explaining the bond market conundrum.

28. One month later, in Bernanke (2005).

29. Global savings, meanwhile, fell from 22.4 percent to 21.5 percent, according to the October 2009 revision of the IMF's *World Economic Outlook* database. We know from this what happened to global investment, because global savings and global investment must be equal as a matter of definition. To the extent that sources like the above indicate otherwise, this must be a statistical discrepancy.

30. Here financial underdevelopment should be construed broadly to include underdeveloped public mechanisms like social security through which households can prepare for retirement. In addition it is important to note that capital outflows from China were increasingly supplemented, and at their peak nearly matched, by capital outflows from oil-exporting countries running current account surpluses as a result of high petroleum prices. For these countries the constraint was not so much the underdevelopment of financial markets as it was limits on how quickly physical investment could be ramped up—witness the 2009 crisis in Dubai.

31. The Great Moderation may have also reduced precautionary saving, there being less need to save for a rainy day insofar as there was the expectation of fewer rainy days. Then there was the growth of the federal budget deficit in the early part of the decade. While there was no one-to-one link between the budget and current account deficits, there is no question about the direction in which growing budget deficits worked. And, given the fall in household savings rates, it kicked in at the worst possible time.

32. Compare Aizenman and Marion (2003) with Aizenman and Lee (2007).

33. This from Craine and Martin (2009).

34. Bandholz, Clostermann, and Seitz (2009).

35. See Warnock and Warnock (2009).

CHAPTER 6

1. There is of course an even greater tendency to invoice and settle in U.S. dollars in the case of the United States' own exports to Canada. The study in question is Goldberg and Tille (2009). Their 72 percent figure refers to the share of export transactions by count.

2. Data are from the Bank's most recent triennial survey, for 2010. Note that the totals for all currencies sum to 200 percent since two currencies are involved in each transaction.

3. This as of the end of 2008. These figures are based on a narrow measure that excludes domestic debt securities issued in a country's own market.

4. This was the episode on which Sarah Palin was commenting in the Facebook post noted in chapter 1.

5. Most of the movement in the dollar's share from year to year reflects valuation effects, dollar appreciation increasing the value of central banks' existing dollar holdings, dollar depreciation reducing them. The IMF also publishes data on reserve holdings net of valuation effects. They show the dollar's share rising sharply in 2003, plateauing thereafter, and falling slowly in the final years of the decade. To be sure, the dollar's share fell in the final months of 2008, at the height of the crisis, as central banks supported their currencies and provided financial markets desperately needed dollar liquidity by loaning out part of their dollar reserves. Disproportionate sales of dollars reflected the fact that many emerging markets whose currencies were hit manage their exchange rates against the dollar and therefore hold their reserves in that form. Central banks in a number of emerging markets sought to relieve their financial markets and institutions of the effects of severe credit stringency—their banks having borrowed abroad, in dollars, and now seeing their foreign lenders delever—by loaning them dollars, which again translated into a decline in dollar reserves.

6. These are the numbers gathered as part of the Treasury's International Capital (TIC) reporting system. Details are in Sobol (1998).

7. An analysis of this tendency is Gopinath, Itskhoki, and Rigobon (2007).

8. This according to the *IMF Annual Report*.

9. These calculations focus on what central bank portfolio maximizes a particular combination of stability and return. See, for example, Papaioannou, Portes, and Siourounis (2006).

10. As noted in chapter 3, allowing foreigners to buy and sell Japanese securities would have made it more difficult to use the financial system to channel funds toward favored domestic firms, the practice that was long a staple of Japanese industrial policy.

11. As of the second quarter of 2009.

12. This is not a surprise, given that the desire to create a European alternative to the dollar was one of the original motivations for establishing the euro.

13. Even excluding intra-euro-area trade.

14. www.independent.ie (October 1, 2009).

15. As described in chapter 4, pp. 91–92.

16. Enlargement of the euro area to include new members would also make for larger euro-area financial markets, but in practice the aspirants are too small to make a difference.

17. Again, according to the IMF and as of the third quarter of 2009.

18. German government bonds have a reputation for stability, but the outstanding stock is only a quarter the stock of U.S. treasuries. Moreover, because many German government bonds are held to maturity by pension funds, insurance companies, and other institutional investors, the market in them lacks liquidity. Other euro-area countries have more bonds outstanding, but they also have deep financial problems. Italian government bonds are the most important euro-area debt securities by value, but Italy's uncertain financial prospects make them unattractive as reserve assets. And whatever problems Italian bonds may have, Greek, Portuguese and Spanish bonds have them in spades.

19. To be sure, the euro area is not be first-ever monetary union and, by implication, the euro is not the first supranational currency. It is not even Europe's first-ever monetary union, Belgium and Luxembourg having shared a currency and central bank from 1944 and also, on a somewhat looser basis, from 1921 until 1940. The Luxembourg franc was forcibly detached from the Belgian franc and pegged to the mark by the German Reich during World War II—which is a reminder that monetary union is not necessarily forever. There were also some limited experiments with currency interchangeability, the Latin Monetary Union and the Scandinavian Monetary Union, in the nineteenth century. But it is the first monetary union made up of a group of such large, economically advanced countries.

20. Ten percent of national income being the difference between 13 and 3 percent of GDP budget deficits.

21. And the International Monetary Fund, which in the end provided a fraction of the bailout loan.

22. That pool could be raised by allocating a certain fraction of the taxes of the member states to this activity, either all member states or perhaps only those with excessive deficits, or else by giving the fund itself the authorization to borrow on financial markets, with the full faith and credit of the member states standing behind its obligations. One proposal for such a mechanism is Gros and Mayer (2010), but there are others.

23. This was essentially what the U.S. government did for temporarily illiquid states in 2009, extending them temporary assistance through the federal budget.

24. This is how the debts of insolvent states and municipalities are restructured in the United States under Chapter 11 of the bankruptcy code.

25. See European Central Bank (2010). It did not however endorse the idea of giving this institution the authority to oversee the restructuring of the debts of insolvent governments, presumably to avoid exciting the markets.

26. Strange (1980), p. 47.

27. As of the end of 2009.

28. This includes those managed by the China Investment Corporation, the sovereign wealth fund that manages a portion of the central bank's foreign exchange reserves. Here I rely on the estimates of Brad Setser, formerly of the Council on Foreign Relations (http://blogs.cfr.org/setser/).

29. Technically this result requires that dollar- and nondollar securities be imperfect substitutes, which is of course the assumption underlying the desire to hold a diversified reserve portfolio. International economists will recognize here the controversy over the effectiveness of sterilized intervention in foreign exchange markets.

30. Reported by Sommerville (2009).

31. See Zhou (2009).

32. See chapter 3, pp. 49–50.

33. $50 billion worth in the case of China, $10 billion each in the cases of Russia and Brazil. But notice the unit of denomination used to express the extent of their commitment.

34. United Nations (2009), p. 98.

35. Countries could conceivably decide to price their goods in SDRs, but doing so introduces an additional element of complexity relative to pricing in them in dollars. Thus it is revealing that OPEC continues to price its oil in dollars despite both the prospective advantages in terms of risk-reduction and potential political attractions of SDRs. Evidence on the risk-reduction advantages to OPEC of SDR pricing can be found in Essayyad and Algahtani (2007).

36. Federal Reserve Bank of New York (1981–82), p. 40.

37. Exchange rate risk can be hedged, of course, but that is yet another additional cost. And hedging markets exist only for relatively short-maturity instruments, where many of the obligations of pension funds and insurance companies extend over long horizons.

38. The origins of this rule are described in chapter 3, p. 57.

39. As we saw in chapter 3, pp. 65–66.

40. See for example Kenen (2010). Yongding Yu, a former advisor to the People's Bank of China, alludes (in Yu 2009) to the possibility of a Substitution Account through which the PBOC's dollars would be exchanged for SDRs as a justification for Zhao's proposal.

41. Then in 2009 the Chinese government announced a policy entitled "the State Council's view on promoting Shanghai to build an international financial center and international shipping center by accelerating the development of a modern service industry and an advanced manufacturing industry."

42. Initially, those select companies were limited to the municipality of Shanghai and province of Guangdong. In mid-2010 state media reported that the program would be expanded to companies in 20 additional municipalities and provinces.

43. See McGregor (2009).

44. Other countries, such as Malaysia, have indicated that they may follow.

45. The announcement in June 2010 by the People's Bank of China that it was increasing the flexibility of the renminbi exchange rate was a first small step in this

direction and another indication that Chinese officialdom is serious about internationalizing the currency.

46. There is another possibility, namely that Asia might one day wish to follow Europe in creating a single regional currency. But China doesn't have to participate in a monetary union in order to achieve the economic and financial scale that is a prerequisite for its money to play an international role. It doesn't have to pool its monetary sovereignty in order for its currency to become a reserve unit. Rather than pushing ahead, in the manner of Europe, toward a regional monetary union, it will prefer to wait, for the longer it waits the greater will be the weight of the renminbi within the region. There are plenty of other reasons why a pan-Asian monetary union is unlikely. The renminbi's own prospects as an international currency are yet another one.

47. Worth $6.7 billion at then-prevailing prices.

48. Indeed, in order to make its portfolio more liquid, the Fund had been already selling gold for more convenient financial assets for years.

49. It is worth noting that not even India has been bucking the global trend of central banks holding a declining share of reserves in gold: in the mid-1990s it held fully 20 percent of its foreign reserves in gold, very much higher than even after the much-vaunted IMF transaction.

50. The technical term for this form of increasing returns is "network externalities," while the name given its self-reinforcing feature is "lock-in." The same argument was traditionally made for the operating system (or word-processing software) of personal computers—that, since it paid to use the same operating system as one's colleagues, there was only room in the market for one operating system. The analogy highlights the limits of the argument as applied to international currencies: when the market grows large and the costs of interchangeability fall, there is room for several alternatives.

51. The analysis in chapter 2 suggests that even for the late nineteenth century this natural-monopoly view is exaggerated. Even then several currencies, not just the British pound but also the French franc and German mark, were used to quote the prices of imports and exports, provide trade credit, and denominate international bonds. While sterling was first among equals, the fact that the franc and mark were also used in international transactions is hard to reconcile with the natural-monopoly view. De Cecco (2009) also makes this point.

CHAPTER 7

1. Described in chapter 3, pp. 42–43.

2. Nasser had originally indicated his interest in obtaining "Chinese arms" to Zhou Enlai in 1955, when the two leaders attended the first meeting of nonaligned nations in Bandang, Indonesia. China itself depended on the Soviet Union for its military hardware, which may help to explain why Dulles had responded so strongly to Nasser's recognition of the People's Republic.

3. Feyrer (2009) shows that closure of the Suez Canal in 1967, as described in chapter 3, had very substantial effects on transport costs and the volume of trade. Clearly, the same was true in 1956–1957.

4. Nutting (1967), pp. 34–35.

5. Richard Newstadt, in his classic study of Anglo-American relations, blames Eden's "muddled perception" of American attitudes on his reliance on Macmillan (Newstadt 1970).

6. Horne (1968), p. 422.

7. As described in chapter 3.

8. The minimally acceptable level of reserves was seen as $2 billion because that was approximately the value of the pounds held by "unreliable" non-sterling area countries, who, it was feared, might demand that the British authorities convert them into dollar at any time. Fforde (1992), p. 543.

9. It was especially risky given the Bank of England's reluctance, on both political and doctrinal grounds, to raise interest rates to defend the pound. The political rationale for restraint was that higher interest rates would create unemployment, the doctrinal one that the postwar consensus among British economists was that monetary policy could do little to affect the real economy and, in particular, the balance of payments.

10. The danger was that if Britain devalued again, only seven years after the last time, the other members of the sterling area might not follow, and with their exchange rates moving, trade and financial flows within the area would be discouraged. And, as Kunz (1991, p. 89) puts it, "The importance of the strength of sterling and the continued existence of the sterling area to the British government in 1956 cannot be overemphasized." The dilemma was that the Suez Canal, which so reduced transport costs between Britain and Australasia, was also seen as critically important to the continued existence of the sterling area.

11. Eden himself blamed speculation by Americans and, strangely, the Chinese. Recall that China had allegedly intermediated between Nasser and the Soviets after Chinese and Egyptian leaders met in Bandang. So here was a case where China did perhaps use its financial weapon (Eden 1960, pp. 555–56).

12. Thus, to exert financial leverage the United States didn't have to actively undermine sterling. It didn't have to sell its holdings. In fact, U.S. government holdings of sterling securities declined only very slightly during the fourth quarter of 1956, the period that coincided with the height of the crisis. It simply had to oppose British requests for support through the IMF. Technically, Britain needed only a simple majority of directors on the IMF board to support its request. But with the Latin Americans and Japanese likely to side with the Americans, cobbling together a majority would be impossible given U.S. opposition.

13. Relative to their own currencies.

14. Cited in Kunz (1991), p. 151.

15. Technically, its quota. Macmillan could also explain that President Eisenhower would ask Congress for approval of a waiver of the $175 million payment due on the

Anglo-American Loan of 1945 and that the U.S. had promised a credit for Britain's oil imports from the Export-Import Bank.

16. The $500 million Export-Import Bank loan followed two months later.

17. Just as they moved away from the pound sterling during World War I, when they grew concerned for its stability (see chapter 2).

18. As described in chapter 3, pp. 51–53.

19. Much as the ECB bought euro bonds in May 2010 when panic threatened to engulf European bond markets.

20. Again, Europe's experience in the spring of 2010 illustrates the risks. The ECB's extraordinary purchases of government bonds were not by themselves enough to reassure investors or prevent movement out of the euro. Reassuring the markets required, in addition, European governments to demonstrate their readiness to adopt serious measures of fiscal consolidation.

21. This according to the forecasts of Auerbach and Gale (2009). Although the Congressional Budget Office's alternative forecasts suggest smaller deficits and debts, the CBO is required to assume that current law remains in place, which history suggests is not always plausible. An illustration of this is the Alternative Minimum Tax (AMT), which is not indexed for inflation or rising incomes and therefore subjects a growing share of households to higher tax rates over time. In practice the Congress has repeatedly adjusted AMT thresholds "temporarily"—something that it will presumably continue to do. Current law also mandates cuts in Medicare reimbursement rates for physicians, whose activation the Congress has regularly deferred. The CBO is required to assume that these cuts are imposed.

22. One out of every five tax dollars for debt service is the implication of U.S. interest rates at normal levels of, say, 5 percent.

23. See the estimates of the impact of foreign purchases on U.S. interest rates in chapter 5, notes 33–35. Recall that each percentage point represents an additional 5 percent of federal tax revenues when the debt-to-GDP ratio approaches 100 percent.

24. While state and local taxes account for another 9 percent of U.S. GDP, this does nothing to get the federal government out of its pickle. State and local governments raise additional revenues, but they are also a source of additional debt. The IMF projects the U.S. general government debt ratio, including state as well as federal governments, as reaching 100 percent in 2014.

25. The projected growth of entitlement spending explains almost all of the projected growth in total noninterest spending, where Medicare and Medicaid drive that increase; they are responsible for 80 percent of the growth in spending on the three largest entitlements (the third presumably being Social Security) over the next 25 years.

26. This is the Fed's so-called dual mandate.

27. Thus, the exchange rate does not appear explicitly in the Taylor Rule (see chapter 5) that economists typically use to think about the appropriate setting for the Fed's policy instrument; the only arguments of the Taylor Rule are anticipated inflation and the output gap.

28. Bernanke (2009). What the chairman actually said was unexceptional. "The foreign exchange value of the dollar has moved over a wide range during the past year or so. When financial stresses were most pronounced, a flight to the deepest and most liquid capital markets resulted in a marked increase in the dollar. More recently, as financial market functioning has improved and global economic activity has stabilized, these safe haven flows have abated, and the dollar has accordingly retraced its gains. The Federal Reserve will continue to monitor these developments closely. We are attentive to the implications of changes in the value of the dollar and will continue to formulate policy to guard against risks to our dual mandate to foster both maximum employment and price stability." But the fact that Bernanke saw fit to comment on the dollar made this passage the most closely observed part of the speech.

29. The phrase is from Calvo and Reinhart (2002). That it is foreign-currency-denominated obligations that encourage governments and central banks to manage their exchange rates in this way is shown by Hausmann, Panizza, and Stein (2001).

30. $200 billion was approximately the value of private and government debts to foreigners coming due in the next 12 months.

31. The Fed at the same time provided $30 billion of swaps apiece to the central banks of Brazil, Mexico, and Singapore, as described in chapter 6.

32. $1 trillion being about 6 percent of U.S. GDP, which was the size of the U.S. current account deficit going into the crisis. With total reserves excluding gold rising at about $500 billion a year and two-thirds of this being in dollars, the corresponding decline in U.S. spending will be a bit south of $500 billion. I return to this below.

33. See Goldin and Katz (2008). In part this reflects the simple arithmetic fact that it becomes harder to raise educational attainment when the latter has reached high levels (more than 100 percent of the population can't graduate from college), but the authors show that there is more at work than just this mathematical limit.

34. This should be thought of as depreciation on a trade-weighted basis.

35. Assuming 5 percent growth of U.S. nominal income (3 percent real growth and 2 percent inflation), this then allows the ratio of external debt to GDP to stabilize at 60 percent, a high but feasible level. Assuming a real interest rate of 3 percent, the United States would then be transferring about 2 percent of its annual income to foreigners to service its external debt. Whether 3 percent is the right figure to assume for the real interest rate is a good question, to which I return. Note that a decline in U.S. spending of 3 percent of GDP is a bit less than $500 billion, which matches the arithmetic in note 32 above.

36. The reason for this is that exchange rate depreciation translates into higher import prices less than one for one. And imports are only a fraction of what American households consume. Federal Reserve Board staff estimate the increase in import prices due to a 30 percent depreciation of the dollar to be on the order of 6 percent. (This is from Marazzi et al. 2005, who estimate an exchange-rate "passthrough" coefficient of 20 percent. Irhig, Marazzi, and Rothenberg 2006 and Corsetti, Dedola, and Leduc 2007 estimate somewhat larger passthrough coefficients, other authors smaller ones. I split

the difference.) With imports also 20 percent of GDP, this suggests a 1.2 percent decline in U.S. living standards. If the prices of domestically produced goods that compete with imports rise accordingly, relative to the purchasing power of American households, then the decline in living standards becomes somewhat larger (and consistent with the decline in domestic spending estimated above).

37. Piketty and Saez (as summarized in Saez 2009) show that the share of national income accruing to the top 0.01 percent of the distribution of earners has roughly doubled, from 3 to 6 percent, between 2001 and 2007. That much of this is attributable to incomes earned in employment in financial services is documented by Kaplan and Rauh (2007).

38. These are 2008 figures, from data published by the Bureau of Economic Analysis. Manufactures actually account for 43 percent of U.S. exports, services 30 percent, agriculture 6 percent, and materials—which are roughly one-third raw and two-thirds manufactured or semimanufactured—the remaining 21 percent.

39. Feenstra and Hanson (2000) estimate the relative importance of capital and labor and of production and nonproduction workers in U.S. imports and exports. Their table 2 confirms that U.S. exports use a higher ratio of capital to labor and a higher ratio of (more skilled) nonproduction to (less skilled) production workers than do U.S. imports.

40. A study showing this is Bernard, Jensen, and Schott (2006).

REFERENCES

Adrian, Tobias, and Hyun Shin (2010), "Financial Intermediaries and Monetary Economics," Staff Report no. 398, New York: Federal Reserve Bank of New York (February).

Ahmed, Shaghil, Andrew Levin, and Beth Anne Wilson (2002), "Recent U.S. Macroeconomic Stability: Good Policies, Good Practices, or Good Luck?" International Finance Discussion Paper no. 2002-730, Washington, D.C.: Board of Governors of the Federal Reserve System (July).

Aizenman, Joshua, and Jaewoo Lee (2007), "International Reserves: Precautionary versus Mercantilist Views, Theory and Evidence," *Open Economies Review* 18, pp. 191–214.

Aizenman, Joshua, and Nancy Marion (2003), "The High Demand for International Reserves in the Far East: What's Going On?" *Journal of the Japanese and International Economies* 17, pp. 370–400.

American Acceptance Council (1931), *Facts and Figures Relating to the American Money Market*, New York: American Acceptance Council.

Auerbach, Alan, and William Gale (2009), "The Economic Crisis and the Fiscal Crisis, 2009 and Beyond, an Update," unpublished manuscript, University of California, Berkeley, and the Brookings Institution (September).

Bandholz, Harm, Jorg Clostermann, and Franz Seitz (2009), "Explaining the US Bond Yield Conundrum," *Applied Financial Economics* 19, pp. 539–50.

Barro, Robert (1979), "Money and the Price Level under the Gold Standard," *Economic Journal* 89, pp. 13–33.

Bellman, Eric, Gina Chan, and Wilawan Watcharasakwet (2009), "In the Black Market, the Dollar Still Rules," *Wall Street Journal* (Asian Edition) (October 29), p. M4.

Bernanke, Ben (2005), "The Global Savings Glut and the U.S. Current Account Deficit," Speech to the Virginia Association of Economics, Richmond, Virginia (March 10), www.federalreserve.gov.

Bernanke, Ben (2009), "On the Outlook for the Economy and Policy," Speech to the Economic Club of New York, New York (November 16), www.federalreserve. gov.

Bernanke, Ben (2010), "Monetary Policy and the Housing Bubble," Speech at the Annual Meeting of the American Economic Association, Atlanta (January 3), www.federalreserve.gov.

Bernard, Andrew, J. Bradford Jensen, and Peter Schott (2006), "Survival of the Best Fit: Exposure to Low Wage Countries and the (Uneven) Growth of US Manufacturing Plants," *Journal of International Economics* 68, pp. 219–37.

Bertaut, Carol C., and Ralph W. Tryon (2007), "Monthly Estimates of the U.S. Cross-Border Securities Positions," FRB International Discussion Paper no. 910 (November).

Brown, William Adams (1940), *The International Gold Standard Reinterpreted, 1914–1934*, New York: National Bureau of Economic Research.

Broz, Lawrence (1997), *The International Origins of the Federal Reserve System*, Ithaca, N.Y.: Cornell University Press.

Calvo, Guillermo, and Carmen Reinhart (2002), "Fear of Floating," *Quarterly Journal of Economics* 107, pp. 379–408.

Chandler, Lester V. (1958), *Benjamin Strong, Central Banker*, Washington, D.C.: Brookings Institution.

Chernow, Ron (1993), *The Warburgs: The Twentieth Century Odyssey of a Remarkable Jewish Family*, New York: Random House.

Chinn, Menzie, and Jeffrey Frankel (2007), "Will the Euro Eventually Surpass the Dollar as the Leading International Reserve Currency?" in Richard Clarida (ed.), *G7 Current Account Imbalances: Sustainability and Adjustment*, Chicago: University of Chicago Press, pp. 283–338.

Cleveland, Harold van B., and Thomas F. Huertas (1985), *Citibank, 1812–1970*, Cambridge: Harvard University Press.

Corsetti, Giancarlo, Luca Dedola, and Silvain Leduc (2007), "DSGE Models of High Exchange-Rate Volatility and Low Pass-Through," CEPR Discussion Paper no. 5377, London: Centre for Economic Policy Research (December).

Craig, R. Bruce (2004), *Treasonable Doubt: The Harry Dexter White Spy Case*, Lawrence: University of Kansas Press.

Craine, Roger, and Vance Martin (2009), "Interest Rate Conundrum," *B.E. Journal of Macroeconomics* 9, pp. 1–27.

De Cecco, Marcello (2009), "From Monopoly to Oligopoly: Lessons from Pre-1914 Experience," in Eric Helleiner and Jonathan Kirschner (eds.), *The Future of the Dollar*, Ithaca, N.Y.: Cornell University Press, pp. 116–41.

Dyson, Kenneth (1994), *Elusive Union: The Process of Economic and Monetary Union in Europe*, London: Longman.

Dyson, Kenneth, and Kevin Featherstone (1999), *The Road to Maastricht*, Oxford: Oxford University Press.

Eden, Sir Anthony (1960), *Full Circle*, London: Cassell.

Eichengreen, Barry and Marc Flandreau (2009), "The Rise and Fall of the Dollar (or when did the Dollar Replace Sterling as the Leading International Currency?)", *European Review of Economic Histroy* 13, pp. 377–411.

Emminger, Otmar (1986), *D-Mark, Dollar, Währungskrisen*, Stuttgart: Deutsche Verlags-Anstalt.

Essayyad, Musa, and Ibrahim Algahtani (2007), "Portfolio Risk Reduction in Oil Pricing: The Case for SDRs," *International Journal of Global Energy Issues* 27, pp. 397–403.

European Central Bank (2010), "Reinforcing Economic Governance in the Euro Area," Frankfurt: European Central Bank (June 10).

Evans, David (2007), "Banks Sell 'Toxic Waste' CDOs to Calpers, Texas Teachers Fund," *Bloomberg News*, www.bloomberg.com (June 1).

Federal Reserve Bank of New York (1981–82), "The SDR in Private International Finance," *Federal Reserve Bank of New York Quarterly Review*, pp. 29–41.

Feenstra, Robert, and Gordon Hanson (2000), "Aggregation Bias in the Factor Content of Trade: Evidence from U.S. Manufacturing," *American Economic Review* 90 (Papers and Proceedings), pp. 155–60.

Feyrer, James (2009), "Distance, Trade and Income—the 1967 to 1975 Closing of the Suez Canal as a Natural Experiment," NBER Working Paper no. 15557 (December).

Fforde, John (1992), *The Bank of England and Public Policy, 1941–1958*, New York: Cambridge University Press.

Flandreau, Marc, and Clemens Jobst (2006), "The Empirics of International Currencies: Historical Evidence," CEPR Discussion Paper no. 5529, London: Centre for Economic Policy Research (March).

Garber, Peter (1993), "The Collapse of the Bretton Woods Fixed Exchange-Rate System," in Michael Bordo and Barry Eichengreen (eds.), *A Retrospective on the Bretton Woods System: Lessons for International Monetary Reform*, Chicago: University of Chicago Press, pp. 461–95.

Goldberg, Linda, and Cedric Tille (2009), "Micro, Macro, and Strategic Choice in International Trade Invoicing," CEPR Discussion Paper no. 7534, London: Centre for Economic Policy Research (November).

Goldin, Claudia, and Lawrence Katz (2008), *The Race Between Education and Technology*. Cambridge: Belknap Press for the Harvard University Press.

Gopinath, Gita, Oleg Itskhoki, and Roberto Rigobon (2007), "Currency Choice and Exchange-Rate Passthrough," NBER Working Paper no. 13432 (September).

Gourinchas, Pierre-Olivier, and Hélène Rey (2007), "From World Banker to World Venture Capitalist: U.S. External Adjustment and the Exorbitant Privilege," in Richard Clarida (ed.), *G7 Current Account Imbalances*, Chicago: University of Chicago Press, pp. 11–55.

Govan, Thomas Payne (1959), *Nicholas Biddle*, Chicago: University of Chicago Press.

Greenspan, Alan (1998), "The Regulation of OTC Derivatives," Testimony to the House Committee on Banking and Financial Services (July 24), http://www.federalreserve.gov/boarddocs/Testimony/1998/19980724.htm.

Greenspan, Alan (2002), "Remarks by Chairman Alan Greenspan at a Symposium Sponsored by the Federal Reserve Bank of Kansas City, Jackson Hole, Wyoming" (August 30), www.federalreserve.gov.

Greenspan, Alan (2010), "The Crisis," *Brookings Papers on Economic Activity* 1, pp. 201–246.

Greider, William (1987), *Secrets of the Temple: How the Federal Reserve Runs the Country*, New York: Simon and Schuster.

Gros, Daniel, and Thomas Mayer (2010), "Disciplinary Measures," *Economist* (February 18), www.economist.com.

Habib, Maurizio M. (2010), "Excess Returns on Net Foreign Assets: The Exorbitant Privilege from a Global Perspective," ECB Working Paper no. 1158 (February).

Harris, Joel (2009), "The Last Great Dollar Crisis," *Wall Street Journal Asia* (December 2), p. 15.

Harrison, Mark (1998), "The Economics of World War II: An Overview," in Mark Harrison (ed.), *The Economics of World War II: Six Great Powers in International Comparison*, Cambridge: Cambridge University Press, pp. 1–42.

Hausmann, Ricardo, Ugo Panizza, and Ernesto Stein (2001), "Why Do Countries Float the Way They Float?" *Journal of Development Economics* 66, pp. 387–414.

Horii, Akinari (1986), "The Evolution of Reserve Currency Diversification," BIS Economic Paper no. 18, Basle: Bank for International Settlements (December).

Horne, Alistair (1968), *Macmillan*, London: Macmillan.

Ihrig, Jane, Mario Marazzi, and Alexander Rothenberg (2006), "Exchange-Rate Pass-Through in the G-7 Countries," International Finance Discussion Paper no. 851, Washington, D.C.: Board of Governors of the Federal Reserve System (January).

James, Harold (1996), *International Monetary Cooperation since Bretton Woods*, New York: Oxford University Press.

Jones, Geoffrey (2005), *Multinationals and Global Capitalism*, New York: Oxford University Press.

Kaplan, Steven N., and Joshua Rauh (2007), "Wall Street and Main Street: What Contributes to the Rise in the Highest Incomes?" NBER Working Paper no. 13270 (July).

Kenen, Peter (2010), "Revisiting the Substitution Account," *International Finance* 13, pp. 1–23.

Keynes, John Maynard (1919), *The Economic Consequences of the Peace*, London: Macmillan.

King, W. T. C. (1936), *History of the London Discount Market*, London: George Routledge & Sons.

Kloten, Norbert (1980), "Germany's Monetary and Financial Policy and the European Community," in Wilfrid Kohl and Giogio Basevi (eds.), *West Germany: A European and Global Power*, Lexington: Lexington Books, pp. 177–99.

Kohn, Donald (2009), "Monetary Policy and Asset Prices Revisited," *Cato Journal* 29, pp. 31–44.

Kunz, Diane B. (1991), *The Economic Diplomacy of the Suez Crisis*, Chapel Hill: University of North Carolina Press.

Laughlin, J. Laurence (ed.) (1912), *Banking Reform*, Chicago: National Citizens League.

Lewis, Cleona (1938), *America's Stake in International Investments*, Washington, D.C.: Brookings Institution.

Lewis, Michael (2010), *The Big Short: Inside the Doomsday Machine*, New York: Norton.

Lindbergh, Charles A. (1913), *Banking and Currency and the Money Trust*, Washington, D.C.: National Capital Press.

Marazzi, Mario, Nathan Sheets, Robert J. Vigfusson, Jon Faust, Joseph Gagnon, Jaime Marquez, Robert F. Martin, Trevor Reeve, and John Rogers (2005), "Exchange Rate Pass-Through to U.S. Import Prices: Some New Evidence," International Finance Discussion Paper no. 833, Washington, D.C.: Board of Governors of the Federal Reserve System.

Marsh, David (2009), *The Euro: The Politics of the New Global Currency*, New Haven: Yale University Press.

Mayer, Martin (1980), *The Fate of the Dollar*, New York: Times Books.

McGregor, Richard (2009), "China Moves to Cut Reliance on the Dollar," *Financial Times* (July 2), p. 4.

McIvor, R. Craig (1958), *Canadian Monetary, Banking and Fiscal Development*, Toronto: Macmillan.

McKinnon, Ronald (1996), *The Rules of the Game*, Cambridge: MIT Press.

Meier, Gerald (1974), *Problems of a World Monetary Order*, New York: Oxford University Press.

Michener, Ron (1987), "Fixed Exchange Rates and the Quantity Theory in Colonial America," *Carnegie-Rochester Conference Series on Public Policy* 27, pp. 245–53.

Mintz, Ilse (1951), *Deterioration in the Quality of Foreign Bonds Issued in the United States, 1920–1930*, New York: National Bureau of Economic Research.

Newstadt, Richard (1970), *Alliance Politics*, New York: Columbia University Press.

Nussbaum, Arthur (1957), *A History of the Dollar*, New York: Columbia University Press.

Nutting, Anthony (1967), *No End of a Lesson*, London: Constable.

Painton, Frederick, Jordan Bonfante, and Thomas A. Sancton (1983), "Europe: The Battle for the Franc," *Time* (April 4).

Papaioannou, Elias, Richard Portes, and Gregorio Siourounis (2006), "Optimal Currency Shares in International Reserves: The Impact of the Euro and the Prospects for the Dollar," NBER Working Paper no. 12333 (June).

Partnoy, Frank (2003), *Infectious Greed: How Deceit and Risk Corrupted Financial Markets*, New York: Profile Books.

Phelps, Clyde William (1927), *The Foreign Expansion of American Banks*, New York: Ronald Press.

Powell, James (1995), *A History of the Canadian Dollar*, Ottawa: Bank of Canada.

Reeves, Richard (2001), *President Nixon: Alone in the White House*, New York: Simon and Schuster.

Rubin, Robert, and Jacob Weisberg (2003), *In an Uncertain World*, New York: Random House.

Rudabusch, Glenn (2009), "The Fed's Monetary Policy Response to the Current Crisis," FRBSF Weekly Letter 2009-17, San Francisco: Federal Reserve Bank of San Francisco (May 22).

Rudabusch, Glenn, Eric Swanson, and Tao Wu (2006), "The Bond Yield 'Conundrum' from a Macro-Finance Perspective," Working Paper no. 2006-16, San Francisco: Federal Reserve Bank of San Francisco (May).

Rueff, Jacques (1971), *The Monetary Sin of the West*, London: Macmillan.

Sachs, Jeffrey (1980), "Wages, Flexible Exchange Rates and Macroeconomic Policy," *Quarterly Journal of Economics* 94, pp. 731–47.

Saez, Emmanuel (2009), "Striking it Richer: The Evolution of Top Incomes in the United States (Update with 2007 Estimates)," unpublished manuscript, University of California, Berkeley (August).

Safire, William (1975), *Before the Fall: An Inside View of the Pre-Watergate White House*, Garden City, New York: Doubleday.

Shleifer, Andrei, and Lawrence Summers (1990), "The Noise Trader Approach to Finance," *Journal of Economic Perspectives* 4, pp. 19–33.

Simon, Pierre-Henri (1957), *Contre la torture*, Paris: Editions du Seuil.

Skidelsky, Robert (2001), *John Maynard Keynes*, Volume 3: *Fighting for Freedom*, New York: Viking.

Sobol, Dorothy Meadow (1998), "Foreign Ownership of U.S. Treasury Securities: What the Data Show and Do Not Show," *Current Trends in Economics and Finance* 4 (no. 5), New York: Federal Reserve Bank of New York (May).

Sommerville, Glenn (2009), "Geithner Tells China its Dollar Assets are Safe," *Reuters* (June 1), www.reuters.com.

Stephenson, Nathaniel Wright (1930), *Nelson W. Aldrich: A Leader in American Politics*, New York: Charles Scribner's Sons.

Strange, Susan (1980), "Germany and the World Monetary System," in Wilfrid Kohl and Giorgio Basevi (eds.), *West Germany: A European and Global Power*, Lexington: Lexington Books, pp. 45–62.

Summers, Lawrence (1998), "Testimony before the Senate Committee on Agriculture, Nutrition and Forestry on the CFTC Concept Release" (July 30), www.ustreas.gov.

Szulc, Tad (1972), "Letter from the Azores," *New Yorker* (January 1), http://archives.newyorker.com.

Tavlas, George (1998), "The International Use of Currencies," *Finance and Development* 35, pp. 46–49.

Taylor, John (2007), "Housing and Monetary Policy," Remarks prepared for presentation to the policy panel at the Symposium on Housing, Housing Finance and

Monetary Policy organized by the Federal Reserve Bank of Kansas City, Jackson Hole, Wyoming (August).

Tett, Gillian (2009), *Fool's Gold: How the Bold Dream of a Small Tribe at J.P. Morgan was Corrupted by Wall Street Greed and Unleashed a Catastrophe*, New York: Free Press.

Triffin, Robert (1947), "National Central Banking and the International Economy," *Postwar Economic Studies 7*, pp. 46–81.

Triffin, Robert (1968), *Our International Monetary System: Yesterday, Today and Tomorrow*, New York: Random House.

United Nations (2009), *Preliminary Report of the Commission of Experts on Reforms of the International Monetary and Financial System*, New York: United Nations (May).

United Nations Conference on Trade and Development (2008), *World Investment Report*, Geneva: UNCTAD.

Warnock, Frank, and Virginia Warnock (2009), "International Capital Flows and U.S. Interest Rates," *Journal of International Money and Finance* 28, pp. 903–19.

Wicker, Elmus (2005), *The Great Debate on Banking Reform: Nelson Aldrich and the Origins of the Fed*, Columbus: Ohio State University Press.

Williams, David (1968), "The Evolution of the Sterling System," in C. R. Whittlesey and J. S. G. Wilson (eds.), *Essays in Money and Banking*, Oxford: Oxford University Press, pp. 266–72.

Yu, Yongding (2009), "Notes for Diaoyutai Dialogue between American and Chinese Economists," unpublished manuscript, Institute of World Economics and Politics, Chinese Academy of Social Sciences (July).

Zhou, Xiaochuan (2009), "Reform the International Monetary System," Speech of the Governor of the People's Bank of China, www.pbc.gov.cn (March 23).

Acknowledgments

M any friends and colleagues contributed to the speedy conclusion of this project. For extensive editorial guidance I thank my editor Dave McBride at Oxford University Press. For comments on chapters I am grateful to Paul Blustein, Jerry Cohen, Richard Grossman, Peter Kenen, Richard Cooper, Menzie Chinn, Jeff Shafer, Ted Truman, Douglas Webber, and Dave Wessel— not to imply that they necessarily were or are in agreement with the result. Two thoughtful editors, Justine Rosenthal of *The National Interest* and James Hoge of *Foreign Affairs*, provoked me into writing the articles that grew into chapters 5 and 6. Scott Moyers helped me to navigate the world of publishing. Cheryl Applewood kept my office and, more generally, my life running smoothly. Menzie Chinn, Marc Flandreau, and Gisela Rua helped with data. Not least, my employer provided a sabbatical year that made it possible to write a book.

And the result, once more, is for Michelle.

INDEX

acceptances. *See* trade acceptances
Africa, 155, 175
agency securities, 124
Aldrich Plan, 23, 24, 25
Aldrich, Nelson, 22–23, 25, 156
Aldrich, Winthrop, 156
Algeria, 42–43, 49
  Algerian rebellion, 155
Alphandéry, Edmund, 93
American Acceptance Council, 182
American International Group (AIG), 98,
  99, 102, 104, 188
Andrew, A. Piatt, 24
Anglo-American loan, 47
Arab-Israeli War, 57
Argentina, 27, 34
Asia, 17, 27, 44, 115, 116, 122, 147, 151, 154,
  155
Asian Development Bank, 145
Asian financial crisis, 114
asset bubbles, 110
Aswan Dam, 154
Australia, 37

bancor, 45–47, 50, 54

bank branches, foreign, 27–28
Bank for International Settlements, 60,
  101, 123
Bank of England, 14, 19, 26, 29, 30, 35, 37,
  92, 195
Bank of France, 37, 43, 52, 84
Bank of Korea, 145, 168
Bank of the United States, 19–22, 23
bank runs, and Great Depression, 34
Bankers Trust Company, 29, 180
banking regulation, role in U.S.
  dependence on British trade
  financing, 16–17
Basel Accord, 100
Bear Stearns, 108, 113, 188
Belgium, 34, 36, 58, 78, 95, 185, 192
Berlin Wall, 72, 88
Bernanke, Ben, 105, 115, 167, 189
Bernstein, Nils, 129
Biddle, Nicholas, 19–22
bills of credit, 11
bimetallism, 12
bipartisan commission, and U.S. budget
  deficit, 166
black market, 2

Black-Scholes model, 105
Blair, Tony, 96
Blumenthal, Michael, 63
BOK. *See* Bank of Korea
Born, Brooksley, 103–104
Brandt, Willy, 72–74, 78
Brazil, 27, 121, 140, 144, 151, 193
Bretton Woods System, 47, 49, 52, 57, 58,
    59, 66, 69, 71, 72, 187
Brezhnev, Leonid, 59
Brown Brothers and Company, 18
Bryan, William Jennings, 19, 35
budget deficit, U.S., 162–167
budgetary policy, U.S., 163
Bundesbank, 44, 53, 67, 74, 76, 78–80, 82,
    89, 90, 93, 94
Burns, Arthur, 61, 64, 77
Bush, George W., 105

Caldwell and Company, 34
Caldwell, James, 34
Caldwell, Rogers, 34
Callaghan, James, 80
Canada, and U.S. dollar, 13
Carli, Guido, 58
Carter, James E., 63, 66, 185
CDOs (collateralized debt obligations),
    98–100, 101, 105, 108, 109
central bank, 2, 45, 51, 54, 111, 127, 141, 142,
    148, 167, 169, 184, 191
    establishment of in U.S., 22–26
    U.S. early attempts, 19–22
Central Bank of the Russian Federation, 135
CFTC. See Commodity Futures Trading
    Commission
Chase Securities Co., 31
China, 3, 7, 44, 45, 49, 51, 115, 121, 123, 135–138,
    140, 142–147, 148, 149, 151, 153, 159–160,
    170, 174, 175, 176, 194, 195
China Investment Corporation, 135
Churchill, Winston, 156
Clappier, Bernard, 81

Clay, Henry, 21
Clay, Lucius, 48
Clearing Union, 46, 47
Clinton, William J., 94, 103
Coinage Act of 1792, 12
Cold War, 48, 71, 88, 157, 182
collateralized debt obligations. *See* CDOs
colonial currency, 9–12
colonial economy, and crop price riots, 10
Committee of Twenty, 62
commodity currency, 9–10
Commodity Futures Trading
    Commission (CFTC), 103, 104
Common Agricultural Policy, 72, 74, 77
Common Market, 71, 75
compensation, regulation of, 109
Connally, John, 59, 60
continental bills (continentals), 11
Continental Congress, 11
Coombs, Charles, 51
credit default swap, 99
Cuba, 27, 31
currency
    colonial, 9–12
    elastic, 26
current account convertibility, 41–42

Davison, Henry, 24, 29, 180
de Gaulle, Charles, 4, 42, 52–53, 58, 73
debt/GDP ratio, 164
deflation, 111
Delors Report, 87
Delors, Jacques, 84, 85, 86, 87–88
Denmark, 77, 91, 187
derivatives market, 103, 104
deutschmark, 44, 67, 68, 76, 77, 79, 82, 83,
    84, 86, 90, 93, 94
Dillon, Douglas, 54
discount brokers, 108
Dodge Plan, 48
dollar
    in 2008–9 crisis, 60–63

crash scenario, 153, 160–167
as currency for international
    transactions, 1, 36, 39, 63, 68, 114,
    121–122
devaluation in 1973, 61–63
early history, 11–12
and incumbency as advantage, 32, 124–125
and international role, 32, 98, 119, 121, 167
as percent of foreign reserve holdings, 123
and rivals, 7–8, 126–130
and suspension of conversion into
    gold, 76
and trade financing, 26–27
dollar acceptances. *See* trade acceptances
dollar peg, 63, 125, 145, 161
dollar reserves, China, 117
dollar sign, origin of, 12
Dulles, John Foster, 154

ECB. *See* European Central Bank
economic health, as factor in geopolitical
    leverage, 177
Eden, Anthony, 41, 155–158
education, U.S., 170, 174
EEC. *See* European Economic Community
Egypt, 34, 154–157
Eisenhower, Dwight D., 48, 54, 154,
    156–157, 170
Emminger, Otmar, 56, 70, 81, 92, 187, 188
entitlements, 165–166
equity tranche, 98, 108
ERM. *See* Exchange Rate Mechanism
EU. *See* European Union
euro, 6, 7, 8, 51, 69, 71, 94–96, 97, 135, 140,
    147, 151
as alternative to the dollar, 88, 127–133
Europe, 3, 7, 23, 24, 26, 27, 31, 47–49, 50,
    56, 60, 63, 68, 70, 109, 117, 121, 127,
    129, 130–135, 151, 154, 161, 164, 166,
    170, 171
monetary union, 69–96, 192
and postwar reconstruction, 30, 47–48

European Central Bank (ECB), 51, 87, 89,
    94–95, 127, 129, 132, 141
European Commission, 70, 80, 86, 130
European Economic Community (EEC),
    70, 72, 74, 77, 78, 80, 88
Monetary Committee of, 92, 186
European Monetary Institute. *See*
    European Central Bank
European Monetary System (EMS),
    82–86, 186, 187
European Monetary Union, 80, 89
European single currency, 69, 70, 72, 74
early interest in, 69–70
motives for creating, 70–71
European Union (EU), 109, 130, 133, 134
Exchange Rate Mechanism (ERM), 82,
    84, 87, 88, 89–93, 129
exchange rate, 36, 39, 60–61, 62, 75, 76, 77,
    79, 89–93, 117, 125, 127, 147, 153, 167,
    173, 175, 186, 191–195, 197,
pegged, 27, 61, 63, 117, 125, 145, 161, 186
exorbitant privilege, 117–118, 119, 122, 134,
    161, 167, 172, 175
as factor in 2008–9 crisis, 4, 98
Valéry Giscard d'Estaing, 4, 40
Export-Import Bank of Japan, 44
exports, U.S., 169–170, 175

Fannie Mae, 114, 118, 124
fear of floating, 167
federal funds rate, 111
Federal Reserve System, 22–26, 29, 33, 61,
    109, 110, 112, 114, 145, 147, 167, 168,
    197
Federal Reserve Act, 18, 25–26, 27
Federal Reserve Bank of New York, 28,
    36, 66, 139
Federal Reserve Board, 25, 29, 50, 61, 110
financial crisis
of 1907, 24, 26, 29
of 2008–9, 97–120, 160, 168, 171
causes of, 98–100, 109–11, 112, 117–120

financial crisis (*continued*)
    and dollar depreciation, 5
    and effects on exorbitant privilege, 4, 118
financial regulation and 2008–9 crisis,
        98–100, 101, 102, 103, 104, 105
foreign acceptances, 32
foreign bank branching, U.S. prohibitions
        on, 17
foreign bonds, default of, 32
foreign liabilities, 4, 114
foreign loans, 3, 33
Fowler, Henry, 56
France, 19, 34, 36, 39, 42–43, 49, 52, 55, 56,
        58, 73, 74, 76, 79, 84, 85, 88, 89, 95, 155
    French franc, 3, 22, 42, 46, 49, 70, 72,
        73, 76, 77, 79, 83, 85, 92
    and "the events of May," 73
Franklin, Benjamin, 11
Freddie Mac, 114, 118, 124
free-silver movement, 19

Geithner, Timothy, 136
General Tariff of 1932, 33
George of Poděbrad, 69
German reunification, 70, 88, 90, 171
Germany, 19, 30, 33, 35, 43–44, 49, 53,
        58, 67, 70, 72–74, 75, 77, 78, 80–82,
        84–85, 86–87, 88, 90, 92–93, 127, 131,
        161, 171, 174, 192
Giscard d'Estaing, Valéry, 4, 40, 56, 74,
        80–82
Glass-Steagall Act, 108
gold bloc, 37
gold market, "two-tier," 58, 59
Gold Pool, 51, 58
gold standard, 14, 19, 35, 52, 69, 182
gold, as international reserves, 147–49
gold-dollar system, 50, 56
Goldman Sachs, 103
Gorbachev, Mikail, 89
Gramm-Leach-Bliley Act, 108
Great Britain. *See* United Kingdom

Great Depression, 33–34
Great Moderation, 110, 115
Greece, 131–133
Greenspan put, 110
Greenspan, Alan, 61, 65, 103, 104, 110, 111,
        114, 118, 189
Group of Ten, 55, 56
Guaranty Trust Company, 18, 181

Hallstein, Walter, 186
Hamilton, Alexander, 12, 20, 23, 28
    Report on the Establishment of a Mint, 12
Hartley, Marcus, 17
Harvard University, and timber
        purchases, 149
healthcare reform and U.S. budget
        deficits, 164
Heath, Edward, 78
Hincks, Francis, 13
House Committee on Banking and
        Financial Services, 104
housing prices and 2008–9 crisis, 100,
        112, 116, 118
HSBC Holdings PLC, 146, 188
Hungary, 148

IAB. *See* International Acceptance Bank
Iceland, 148
immigration policy, 165
income inequality in U.S., 173, 175
India, 50, 121, 148, 151
infrastructure, U.S., 170
interest rates, 112, 114, 118
International Acceptance Bank (IAB), 30
International Banking Corporation, 17, 28
international currencies, multiple, 150–152
International General Electric, 35
International Monetary Fund, 6, 39, 47,
        55, 56, 62, 65, 132, 134, 137, 138, 139,
        140, 141, 142, 148, 155, 157, 159, 169
international monetary system, 121–122,
        150–152

Iran, 66, 67, 123, 153
Ireland, 77, 95, 139, 188
Israel, 155, 157
Italy, 52, 58, 78, 80, 90, 91, 92, 94, 130

Jackson, Andrew, 21
Japan, 44, 45, 47, 48, 50, 67–68, 121, 123,
     127, 130, 151, 167
Japan Development Bank, 44
Jeckyll Island, 24, 25, 29
Jefferson, Thomas, 11, 20
Jenkins, Roy, 80
Joachimsdollar, 11
johannes, 11
JP Morgan & Co., 106

Kemmerer, Edwin, 30
Kennedy, John F., 54, 55
Keynes Plan, 45–47
Keynes, John Maynard, 33, 41, 136
Kissinger, Henry, 60, 128
Kohl, Helmut, 85–87, 88, 91, 94
Kohn, Donald, 110
Korea, 114, 144, 168, 183
Kuhn, Loeb and Co., 23

Latin America, lending in, 31
Latvia, 148
Lazard Frères, 18
League of Nations, 30–31
Lehman Brothers, 102, 128, 161
lending boom, 113
Lindbergh, Charles A. Sr., 25
living standards, U.S., 171
London, as international financial center,
     14–15
London gold market, closing of in 1967,
     58
Long-Term Capital Management
     (LTCM), 104, 106
Louis d'or, 11
Luxembourg, 74, 93–96, 192

M.M. Warburg and Company, 23, 30
Maastricht Treaty, 89, 91, 92, 95
Macmillan, Harold, 156, 157, 158
MacVeagh, Franklin, 24
Madison, James, 20
Major, John, 96
manufacturing industry, decline in U.S.,
     173
Marshall Plan, 48
mathematical tools, use in managing risk,
     104–108
McDougall Report, 187
Medicaid, 166
Medicare, 166
Meriwether, John, 106
Merkel, Angela, 131
Miller, G. William, 64, 66, 110
Ministry of International Trade and
     Industry (MITI), 45
Minor, Clark H., 35
mint, in early U.S., 9, 10, 11
Mintz, Ilse, 31
MITI. *See* Ministry of International
     Trade and Industry
Mitterrand, François, 83–84, 86, 88, 89
Monetary Committee, of European
     Economic Community, 92
Moody's, 99
Morgan, J. Pierpont, 18, 22, 24, 29
mortgage interest rates and 2008–9 crisis,
     112–114, 118
mortgage-backed securities, 98

Napoleon, 27, 43, 69
Nasser, Gamal Abdel, 154–157
National Bank of Denmark, 128
National Banking Act of 1863, 18
National Citizens League for the
     Promotion of Sound Banking, 24
National City Bank, 24, 25, 27, 28
National City Company, 25
National Monetary Commission, 22, 25

National Reserve Association, 23, 24
Native Americans, and colonial trading, 9
Nazis, 72, 83
Netherlands, 33, 36, 58, 76, 77
New Century Financial, 188
New Economic Program, 60
New Zealand, 37
Newton, Sir Isaac, 12, 14
Nixon, Richard M., 55, 59–61, 74, 76
Norman, Montagu, 30, 35
Norton, Charles, 181
Norway, 72, 77, 149
Nutting, Anthony, 156

Obama, Barack H., 172, 185
oil pricing, 2, 6, 123, 157
Okun, Arthur, 65
OPEC (Organization of Petroleum
    Exporting Countries), 63, 65, 66, 123
Open Market Committee, 66, 111
Organization of European Cooperation
    and Development, 50
Organization of Petroleum Exporting
    Countries. *See* OPEC

Palin, Sarah, 6
Papandreou, George, 131
paper gold, 54
Paulson, Henry, 104
pegging. *See* exchange rates
People's Bank of China, 117, 135, 184
pesos, 10
piracy, 10
Pöhl, Karl Otto, 87, 88
Pompidou, Georges, 73, 74, 76, 77, 79
Portugal, 11, 93, 95

Queen Elizabeth, 58

rating agencies, 99, 101
Reagan, Ronald, 185
real assets, 149

rediscounting, 19
renminbi, 6, 7, 8, 33, 45, 49, 143, 144, 145,
    147, 151
Report of the Technical Group on
    Indicators, 62
Reserve Bank of India, 148
reserve drawing rights, 56
RiskMetrics Group, 107
Roosevelt, Franklin D., 41
Royal Mint, 14
Rubin, Robert, 103–04
Rueff, Jacques, 40, 52, 69
Russia, 106, 123, 127, 134, 135, 137, 140, 151,
    155, 162

Saudi Arabia, 65, 123, 139, 186
savings glut, global, 115
Schäuble, Wolfgang, 133
Schiller, Karl, 53, 73, 77
Schmidt, Helmut, 78–82, 186
Scholes, Myron, 106, 107
Schulmann, Horst, 81
Schultze, Charles, 65
SDRs. *See* Special Drawing Rights
Securities and Exchange Commission, 107
seignorage, 4
sequins, 11
shadow banking system, 105
Shanghai, as international financial
    center, 45, 146
Single Market, 86, 87, 90, 109
Smithsonian Agreement, 61, 66, 77
Smoot-Hawley Tariff, 33
Snake in the Lake, 78
Snake in the Tunnel, 78, 81, 82
Social Security, U.S., 165
Soros, George, 90, 92
South Africa, 39, 53, 55, 185
Soviet Union. *See* Union of Soviet
    Socialist Republics (USSR)
Spain, 10, 93, 95
Spanish dollars, 10, 12

Special Drawing Rights (SDRs), 6, 56, 65, 137–143
spending, unfunded and U.S. deficit, 163
Stability and Growth Pact, 130
Stabilization Fund. *See* Clearing Union
Standard & Poor's, 99
sterling, 22, 26, 32, 33, 35, 36–37, 40–42, 54, 57–58, 62, 65, 78, 87, 90, 91, 96, 126, 129, 157–59, 160, 165
    depreciation of, 35–36, 58
    pegging to dollar, 27
Stiglitz, Joseph, 137
Strauss, Franz Josef, 73
Strong, Benjamin, 24, 28–30, 180
subprime crisis, 101
Substitution Account, 65, 142
Suez Crisis, 57, 154–157
Summers, Lawrence, 102
Sweden, 36, 91, 128, 130, 139, 187
Switzerland, 36, 126

tail risk, 111
Taiwan, 154
tax cuts and U.S. deficit, 163, 168
Taylor Rule, 111
Taylor, John, 111
Tech Bubble, 110, 111
Terceira Conference, 76
Thatcher, Margaret, 49, 55, 87, 88, 90
Tier 1 and Tier 2 capital, 101
tobacco, as legal tender, 10
Tokyo, as international financial center, 45
trade acceptances, 15, 18, 23, 26–28, 30, 33, 180
    and American Acceptance Council, 28
    obstacles to growth of, 27
trade credit, American difficulties with, 18
trade deficit, U.S., 170
trade financing, 14–17
    American difficulties with, 15–17, 18
    and Britain's early dominance, 15
Treaty of Rome, 156
Trichet, Jean-Claude, 92

Triffin Dilemma, 49–51, 137
Triffin, Robert, 49
Truman, Harry, 41
Turkey, 129

U.S. dollar. *See* dollar
U.S. treasury bonds, 4, 106, 140
Ukraine, 148
United Kingdom, 17, 33, 34, 39, 40, 41, 45, 65, 67, 77, 78, 80, 90, 91, 96, 126, 130, 158, 177, 183, 187
United Nations, 137
United Nations Relief and Reconstruction Administration, 47
United States Bank of Pennsylvania, 21. *See also* Bank of the United States
Union of Soviet Socialist Republics (U.S.S.R.), 53, 71, 73, 89, 182, 184, 185, 194

Value at Risk (VaR), 106, 107
Vanderlip, Frank, 24, 25, 27
VaR. *See* Value at Risk
Vichy Government, 52
Volcker, Paul, 66, 67, 110, 111, 139
von Mises, Ludwig, 52

Waigel, Theo, 93, 95
wampum, 9
Warburg, Paul, 23, 28, 30
Werner Report, 75
Werner, Pierre, 75
White Plan, 47
White, Harry Dexter, 46–47
Wilson, Harold, 58
Wilson, Woodrow, 25
World Bank, 145, 156
World War I, 26, 33, 42, 69, 196
World War II, 7, 39, 42, 45, 47, 55, 70, 89, 93, 121, 133, 134, 157, 177, 192
yen, 44, 45, 67, 68, 127, 139, 144

Zhou, Xiaochuan, 137, 142–143